The Lover's World

Alice B. Stockham

The Lover's World
A Wheel of Life

Edited with an Epilogue
by Heinz Schott

BoD – Books on Demand

Bibliografische Information der Deutschen Nationalbibliothek:

Die Deutsche Nationalbibliothek verzeichnet diese Publikation
in der Deutschen Nationalbibliografie; detaillierte bibliografische
Daten sind im Internet über www.dnb.de abrufbar.

Reprint of the First Edition:
Alice B. Stockham: *The Lover's World. A Wheel of Life.*
Chicago: Stockham Publishing Co., 1903
Cover photo:
Dandelion in the Kottenforst near Bonn, Germany
(H. Schott, 2018)

SCHOTT's NEUE BIBLIOTHEK / 5

© 2019 Heinz Schott
Herstellung und Verlag: BoD – Books on Demand, Norderstedt.

ISBN: 9783749432271

GREETING

THE LOVER'S WORLD, in its entirety, is a treatise on Love and the appropriation and mastery of sexual energy, the use of passion and creative force.

Very early in life, as a medical practitioner, through heart experiences of many, the author was led to take a deep interest in this subject. Men and women were digging their graves with the spade of ignorance. Later her world enlarged, the audiences who listened to her private and public lectures, who read her books, became her friends and correspondents. Through personal interviews and letters she has reached the heart of the world; she has listened to the sad refrain of broken hearts and wretchedness as well as the jubilant song of victory. Hundreds of volumes have been read, long journeys have been taken in order to obtain practical wisdom that could lead people from the bondage of ignorance to the freedom of knowledge.

The Lover's World, garnered sheaves from the wisdom of books and life's experiences, is now returned to the heart of humanity.

The fundamental principle of life must show forth in application, must lead one to so order every detail that it shall harmonize with all activities. It is fitting and important to learn the art of beauty and polished manners, to have the knowledge of making an artistic home, to have kindly association with friends and neighbors, to live the perfect conjugal union, to procreate children of beauty and power; all of these are a fulfilment of love.

After all study and research one comes to the conclusion that perfect sexual control is obtained through a perfected manhood and womanhood. The sexual life is a part of the entire life, so as the Lover's World deals with all stages of life, is a Wheel of Life, each chapter, each precept, directly or indirectly, is intended as a help to mastery. One can not separate and perfect the sexual life by itself. One must have a philosophy upon which to base conduct and learn to govern life by that philosophy.

The Lover's World teaches that man is a living spiritual being, a soul which he may, if he will, train into effectiveness. It becomes, through knowledge, dominant over every function, and man as creator controls his creations. In the union of love and wisdom, faculties are no more perverted but consecrated to fullest use.

Thus the Wheel of Life with its hub — kosmic mind, its spokes — thought and sense perception, its felloes — outward manifestation, all unified, become a harmonious whole — love, life and intelligence manifesting in will and activity.

Intellect, emotions and passions are trained into service. Strength supplants weakness; knowledge, ignorance; and spiritual consciousness is awakened. The heart life, the real life, becomes manifest in thought, word and deed.   A. B. S.

TABLE OF CONTENTS.

CHAPTER IV.

ROMANTIC LOVE.

CHAPTER V.

THE LOVER — MAN.

CHAPTER VI.

THE LOVER — WOMAN.

CHAPTER VII.

PASSION — WOMAN.

CHAPTER VIII.

PASSION — MAN.

CHAPTER IX.

MARRIAGE.

CHAPTER X.

APPROPRIATION AND MASTERY.

CHAPTER XIX.

RECREATION.

CHAPTER XX.

SLEEP.

CHAPTER XXI.

DRESS.

CHAPTER XXII.

BEAUTY AND ITS POWER.

CHAPTER XXIII.

COURTESY LOVE'S LANGUAGE.

CHAPTER XXIV.

CHAPTER XXV.

DON'T WORRY.

CHAPTER XXVI.

FREEDOM OF CHILDHOOD.

CHAPTER XXVII.

FROEBEL'S LAW OF UNITY.

CHAPTER XXVIII.

BOY LOVER.

CHAPTER XXIX.

GIRL LOVER.

Sweet Sixteen.— Original Ideas.— The Maiden a Century Ago.— Sex Differences Disappearing.— Motherhood Demands Vigor.— The Maiden Loves.— Love Unchangeable.—The Maximum of Love.— Outlets for Activity.—Arduous Tasks.— Original Entertainments.— Soul Victories.— Helen of Troy.— Lucretia Mott.— A Block of Marble.
238 - 247

CHAPTER XXX.

THE AWAKENING.

Faith and Knowledge.— Esse and Existo.— Conversion.— Spiritual Consciousness.— Initiation.— Brotherhoods and Mystic Orders.— The Ways Are Many.— With or Without Creed.— The Day of Deliverance
248 - 253

CHAPTER I.

LOVE AS LAW.

Without the law of love the universe would cease to be.

Love is the supreme power of the universe. It is the attracting and impelling force that holds stars and constellations in orderly relation. Through love atom is held to atom to produce stone and sparkling gem; through love in its dual expression plant and animal life are perpetuated. In all creation, in stone, plant and animal, love is the power, law is the process, and manifest life is the result.

Man includes the principles and properties of all life; he is the indestructibility of the rock, the beauty, pliancy and radiance of the plant, the eagerness, alertness and courage of the animal. But he is more than all these, he has a higher consciousness that renders it possible for him to be a lover in a more exalted sense than plant or animal.

Man's life is impelled and ordered by love; but the ability to be conscious of it, to train his thoughts in harmony with it, to appropriate it to daily use, is a measure of the difference between man and the animal. This power and ability of man by which also he is conscious of infinity, and of himself as a spiritual being, is the basis of all theories of life, the teachings of sages, the fundamentals of all creeds.

The philosophy and religion of the ages unite in teaching that there is a life within a life. Kant's Noumenon, the Thing in itself, is back of all phenomena. " The world of Noumena is fundamental and determining. The world of Phenomena, the sensible or objective world, is derivative and dependent, while the two are organically one. The sensible world is the manifestation of the intelligible world, the noumena which are present in and identical with the sensible world, are revealed as a world of spirit. The human spirit finds itself as a dependent center of an ideal life, which is supported in the last resort only by a divine life."

" Being is not simply inertly existing in space; no such existence, considered absolutely, is known or knowable. Being is doing, and doing is in the first and last resort, the operation of Spirit. The activity of Spirit is Life."

Fichte's " Infinite I " is absolutely independent, while all is dependent on it. The object must correspond to the " I "; its absoluteness demands this.

Hegel gives a philosophy of idealism, as one writes: " He gathers in the vineyards of the human spirit the grapes from which he crushed the wine of thought. His Idea is the absolute spirit, self-determined, therefore free; independent, therefore infinite. It is the efficient force of the universe, not blind, but intelligence and will. The universe is the process of the absolute; in religious language, the manifestation of God. In the background of all the absolute is eternally present. The rhythmic movement of thought is the selfunfolding of the absolute. God reveals Himself in the logical idea in nature, and in mind. That which is called the noble, the excellent, the perfect in human character, is nothing else in effect than the veritable essence of spirit, the Moral and Divine principle which manifests itself in man. "

Hegel's philosophy is realism as well as idealism, and never quits its hold on facts.

Froebel's Unity is " self-consciousness, self-intelligencc, self-acting law manifesting in diversity. Everything is of Divine Nature and origin. "

The purpose of Man's existence, of all existence, is to express God, the spiritual. Only that which holds within itself the *living spirit* can become manifest. (See Supplement *a*.)

The Christ of Christianity is the Divine Spirit, awakened in man, the spiritual kingdom consciously revealed in the heart of man as a kingdom of conquest and power.

What is this Noumenon, this Idea, this Unity, this Christ ? Is it not love manifesting in the heart of man ?

We have many schools of philosophy, all expositions of man's soul life and demonstrating his spiritual power; in all and through all is a golden cord of unity which is love.

The consciousness of the redeeming power of love awakens the soul to its possibilities. It is the finding of the Christ in one's self — a knowledge of the heart-life of man.

One may have been led to love's awakening through the teaching of theology; through an idealism of philosophy; from seeing the unity of all life in mountain, brook and stone; it may have been revealed in a message from the East; the question need not arise how and where he obtained it; but if he has the larger grasp of life, if he knows the inclusiveness and dominance of the spiritual life, he is a lover from love's own world. He is in the world but not of it; he sees with new eyes, he hears with new ears, and his speech is that of a new man.

Be not dishearted, O man ! If this illumination seems fleeting, one glimpse only, no matter how brief, is proof of the possibility of more extended experience. The triune man, spirit, soul and body,[1] is so constituted that every part must develop in harmony with every other part. So, when love calls and love lures, be still, O soul, and listen ! Cease the babbling of tongues, the hastening to and fro of thoughts, and let love kindle the creative fire, until the ocean of thought is calmed and all life shows forth in symmetry; and beauty.

----

1 Throughout this work the word Spirit is used as the source, the kosmic force or divine nature.

Soul is spirit in action and includes intellect, emotions and sensations, — "Individual personal e xistence. "

Body is manifestation, the visible vehicle of soul expression.

Thus day after day love walks hand in hand with wisdom and man becomes a lover in his world;

A lover of himself,

A lover of his family,

A lover of friends,

A lover of the race,

A lover of all living creation.

As a child of love, as youth or maiden, as husband or wife, as father or mother, one is always the lover.

Nay, the affections are for all; and he, or she, has most of life, who has them most.

CHAPTER II.

LOVE.

Angels call it heavenly joy;
Infernal tortures the devils say;
And Men? They call it *love.*

In love, divines, poets and sages have an inexhaustible theme. Artists have pictured it, authors portrayed it, and novelists revealed its many-sided manifestations. Still, the beauty, power and service of love are as yet scarcely known.

Love has no adequate definition; all of its synonyms are tame and unsatisfactory. Affection, fondness, attachment and many others are included in the one grand Saxon word — LOVE.

Love is the manifestation of the God-life in man, the fulfilling of the law. There is only one love, but it is diverse in expression, and for convenience may be considered as: Kosmic love, Self love, Romantic love, Conjugal love, Parental love, Social love.

A constructive, potent thought is love impelling, pushing forth in manifestation. Intellect and intuition unite in a germinating process; this union is a fecundation or conception.

Intuition, the feminine, knows, perceives, desires; it hears in the silence messages from the Absolute; intellect, the masculine wisdom, applies wires, receiver and transmitter, thus converting the messages into veritable creations.

As both masculine and feminine are equally essential for a creation in physical life, so in the realm of spirit, that thought creations may not be abortive, a complete union of the feminine and masculine qualities of mind are essential.

The man who does his work through reason and research; who analyzes, compares and infers, if he has not times when these faculties are coupled with insight — the impression or leading from within — labor may prove in vain. On the other hand, the man who is governed by intuition, who follows his impressions, is likely to run hither and thither; he makes many beginnings, but few completions, is full of visions and prophecies of the new time, but fails to put them into execution.

To make kosmic love effective, there must be nuptials in the soul; it must not be mere lovemaking, a singing of songs and dreaming of dreams, but a controlled conjunction of love and wisdom. This is the immaculate conception in the soul, typified and symbolized in song and story — a worthy theme — as it is the greatest and highest of all experiences. It is appropriately called the *new birth,* for it is the soul's perception of its own greatness, of its inner powers, producing an ecstasy or illumination.

As the buried gold is delved from the earth and utilized, as fire hidden in coal becomes fuel for furnace and foundry, so man may manifest in power the strength and efficiency of love.

The great central fact in human experience, is the coming into *vital, conscious realization* of our one-ness with infinite Love, and the opening of ourselves freely to its divine inflow.

CHAPTER III.

SELF LOVE.

Self reverence, self knowledge, self control, these three alone lead life to sovereign power.

Self love is a natural manifestation of kosmic love. Self love, though ordinarily decried, is inherent in the mind of man and is the essence of self preservation.

In the consciousness of the oneness of all life, the divine self, that is the image and likeness of God, is a revelation of man's possibilities. This is the power and strength of inspiration; this is the foundation of true character. Who knows this has faith, courage and endurance; when he manifests these in efficiency, in bravery, in accomplishment, he receives the commendation and blessing of himself and friends. He trusts himself because of his possibilities. His influence, his attainments, his successes are due to confidence in himself. Consciously or unconsciously he draws from the divine source of his inherent nature. One often needs to cultivate self appreciation, to develop confidence and daring to express this nature.

This is not self adulation, self gratification, love of approbation, vanity and pride, which are merely perversions of self love, prolific weeds in the garden of life to be reclaimed and wisely utilized.

To change a crab-apple into a maiden's blush, a thorn into a fig tree, a briar into a rose, requires the application of principle. A gardener removes from some secluded corner an old-fashioned rose bush; he cuts and prunes it, leaving only a single brown stalk and the living root. He digs a deep hole, placing in first clay, then a soil composed of sand, manure and leaf mold. The place chosen has no shadow, no umbrageous neighbor to demand sustenance from the soil. He carefully plants this old bush, spreading every rootlet and tendril with skill.

From a florist he has procured buds of a spreading rose tree whose perennial blossoms are noted for beauty and fragrance; with a sharp knife an incision is made in the old stalk, and into this is inserted the new scion, effected in such a way that the life sap of the old will come into contact with the sap of the new and form a union. Faith and hope portend a glad fruition of his labors.

Mark the process; the ever-present life of the old plant is preserved, but its manifestation is changed by the infusion of a new life. The inherent force of the rose life, always good, always potent, is directed by the ingenuity of man. It is no more an unsightly shrub, cumbering the ground, but becomes a thing of beauty to gladden the heart of all who behold. The inherent life is reorganized and is redeemed by the transfusion of new rose blood; and through the alchemy of nature the bush is reclaimed, and behold it is no more a weed.

The symbol is good, but, like all symbols, incomplete. The self-lover is his own gardener, and the weeds of his nature are transformed through a recognition of his real nature, through a knowledge that every soul according to kosmic law is imbued with all faculties and possessed of all possibilities.

That he is an image and likeness of God is not merely a trite saying; it is founded upon truth, and man's appreciation of the truth makes it not only possible but demonstrates the necessity of self love.

The self-lover sees God not only in murmuring brooks and running streams, but beholds him in him-self, a potent force, omnipotent and inexhaustible, Man in his nature possesses the coherence of rocks, the beauty of plants, virility of animals, the force of water; he also possesses self consciousness, *he knows that he knows*, and by this knowledge he is able to relate himself to deific force. Wisdom has become united to love and joined to intuition. He lives and has knowledge of life; he is not only governed by the power of attraction, kosmic love, but through knowledge, through the will to command, that force becomes creative and constructive. It serves him in all the activities of life. He becomes master, and all his forces wheel into line and are subservient to his demands through obedience to law that impels all things in a certain orderly manner.

The self-lover is the normal man, the one who trusts and confides in his fellows, but most of all trusts himself; who plants the rootlets of his being in a soil of richness and fertility; who waters them with the sunshine of hope and faith, and most of all, engrafts upon the old stalk the bud of a regenerative life, a life that has cognizance of its own divine nature; he supplements all the possibilities of the old nature with the fragrance and bloom inherent and dormant in the grafted bud.

This is regeneration; the result is:

Confidence in one's genius,

Evolution of intuition.

Courage of individuality,

Mastery.

The self-lover has confidence in his own genius, his own intellect; indeed, in all his faculties. He trusts the *self* that is ever pushing forth into bloom and fruitage. Self love, self appreciation is that which makes one bold to venture and renders achievement possible. He becomes the rose tree that requires neither stake nor trellis. Does he contemplate a new venture, a journey, business or a life partnership, he knows that intellect and intuition united can make no mistake, that wisdom joined to love gives understanding which straightens tangles, solves problems and overcomes difficulties.

Self confidence begets confidence, so that one ascends mountain heights with determination and exultation. A bitter, overwhelming experience to-day, becomes to-morrow the actor's make-believe or a child's pretense. Each victory makes a future conquest less difficult; the soul mounts the Alpine summits because there is no hint of weakness or vacillation.

Self love is a congenial soil for the development of intuition. One sees, knows and has impressions, the infinite breathes into the finite maturity of judgment and quick responsive decisions. Man does not weigh and reason, for the intuition inspires the thought, quickens the work and impels the deed. There seems no formative stage; results are accomplished, plans are fulfilled, and dreams become created things.

The self-lover has courage of individuality. As no two rose bushes are alike, no one blossom is an exact counterpart of the other, no tree mirrors its fellow in the still water; so of individuals, though one in spirit, yet diverse in manifestation. One star differeth from another star in glory.

Man is not a baboon, to imitate his neighbor, monkey, nor a parrakeet, to babble the speech of parrots. Neither is he merely a thought of Deity or a spark of Infinity — he is rather a stream from the ocean, possessing the qualities of the large body, having limitations that give character and differences.

Does every stream seek the same channel, the same mountain side, the same valley, the -same ocean bed? The Amazon and Mississippi are both mighty and majestic, but in their might and majesty are individual and remarkable for unlikeness. Independent and great minds have no patterns to follow; like oriental rugs, each one is a special conception, varying in hue, color and quality, and yet each has its value.

The self-lover does not build a house, cut a garment, attend a church, join a club to be in fashion. He is self minded and self witted. His speech, his house, his clothes, his activities, bespeak that wit and outpicture that mind. His character is founded on a self made plan,

25

and yet it is no distortion of the original image. The self-lover molds the clay out of which his character is builded, he mingles the colors in a fashion of his own to paint his likeness. The God life manifests in infinite variety, and the self-lover permits this manifestation to build for him a character unlike any other man, a character that exalts the human in the divine and recognizes the divine in the human.

The self-lover is master of his own life. Through a trust in innate powers, a knowledge of his possibilities, he overcomes the foes to progress — fear, weakness, inertia and insincerity.

The self-lover is lithe of body and limb, steady of nerve and strong of muscle; he has health and endurance; his inspiration and expiration represent the breath of life and are a counterpart of his aspirations; his mind is alive, alert and knows not weariness, while his spiritual consciousness is awake to divine realities. He evinces power, courage and efficiency, according to self evolution.

The righteousness of self, the stability of self, the invincible power and courage of self is demanded by the self-lover; according to that demand fulfillment follows.

To entertain no possible fear or doubt about the upshot of things —to be *yourself,* to have measureless trust; perhaps that is best of all.

CHAPTER IV.

ROMANTIC LOVE.

Love which is sunlight of peace —
Age by age to increase
Till anger and hatred are dead,
And sorrow and death shall cease.

Souls that are gentle and still
Hear the first music of this
Far off infinite bliss.

Romantic love is the love of ideality; it is born of emotion and sentiment; it is the passion conceived for the opposite sex; it is the fairy story of life and is undoubtedly the outgrowth of race development; it is a human manifestation of kosmic love.

Romantic love sees reflected in another the thoughts, feelings, aspirations, ambitions and accomplishments of his own soul; the loved one becomes the looking-glass of the lover.

Successive ages have evolved emotion and sentiment, which in their forms of expression culminate in romantic love. This is an outgrowth of conditions and environment; at the same time it is an important factor in civilization. It is an element in the evolution of man from the animal to the spiritual life.

(See Supplement *b.*)

Among the primitive races romantic love was not known; among aboriginal tribes to-day it can not be found. In some countries that stand high in art, literature and philosophy, the sentiment known in the West as love is very rare. This is true to a greater or less extent in any country where marriage is contracted by a third party, where royalty, aristocracy or caste governs the relationship.

In India a ceremony that may be called a betrothal occurs very early, often before the children are ten years of age. I witnessed the marriage of a Brahmin youth who was but sixteen and the girl he married was only ten. There was great deference not only to the date, but to the hour and moment defined by an astrologer. Three days previous to the ceremony there was feasting, dancing by nautch girls, burning of innumerable lights and all that accompanies a brilliant oriental festival.

When the high priest pronounced the words that made the bond indissoluble, the mother and a friend held a chuddah between the boy and girl so that they could have no glimpse of each other. The ceremony being completed, the boy returned to the hall of feasting; the girl was carried to her own home in the arms of her uncle, not to meet her betrothed until after there should be signs of maturity; he would then call for her and a final ceremony would be performed and she would behold his face for the first time.

Most writers define this first ceremony as the marriage, but it is only the betrothal, and the marriage takes place when the young man claims his wife; but picturing it at its best, what sentiment, what romance enters into a union like this! Yet, if astrology is unerringly true and its calculations are implicitly followed, then the chances of affection, of an attachment in the conjugal relations, may not be more uncertain than in a union determined by money or position.

In the Orient there seems an entire absence of sentiment in the home relations. Love, as known in the West, never enters the heart of man or woman. Their philosophy decries emotion. It has perfect contempt for Western literature, Western thought and Western customs that are steeped and dyed in romantic love.

In Hindu literature we often find allusions to woman, but if one understands the symbology of that literature, he will most likely find in its interpretation the experiences of the soul and not a reference to material conditions.

It is taught that affection, desire and ambition should be stamped out. The Nirvana of power is emotionless and passionless, while in the West the soul's higher knowledge often comes through the education given by the senses and affections, through the right appropriation of every faculty and function. The soul, through the sense of hearing, listens for heavenly harmonies, through sight views the radiance of all nature, through its love it learns to love divinely. From sense and spirit, the warp and woof of life, is woven a garment of light and wisdom.

Many of the old stories founded on passion and love recount the struggles and victories of the soul; the story of Eros and Psyche, of Helen of Troy, the Vita Nuova of Dante, and the passionate songs of Solomon, are examples of language symbology adopted by ancient and medieval writers; they are not romances representing the varying relationship between men and women, but rather struggles of the human to embrace and possess the divine. One seeking for higher knowledge and striving for spiritual consciousness, sees in these the struggles and experiences of his own soul.

Romantic love finds its fullest expression in modern literature and art, every phase of passion being portrayed by pen and pencil.

Shakespeare, the king of artists, gave such an impetus to romantic love in literature that all love romances pale in contrast with the resplendencies of his productions.

Since Shakespeare's brilliant example, there are few works of fiction not colored and enriched by a portrayal of the emotions of love, by the heart experiences of men and women. Has this no significance in race evolution? Through love one comes to know love; through the emotions and passions of human life one is led to a consciousness of the deeper, richer and diviner life that sees all and knows all. The horizon is widened, the perceptions are enlarged, the intuitions awakened and unity born of the divine revealed.

Tolstoi says: "Art should be a vehicle wherewith to transmit religious, Christian perception from the realm of reason and intellect into that of feeling, and really drawing people in actual life nearer to that perfection and unity indicated to them by their religious feeling. The soul activity of the artist speaks through his work to the soul of the beholder, and the emotions thus aroused create a connecting link to the One Life, the Infinite in man.

The Divine Life has always been, but man as an animal is unconscious of it; through a long process, through the education of experience, of joy and suffering, and most of all through his loves, he comes to recognize the love that is universal, to know the unity of all life and his own inseparableness from this, the kosmic life.

We call the love of friend, the love of child, the love of man or woman emotional love. The religious teacher or philosopher often counsels us to stamp these out and know only the divine; but are not these the very gateways to infinite life? They have their origin in the kosmic forces and they awaken the human perceptions to the deeper spiritual life, thus leading to a realization of Universal life.

Love when it is only the impelling of natural attraction, is kosmic through emotion, feeling and desire it leads to soul illumination.

Romantic love through the finer sensibilities and perceptions enables man to feel and know and use the *all,* the kosmic love.

Whom do you love — father, mother, child, husband, wife? This is good, this is right, but through these loves you must know another — the one Absolute; you find the Christ, and this Christ love is the interpretation of the law, is the gospel of humanity.

If I have all faith so that I can remove mountains and have not love, I am nothing.

Love is strong as death; jealousy is cruel as the grave; the coals thereof are coals of fire, which hath a most vehement flame. Many waters can not quench love, neither can the floods drown it; if a man should give all the substance of his house for love, it would utterly be contemned.

CHAPTER V.

THE LOVER, MAN.

Yet thro' that one, as thro' a glass
The world I seem to see;
And like an image stands that one
Of all the world to me;

And through that inspiration given
As through some morning sun,
I sing, and write, and act for all
Best when it serves for one.

Romantic love creates in the mind of man pictures of ideals, it develops the imagination, and through it soul growth follows that enhances happiness. The lover's world may be seen through magnifying glasses, but the view gives him pleasure. The sun shines more brightly, the grass is greener, flowers are more brilliant and varied of hue, men more just and women more lovely. The lover sees all the world through the eyes of love. '

An emotional man, by the time he is ready to marry, may have been in love many times. Each girj has seemed to him the only one; he has carried her in his heart in day and night dreams, and well may he now ask if philosophy and science have means of guiding him so that he may make no mistake.

Shall he seek the aid of phrenology, which professes to delineate faculties that prove harmonious? May not the stars, through astrology, reveal their secrets to aid his aspirations? Have psychometry and clairvoyance no certain aid in guiding man to choose the one girl from all his acquaintance ? Can he in any way be instructed to choose a companion ? Can these eyes; can this brain, giddy with exaggerated joy, be entrusted with the choosing of a wife ?

Naturally, every man desires that the woman he seeks for a life-long union shall be one to whom he will give and from whom he will receive happiness. In seeking that happiness he may have found that true satisfaction comes not only by giving and receiving, but by growth, by development of powers that increases capacity for the world's demands. The union of feminine and masculine in marriage is a union of qualities that are thus made more effective in service. Man does not seek alone personal happiness, but he believes that this copartnership will bring strength of character and spiritual un-foldment. He not only demands this for himself, but desires it also for the one sought. He looks in the united life to make better use of his creative powers, writing better sermons, painting better pictures, and that she, too, shall become more accomplished and brilliant in a chosen vocation. She is not to abandon music, a profession or business to become the housekeeper and administer to the physical life of her husband — incidentally this may be love's province; what marriage is to do for the unfoldment of her powers is all important; largely speaking, she is a soul seeking soul's evolution, and united love has a mission toward the accomplishment of that evolution.

Equality seems the best intellectual test to apply to the selection of a life partner. It is not equality of station that money can buy; not equality in education, mere gathering of school-book facts and figures; not equality in ability to row a boat, ride a wheel or wield a golf stick; any or all of these are good for acquaintance or friendship; it is rather equality of perception and discernment, an equal outlook on the affairs of the world.

Man has ceased to seek in a companion one to make a fine setting to his establishment, a mere accessory to his possessions, much as he procures a yacht or racehorse; he has ceased to look for a wife that shall only reflect his glory and renown, that is willing to live in a passive world as a satellite.

He does not look for one who will be cook, laundress, seamstress, scrubwoman and nurserymaid for the sake of being a wife; he looks no more for a toy or slave, for a doll or drudge; but he seeks his equal — a woman regal in her own right, who with him has traveled a like road of experience, has similar desires and aspirations, and whose love is willing to take the chances of station and fortune.

It is well that there should be an agreement on religious and political proclivities — these come very close to every heart, always bearing in mind that freedom of thought may result in change of opinion.

Do you love me? — hold me free! —
Love's sweet proof is liberty.

Man need scarcely be deterred from marrying one who has not health of body or physical charms; all other things being equal, he may well know that love and harmony are best promoters and restorers of both health and beauty.

Women who have been delicate and sickly, through a congenial marriage and a right understanding of its privileges, blossom into health and robustness. The consumptive loses the hectic flush, the nerves their morbid sensibility, while the joy of health is manifest in agility, strength and endurance, love being both elixir and tonic.

Man has a right to seek in a woman one who will in every way bring him joy and satisfaction, who by her education and accomplishment may contribute to his development, to his success in a chosen pursuit; at the same time the true man never loses sight of what the fulfillment of love will do for the chosen woman. Her needs, her advancement in an occupation, her soul growth are with his own well considered.

The choice is not made by ordinary standards. A man knows that station, intellectual acquirements and physical accomplishments are only accessories to a soul union. Realizing that there must be a true spiritual relationship, he probably has his surest guide in his own intuitions; alone and in the silent moments of the soul the true answer will come. The rushing, hurrying thoughts are stilled, questions are hushed, the interior faculties are awakened, perceptions are quickened; in the stillness his answer is received.

He can not test himself by seeking the society of many girls. As one rose differeth from another, so every woman has a beauty, an individuality of her own. He loves all the roses of the garden, from the old-fashioned blush rose to the American beauty; the one he selects to wear always closest his heart is the one whose radiance of color, beauty of form, as well as delicacy of perfume permeates fully his own soul; the one whose memory can not be effaced by time, distance or associations. The answer in the silence reveals this chosen one.

Carpenter says: "The aim of love is non-differentiation, absolute union of being; but absolute union can only be found at the center of existence. Therefore whoever has truly found another has found not only that other, and with that other himself, but has found a third; that third is the ONE the Absolute."

> Said to Wamik one who never
> Knew the lover's passion — "Why
> Solitary thus and silent,
> Solitary places haunting,
> Like a Dreamer, like a Spectre,
>   Like a thing about to die ? "
> Wamik answered —" Meditating
> Flight with Azra to the Desert;
> There by so remote a Fountain
>   That, whichever way one travell'd
> League on league, yet one should never
> See the face of Man; for ever
> There to gaze on my beloved;
> Gaze, till Gazing out of Gazing
> Grew to Being Her I gaze on,
> She and I no more, but in One
> Undivided Being blended.

All that is by Nature twain
Fears, or suffers by, the pain
Of Separation: Love is only
    Perfect when itself transcends
Itself, and, one with that it loves,
    In undivided Being blends."

                        — Jani

CHAPTER VI.

THE LOVER, WOMAN.

How did she know his heart was hers?
He spoke no word
Of love to her; how did she know
That when she passed or touched him — so —
His pulse was stirred?

How did she read his secret thoughts.
And never err?
How did she know her glances thrilled
His soul ? That all his heart was filled
With love for her?

A free woman's privilege is to choose her husband. Custom and tradition have proclaimed that she waits to be chosen. She is not to express her love in word or action, but rather she must make a pretense of indifference, no matter how ardent her affection, how deeply the heart is interested, must act a lie about that which most concerns her life interest. (See Supplement c.)

Time was when if a girl was not chosen, she could only sit in a chimney corner and be aunty to somebody's children. It was the only respectable occupation open to her. She still waits to be chosen, but if the right man does not appear, she may enter any vocation of profit and usefulness. Art, literature, science, philosophy and philanthropy all afford ample fields for utilizing her talent and education. Equally equipped she follows any pursuit side by side with man, with equal hope of success; but in that which is nearest to her heart, which lays the foundation of home, she must forever be receptive and at the same time secretive; she must make no demonstration of her love.

" For why should woman, any more than man, play dissembler, with so much at stake?"

The romance of literature and experiences of life are full of the tragedies of hidden love. To-day a brilliant young lady is consigned to the tender mercies of a hospital for the insane, who for four years had carried deep down in her heart a passion for a young man whose acquaintance and association had simply been the manifestation of friendship. To-morrow a sweet, sad-eyed woman will lose the hectic flush on her cheek and her friends will listen to the earth falling on her coffin, her heart stilled by unexpressed emotion.

According to Drummond, love is the outgrowth of desire for offspring, and to woman comes naturally the greater care and responsibility of children. With- these considerations, together with her quicker intuitions, it would seem that justice to coming generations demands that she choose the lover who is to be her husband and eventually father of her children.

In animal life most females take advantage of their freedom to make a choice of mates. (See Supplement *d*.) Bulwer, in " The Coming Race," and Sargent, in " The Woman Who Dared," represent woman as wooing the man, taking the initiative in love matters. Is this a prophecy of the province of the new woman ?

The new girl that is to be the new woman, full of the very best that life can give, will not trust her happiness to the mockery of traditions. The modern woman, with her clubs, her debates, her freedom of action and costume, is forming a public opinion of her own at an amazing rate. Education broad, free and liberal, is now within reach of every young lady. She has not been slow to take advantage of it. Already more girls than boys graduate from high schools. This alone gives them accomplishments beyond any public education that was within reach of women one hundred years ago. Many of our best colleges and universities are co-educational, besides numerous institutions, controlled and operated by the very best talent of the age, are dedicated to the education of young women. These include in their studies, languages, art, literature, philosophy and many specialties. Most of the State colleges and polytechnic schools introduce a scientific course in household economics, while not a few are giving special training in studies that prepare for wifehood and motherhood. Who knows but that the young man of the future will be knocking at the doors of woman's colleges for the better or special opportunities they may afford. (See Supplement *e.*)

Added to all this is the advantage of innumerable clubs for women. The mother's clubs alone, organized in every town and hamlet of the country, are fearlessly handling subjects pertaining to practical life, while clubs and societies devoted to art, music, literature and philanthropy, as well as the organizations accessory to every church, are a great outlet to the talent and energy of the members. Every woman is given an opportunity to develop latent faculties, while thought and speech become free from the shackles that custom may have imposed.

In the evolution of woman she will be able to utilize this intellectual development, guiding it with her instincts and intuitions, and in time dare honestly to express the love that is uppermost.

In her study of ethics, or in the awakening of the inner or soul life, she learns that she must be honest; she can not lie, even to herself. Knowing her own heart, the law of life demands a declaration of that love. True love makes its own declarations; like the boy in school, it whistles itself.

The new man, with his intuitions quickened, his spiritual life awakened, will gladly accept this love as an honest tribute to his manhood. Perhaps the most perfect unions are those where proposals never have to be made, where the life of one is united to the life of the other as naturally as chemical elements unite to form a new product.

The heart love of a woman honestly expressed can never be unwelcome to a true man.

A young woman in love, even under the bondage of conventionality, has many resources. She may act the truth of her soul, although her tongue is bound by traditions. She may resort to gifts that are not considered keepsakes; flowers and fruit are always permissible. These are friendship offerings and yet may be construed as the language of love. A card or booklet on Easter or Christmas may also be a testimony of friendship, with a hint of deeper meaning.

Has she the privilege of preparing his food, even occasionally, she may cater to his taste, doing her best.

Accomplishments in cooking mean much to every man. The saying that the road to a man's heart is through his stomach, has a truth in it. Taste, as well as sight and hearing, is an esthetic sense; it is an art to gratify it. As one makes the nutrition of the body a science, then to please a man's taste becomes both an artistic and scientific accomplishment.

Some of the wealthiest and most cultured ladies of the land have made a special study of cookery; they have become famous for the cuisine of their own household, and are often in demand for directing the menus of special functions, dinners, receptions and banquets.

Cooking school and demonstration teas may serve a purpose in many and varied interests of life, while a heart that is won through perfection in this practical science may be ever grateful for the innocent finesse.

A girl may choose her reading and recreations, her studies and amusements to accord to the taste of the young man she loves. This is far better than in a forlorn way mourning unrequited affection, or in the bitterness of resentment employing the stinging weapon of sarcasm. Love leads the way to conquest.

Be natural; be industrious. Fill your life with activities. Take up some regular pursuit or study and become master of it. Be open, frank and cheerful. Avoid boldness and intrusiveness, also the opposite — reticence and the sulks.

Remember, love may not be compelled; remember, too, that you may have idealized him you love. In marriage love that is romantic only is soon shattered. If you have not deep down in your soul found the third, the *One* Absolute, as Carpenter says, you may be seeking an idol. So strive for unity with the One life; seek the poise of true being and it will be given you to know if the love you so greatly desire is shadow or substance.

Remember, also, that what is good for him is good for you, whether your lives take separate paths or one; if it is his happiness to join hands with another, it is your happiness to have him do so! The experience may be a means of soul growth, and the deeper meaning it has to you the greater development you will derive from it. The time will come when you will recall the experience with joy.

Under the restraints and formalities of present-day customs, it is not at all unusual for a young lady to conceive a dislike toward a young man that shows a preference for her. As schoolmates, as friends and comrades, they may have had a pleasant relationship. The society of each has been mutually agreeable, but at the very moment that she is satisfied that she is singled out for special favors and attentions — the attentions of a lover — she, by some strange mental process experiences a feeling that is entirely opposite. She can not analyze this. When away from him, she reasons about it and endeavors to know her own heart: "We are good friends; why does he seek to be aught else, and then and then ——." Well, likely, she can not tell more. The truth probably is that she has built up an ideal and has never thought of this friend save as an every-day sort of fellow, and though she may be an every-day sort of girl, she resents the special attention. She may think also herself too young for a lover, or there may be another who holds the key to her heart.

Friendship's demands require that this feeling be held in abeyance. Go down deep into your heart — find the quiet place — the place not swerved by emotions; your intuitions will guide you aright.

Never for a moment forget to be polite. One who regards the feelings of another knows the pain and joy of that heart. Knowing this, if love can not be given for love, justice and kindliness will rule every act. Search your motives, be honest with yourself, be honest with him, and you will surely be just to him who loves you.

A lover chosen by relatives, friends or a professional may be the one of all most desired, the one long looked for. A free woman naturally rebels against having a husband provided by any means that limits her freedom of choice. To her the methods savor of barter and trade. The innate revolt against a traffic in souls, a money or position value placed upon herself, is so repugnant to the true woman that the best man in the world so presented to her may appear as a distortion of human nature. His angelic side is entirely hidden. If marriage is to be a bondage in which the best qualities of a woman's soul are prostituted, she prefers to make the choice herself. Fathers and mothers having wide experience and a large acquaintance, with the interest of a daughter at heart, do not always choose for her unwisely. They may have sought the emoluments of riches and station, but at the same time they may not have forgotten to look for character and intrinsic worth.

Young men of wealth may be the chosen of the earth. Certain it is that they have had opportunities to develop their talents, and, too, ma/ be blest with the deeper heart experiences that are beyond all riches and honor.

So, be not too hasty in closing the door of your heart to the one that has been brought into your life for the purpose of marriage. At the same time be not too eager to accept a proffered offer. Having wealth and personal charms, and knowing that you are sought for these, then be sure that the heart's wealth is equal to material wealth, that the soul's greatness is commensurate with the social position that has been a measure for a life union.

To marry in direct opposition to parents and friends is hazardous. It should at least be deferred until one knows that the heart is not blinded with emotion; that it is only a romance for a day. To leave father and mother, who have always devoted their love and life to you, to make a new home with one you have known but a short time, with their consent and blessing, means a great deal; but without their benediction, one's life is cast from its moorings. The new love anchor must be very secure that the barque be not stranded in the storms of life. The circumstances must give a strong argument in favor of a union to consider it for a moment in opposition to the better judgement of those whose love was born with your birth. Ordinarily, the history of such unions is the history of broken hearts, of wretched lives, terminated by breaking up of home, separation from children and the tragedy of a divorce court.

It must be a brilliantly happy life that could in any way compensate for the sorrow and anguish given to parents.

Long ago Miss Mulock said: "I believe that a right love teaches people to think of others first and themselves afterwards."

A true love given and received is its own guidance. It opens wide the portals of intuition and intelligence; it combines justice and tenderness and makes its own rules of etiquette and conduct. It is not only a love of fellowship, a love for each other, but being of the nature of kosmic love, it becomes creative and inventive; like unto the sun it gives light and warmth to all within its radius. It is as impossible for this love to be for *two alone*, to be centered and walled into their hearts, as it is impossible for the sun to discriminate or choose those who shall be benefited by its shine.

Each day, life and its possibilities enlarge; thought and speech are freed from restraint, and yet the speech of silence often expresses more than the speech of words; soul answereth to soul, heart to heart; joys are too sweet and too deep for utterance.

In united affection the lover's opportunity for accomplishment can not be estimated. Selfishness is changed to selflessness, and becomes the love that rejoices with those who are glad, and weeps with those who weep. It is a centrifugal force originating at the center, but ever developing and reaching out to a wider circle.

Love is automatic and by its very nature a perpetual motor; two centers in union form an ellipse and by their own inherent power become constructive. The two do not sit looking in each other's eyes, eager for adulation and praise, absorbed in plans for self pleasure; rather the consciousness of the new life within themselves gives still another consciousness, and that is of the world without. Relatives, friends, the weak and unfortunate, all, all are recipient of love's ideals. The more inclusive this love the more truly is it a breath of the Infinite, the more it radiates in peace and power for all.

The grand passion, Love, sets on fire all the stubble of mentality.

CHAPTER VII.

PASSION — WOMAN.

Sexual desire is Love declaring itself through the generative function. Through sex, love expresses duality in all things and is the uniting and combining power revealing strength in the rock or magnet and beauty in the opal or diamond.

Passion is the speech of love. In human life it is inherent and symbolizes the heart-cry for the union of masculine and feminine. It represents fecundating power; born of the soul in consecration, it may germinate soul qualities.

Sexual instinct is the primal motor for reproduction. As evinced in passion, it must be recognized as life crying for life; it is the language of the soul seeking perpetuity. *It is not of the flesh.* Body can not reproduce itself. All processes originate in the deeper or spiritual life. Procreation is not an exception. To speak of sex instinct as lust of flesh traduces that which gives life. Man is begotten of love, not of lust.

Womanliness is sex expression, the grace of passion; beauty, comeliness, loveliness, vivacity, are the outpicturing of a harmonious sexual development.

The attractive woman, the one who awakens love in many hearts, "the queen in society," is the woman who in her form, in every movement, in her conversation, radiates love naturally through passion.

Passion belongs to the well-balanced, well-developed, healthy woman as much as to the healthy man. Passion may be called a gender sense, a feeling, a calling for the opposite sex, and is no more to be repressed and blotted out than the senses of sight and hearing.

Sexual instinct has no analog. It has been compared to the desire for food and drink, but this simply is a demand for sustenance, a want created by the process of nutrition and waste.

The self-consciousness of many girls, the shrinking attitude of concealment, is largely due to repression from and through erroneous thought. Cold virtue freezes out the blossom of womanhood. Thoughts traducing sexual functions cause disease of body, produce inharmony in physical processes that rob woman of beauty. A woman naturally desires motherhood; the maternal instinct is deeply implanted in her life; but by a strange contradiction she often has an abhorrence for sex expression. Almost as deeply engraven as the maternal instinct is the thought of uncleanness attached to the passion that begets life. The act that produces a child is one of carnality. Secretly she holds an abhorrence of men, and erroneously believes that a passionless life is one of virtue. By holding to thoughts of uncleanness regarding sex life, she puts a blighting touch upon all the processes of generation. The one mistake in all nature's wonder-working plans is human procreation!

Plants fructify through a union of pollen and stigma; birds and beasts procreate after a divine plan; but man, surpassing all in reason and intellect, produces in degradation and defilement. The begotten may be all right, but the begetting is an error.

(See Supplement *f.*)

Even a thought of sex life has been considered immodest and un-womanly. Ignorance has been mistaken for innocence and all knowledge of the creative functions has been withheld, while a woman's life has been a demonstration of the *think not* and *do not* philosophy; books of etiquette are full of mannerisms that kill. Do not run, do not laugh, do not talk aloud, do not bow or speak first to a gentleman, and of all things do not whistle. These are born of the idea of repressing natural energies and blighting natural tendencies, of a mistaken idea of virtue.

The nun's vow and the maiden's sexless virtue alike are morbid conditions; they are the outgrowth of the race condemnation of the sex life. In ignorance suppressed passion has been considered woman's virtue; she must be *cold as snow and chaste as ice.*

Women of piety and philosophy have demanded destruction of sexual instinct; that passion, the sin of inheritance, must be stamped out; the desires of the flesh must be killed; the consequence is disease and disorder of the very citadel of life, while many go to their graves childless.

What other result than disorder could be expected when no other quality has been attributed to passion than baseness and animality? The strongest impulse of woman's life is the begetting of offspring, and to condemn the impulse that creates stabs the heart of life; it scars and seams the soul. What burning words can be uttered to make this seem a truth to woman? The history of passion is the history of the race; it is not the product of sentiment and emotion. Stimulating food, some forms of recreation, artificial and luxurious living, may have perverted passion, but more surely abnormal sex expression has come from the impurity and disloyalty of mind toward it. Suppose an individual should begin thinking a mistake had been made in creating a tongue to perform the function of speech. He carries this thought day and night; he strives to make the tongue useless by becoming speechless; the blood vessels and nerves soon set up a rebellion, causing pain and inflammation; then follow cautery and salves, pills and powders; later a cancer or tumor lead to the last act of the drama.

This is only the possible result of one man's notion. Now, suppose that all people carried a similar thought. Tongues are vile, tongues are the fathers and mothers of slander and lies; tongues lead to delusion, and on the whole it is a very great mistake that man is born with this organ of defilement. The power of thought would be evinced in palsied tongues, in tumors, cancers and diseases never before known.

By a like decree of erroneous thought, by a wholesale condemnation of the manifestation of sex energy, the sexual organs have been deprived of natural inherent functions. Many disorders of women arise from this repression, such as mania, hysteria, menstrual ailments, displacements and tumors. We, as a race, have degraded the seed and germinating power of life, have polluted the very fountains of existence, and then stand aghast at the wrecked foundations.

Woman must change her thought. Passion should not be repressed, but rather awakened and redeemed. She must learn to bless sexual life and all that is connected with it; she must reverence that which gives life, that which stands for force, energy, invention and creation; she must search the recesses of her soul and see that this tradition of uncleanness is eradicated — seed, root and branch.

Arouse dormant mental energies; sing songs of exultation; write jubilant poems; engage in deeds of heroism. If duties and labors have been irksome, put love into them; *practice the virtue of joy;* love life and all that it brings; assume an attitude of strength and endurance. It is a rallying of all the forces, amental march to victory.

Observe times of quiet, letting go all strain of mind, relaxing every part of the body. *Still the mind.* Forget self and let the love-life go out for others. Demand harmony and perfection of spirit, soul and body. Words like this have power: " I have strength and life in every part of my body, every fiber vibrates with health, every nerve thrills with the joy of living." Should this attitude of mind be followed by a thrill passion, at first it may be attended by fear, especially if it is a new experience. There is nothing to fear do not dwell upon it, but rather in quiet seek perfect peace, assuming that it is a natural good and that you will be led to use this gift of life in wisdom.

As latent powers develop, the time will come when it will be best to appropriate this creative energy jn the various pursuits of life. One must distinguish between appropriation and repression; one is positive and the other is negative; one is use and the other abuse. One is a command of life's force and energy, the other a sacrifice of them. One includes the virtue of doing, being and mastery, of finding that all faculties have their rightful place, all functions by nature express health and harmony, and the other is the perversion of these faculties.

Remember always to have faith in life, for in the fruition of that faith is health, peace and power. All sexual perversion may be remedied by

RIGHT THINKING.

Thoughts are creative; the control and concentration of thought gives power and direction to all forces. A little earnest, honest practice will prove the statement: " I am not a child of evil; I am not begotten in sin; I am a child of light; all my inheritance is from the union of wisdom and love; truly I am a child of wisdom and love; thus that which gives a sign of this union — the sexual instinct — is good and not evil, is a force of life the strongest and surest evidence I have left in my consciousness; *it is life;* I hold it in my thought as life; I welcome it as the insignia of life."

The response comes; thought harmonizes functions, and that which seemed an enemy becomes a powerful ally; it radiates and thrills the entire body; it stimulates the intellect, awakens the emotions and quickens the perceptions, vivifying both consciousness and intelligence. We must know that life is a stream of love, and through conscious thought may be changed from pollution to a river of purity, and all its force and activity appropriated in a Godlike manner. What this knowledge is to man can not be calculated. Woman, it lifts from serfdom to royalty.

The Christ in woman must redeem man from the sexual fall. As she has been the greatest sufferer from the perversion and degradation of sex life, may she not in clear vision and illumination be the inspired savior that shall lead to purity and power.

48

As sufferings and diseases untold have arisen from sex perversion, so in the light of knowledge, creative life may be trained into power and efficiency. Through reverence of this kosmic force, one restores it to its rightful place and it becomes a potent factor for both physical and spiritual unfoldment. It is life of the God-life, power of the God-power, and as one wills, it becomes a factor in soul illumination. This is the secret of secrets, and if this page does not reveal it, some other page may make known its power and potency.

Every woman is rightful heir to the glory of womanhood; the crown is hers by divine inheritance; according to her claiming, she molds her life into perfection and mastery.

CHAPTER VIII.

PASSION —MAN.

Wherever science goes, the purifying breath of spring pervades and all things are re-created.

Man's consciousness of love enables him to reverence all functions that represent the love nature. Conception and birth, the wonder miracle of life, are the direct results of the attractive power of love, a manifestation of kosmic love. Man's greatest fall has been through the idea of debasement and pollution of the functions that produce life.

In the kindergarten and home the child is reverently taught the laws of generation in flower and plant; he is filled with delight in getting knowledge of the family life of insect and bird; his greatest happiness is in representing in his plays and games the papa and mama bird and their dependent babies. His daily life is filled with the joy of it.

The youth is instructed in wonders of procreation and reproduction in the barnyard and kennel. Neither child nor youth puts any vulgar construction on these physical processes; he sees only the wonder-working law. (See Supplement *f* 2.)

Is it not possible that the same wonder-working in the life of man may be so taught that all the processes of life shall be looked upon with reverence and purity? May not the sex life be so associated with love life that it shall be redeemed from the degradation given to it by false teachings and traditions? The struggles and discords of family and society, as well as diseases of the body, are largely due to the debasing thoughts ordinarily held regarding sex-life. False ideas, wrong conceptions, are the cobra's venom, deadening and destroying physical processes.

Dr. A. J. Ingersoll teaches that *all* diseases are the result of a wrong attitude of mind toward the creative powers. He says: " Disease originates in unregenerated sexual life." He declares that we should not seek to suppress passion, but should desire Christ to redeem it. He more fully explains that we consecrate our intellects, our strength, our being, to the Christ, but that we must make a special consecration of passion. To do this, all condemnation and debasement of the functions and expressions of sex must be removed from the mind. The race thought has produced this uncleanness, and it can be cast out only by a special consecration; one must devote this power, which is life itself, to the best uses of life.

Havelock Ellis, in the introduction to " Psychology of Sex," says: " I regard sex as the central problem of life. The question of sex stands before the coming generation as the chief problem for solution. Sex lies at the root of life and we can never learn to reverence life until we know how to understand sex."

What Dr. Ingersoll teaches as a religion remains to be demonstrated philosophically and scientifically. In the truth and verities of life, religion and science clasp hands. Religion sees by faith and lives the life; science, through analysis and reason, proves the truth and possibility of that life. Religion teaches one to give back to God what came from God, to consecrate to God's work the force that begets and perpetuates life. Science demonstrates that back of all expression of life is a principle, an energy unrevealed by microscope or scalpel, known as mind or kosmic force.

The material universe exists because there is a cause for existence. Reason and analogy teaches that nothing is produced without a producer. The *esse* of life is being, while existence, *existo,* is a coming out of — is the expression of being — it is being in activity. Spirit becomes active in and through its creations. Man in his own work illustrates this: an inventor is the cause of an invention. The invention may be dormant a long time in his mind, but by and through activity of thought it becomes a machine, an invention.

So the Spirit, the God-power of the world, through activity, through a process of law, manifests in creations. In Man's ability to become conscious of this *all* power, *all* intelligence is his source of redemption. He may name it what he pleases; as we have before said it may be the Noumena of Kant, the Infinite I of Fichte, the Idea of Hegel, or the Christ of Christians. His knowledge of his own spiritual life and the unity of that life with kosmic or deific force gives to him renewed power. This unity is rightly named a new birth; in short, it is conversion; it gives to man new perceptions, new ideals, new meanings in all things. This awakening, redeeming power is in no way more apparent than in the sexual life. As this has been dragged to deepest degradation, so in its rightful place as the most potent God-force, it becomes man's most active, most powerful and most reliable source of his energies and activities.

All man's functions and faculties, all emotions and desires, are good. Nothing is intrinsically bad; an evil tendency is a perverted faculty. *A weed is a plant out of place.* The grass that makes the velvet lawn so delightful to the eye becomes a weed in a bed of roses; the morning-glory, so delicate in color, so prolific in bloom, is a weed in a cornfield; so of the man who walketh in paths of destruction, in whom seemeth no good, his errors are perverted faculties; the morning-glories are a tangle in his cornfield, and the rootlets of the shining grass blades are distorting the rose (or love) life of his nature.

The province of the LOVER'S WORLD is to teach the transformation or regeneration of the sexual life. Creative energy is to be used, not abused. Passion is good, not evil; it is the insignia of life, of the ability to create. In realization of love, the essence or the God-life in sexual functions, we control and generate power to do and to be.

Man speaks of falling when a demand comes for sexual expression.

What has he fallen from? What into? Does God fall when he brings forth? Behold the waving corn! Does it fall when the pollen fertilizes seed? Is it not God-like to create? Does only man sin when impelled by creative force?

Man may glorify passion and the creative act more than beast, bird or flower. By reason of his intellect he may appropriate and transmute it. But how ?

Never by traducing in thought or word the miracle of miracles that brings forth life. The creative act in the mind of man must be redeemed from all uncleanness, all hint of any degradation attending it.

Repression and asceticism are born of the stigma that man has put upon his creative powers. In his fullest conversion there is not only appropriation of this life-given impulse, but he will reorganize his right to the joy it brings. It will not be joy of " eating stolen fruit," but the pleasure of inherent right.

The bird trills his song as an expression of the joys of fecundation; man, too, in the knowledge of a renewed sexual life, may rejoice in its activity; as he was blind, now he sees; as he stumbled in the shadow, now he walks glorified in the sunlight. The very forces that to him were evil become the light to lead the way.

In athletics he may have been captain and victor; he may have followed a regime of diet and hygiene, and sincerely desire the life of the highest morality; he may have experienced deep religious conviction and consecration, and yet after all this he is confronted with what seems to him a demon, and not unlikely settles into the world's teaching of " physical necessity." It is a continual warfare and the heart's desire is not followed by fruition. There is power in passion, and it is man's privilege to put himself in possession of this power. Through knowledge of spiritual law, through science of life, one possesses the key to Sexual Mastery.

He gains great help by knowing that all of God's works are of God; but added to this, science is now proving that every one may, through special training, control passion; he may be master and director of this vital energy. This is through the knowledge that a universal law in nature is at man's command — a law or principle that may become effective through application and experience; this is the law of

ACTIVITY AND REPOSE.

All nature is made up of opposites, animation and inertia, the inner and outer, the positive and negative; two forces, the centripetal and centrifugal, the uniting and dividing, a letting go and taking hold; the impelling and pushing of the vernal bud and the dropping of the decayed leaf; the fulness and activity of day following the rest and quiet of night; the summer's resplendent vegetation on the footsteps of the icy silence of winter; insects and animals illustrate the life of action and repose — the busy, hum of bees in sunny days and the indolent life in the hive of stored treasure, the activity and alertness of beasts against lethargy and hibernation.

All man's forces may be controlled and perfected through knowing this law of opposites. Creative energy thus becomes subject to his command, and passion is converted into power. It is by a conscious

WILLING AND LETTING.

One wills not to will; he loses his life that he may gain it. The giving-up is followed by mastery. Intellectually, consciously, he loosens the rootlets of thought; he obliterates them; the mind becomes the fallow ground, freed from stubble and weeds, for the impelling, generating power of kosmic love and life. Apparently soul is united to or knows deific principle; this union is soul fecundation; a new birth and quickening follow.

This control, the mastery of passion, may be made effective at any time and in any situation. It is a realization in the soul-silence of the active power of kosmic force and love, a transformation of creative energy into soul activities.

That which called through the physical is answered from whence it came, in the spiritual. It is answered through an application of law; a step is gained in the knowledge of forces and how to use them. By watchfulness, persistence, by holding the right attitude of thought, by repetition of formulas [see footnote 2] that build and create— the. victory is won. The soul is full of peace, but it is the peace of power; rest transformed to activity. " The days of struggle are over; he blooms like a flower; he bears fruit like a tree. God is in him and all the world is with him."

It is not the annihilation of passion, the killing out of desire — a crucifixion — it is rather a redemption and consecration. In the heart lust has been changed to love, and a new life is begotten, a life full of promise and fertility.[2]

With this knowledge man holds the secret of health and longevity in his hand. New energy permeates every cell; all processes become adjusted to a natural order and the transfusion of sex energy becomes the elixir of health.

Power through repose has been taught and practiced by many professors of physical culture, but if they know that the mastery of the sexual life accomplishes the greater results, they have not so declared it. They have been silent regarding this important factor in physical development.

Every man and every woman can learn through controlled thought to harness this natural, universal energy, and from being a thorn in the flesh a cause of disease and disorder — it can be made a most potent force for life and power.

Passion and its noble strong seed seek a rich, holy family life, that builds a nation that is the basis of a nation's honor and bringer of a nation's brotherhood, and protests against the blasphemies of immorality.

---

2 See chapter on Appropriation and Mastery.

CHAPTER IX.

MARRIAGE.

- Love comes by fulfilled conditions rather than by commands obeyed.

Marriage is the heart's acknowledgment of a union between one man and one woman. It is kosmic Jove vitalized and made consciously intelligent by ideal or romantic love; the product is *conjugal love,* a veritable union of spirit, soul and body.

One purpose, one accord! Surely, surely the twain are one! Confidence and trust beget rest and peace; wishes are fulfilled, desires attained, hopes realized.

Finck may be right in saying that romantic love is impossible after marriage; the relation of romantic love to conjugal love is as a dream to reality.

Romantic love, through emotion, joy, feeling, awakens kosmic love and blends with this, effecting a new product which partakes of the characteristics of both, still unlike either. This is conjugal love.

Conjugal love is rest, is satisfaction; it is the deep, still river after it has passed the foaming rapids and the swirling whirlpool, and yet it is not the stillness of inaction; efficiency and success follow the union of forces.

The marriage ceremony is a public acknowledgment of a union of hearts, a union already established. It is a ceremony of inauguration, an adjustment to legal enactments that are the outgrowth of usages and wise thought. This ceremony, whether one of royal pomp or performed in curate's study, is a simple symbol representing the soul speech of two already united.

The form of marriage is man-made; its intent is to protect nature in her plan; in a way it is a free restraint, a chosen guardianship, the united pair becoming the wards of authority and society. This authority and guardianship can not well be annulled or defied until selfishness in the human heart is replaced with love, until man manifests the inherent divinity of his nature.

The true inner marriage, the heart's acknowledgment of a union, is a sacrament; the outer marriage, the form and ceremony, is a contract. Any number of rings, church rites or state certificates can never add to or take from the heart sacrament. These are simply a language to tell relatives, society and all of soul nuptials, and the response of those bidden to the feast of rejoicing is significant of social unity.

The natural kosmic attraction between male and female is the inherent propelling force for united lives. It is as strong as life itself. Conjugal union is nature's plan for perpetuity.

In marriage, as in all phases of life, experiences are so varied, circumstances are so widely different, the silken skein of love that united hearts become so knotted and tangled that sometimes it is difficult to find the end that will unravel the intricate mass.

We must realize that it is a silken cord. Silk symbolizes fineness, durability, strength and life, and these qualities are its saving grace. The tangles are error in conduct, the result of ignorance, the mixing of inharmonious colors; the cord is silken, however, and through patience, little by little, the tangles may be straightened. The love that is the life of the cord must show the way.

In marriage, love must be altruistic; never seeking self pleasure only, ever willing to give and receive. There are no wills demanding submissions, no male or female rights imposing obligations, no physical necessities demanding fulfillment, for together at the very altar of consecration they have found the *One* absolute being of their existence. The God-love of their souls is the unchanging center of united lives.

Every physical union must be a realization of the beauty, power and radiance of this divine center; it is a renewed consecration and at the same time a creation. In perfect consummations local sensations become secondary, and the joy of propagation is in spirit only. This happiness in its fulness may not be a sudden attainment. It may require time and patience for fulfilment of the law. It is not easy to meet all individual demands. The greatest difficulty is that there are two parties in the case, and oftentimes one seeks knowledge and the other scorns it.

The strong urgency of the sexual act has seemed to grow with civilization. Returning to the simplicity of nature, with the knowledge of life that religion and science bring us, may we not hope to develop mastery and control of this as of every other function? (See Supplement *g.*)

This mastery and control will arise from recognizing the source and use of sexual activity. In the deepest recesses of the soul of both husband and wife, must be found no revolt against the processes that produce life. Love's consummation in marriage should be attended with pleasure. Life is a joy; to beget life is a divine mission; to procreate either physical or spiritual children is the impulse of inherent forces and should give enjoyment.

One gratifies the eye or the ear; one views a fine landscape or painting for pure sensuous delight. One listens to music for personal gratification only; if one receives from it an illumination, a spiritual uplift, so much the better — that is gain; if the sense of sight, hearing or taste may be gratified, why may not the experiencing personal pleasure in the union of soul to soul, heart to heart in sexual union be considered equally natural and justifiable?

One views a picture that stirs the heights and depths of the soul with thrills of happiness — self-happiness. A controlled union can not be as much for self as the enjoyment of a poem or picture.

In this consummation real, deep pleasure is impossible without altruism — a thought of one for the other. Inherent in this embrace is the God-given power to grow, to reach out for more joy and more power.

Sex passion has no likeness, no exact equivalent in any other human experience. Its universality, its object and its cause all point to a high office, viz.: creation. What more lofty or dignified, what greater privilege than to be a creator! To give life of body or life of spirit is man's greatest gift; and why should it not be a joy, a self joy? When the romantic love of courtship has passed to the conjugal love of marriage, it should be a joy to symbolize that love.

Love and confidence have long since banished fear. Neither husband nor wife seeks to rule the other; there was no bill of sale with the marriage certificate; knowing that " God's plans like lilies pure and white unfold," they rest in the soul embrace, accentuating the confidence of courtship days. The sweet joy thrilling and surging the deepest life may not demand or reach bodily expression, but it is water and dew to the stirrings of the soul, a sufficient promise that aloneness shall be nevermore. (See Supplement *h.*)

In the relation of wife, new phases of the sexual functions are presented. The maternal in her soul seeks expression, answering joyfully to the paternal in her husband. She knows that in the new relation nothing is demanded but the outcome of natural law, and that nature is a kindly protector, originating no methods of procedure that are not pleasant and practicable. Already she has banished from her mind the idea that ignorance is innocence and that repression is virtue. She knows that passion is a symbol of creative energy, is a sign of one's copartnership with God in reproduction.

To listen to the voice of passion, to have it under control, to experience its pleasures, to appropriate to legitimate uses, are lessons the wise woman newly wedded seeks to know.

Love lures and listens for the joy of begetting, and souls attuned to infinite harmonies elect the begetting. If a child, its soul may have been long nurtured and fostered in soul embrace before physical procreation takes place, before there is right adjustment for conception. If the begetting is on other planes for the many purposes of life, the power of controlled sexual energy is especially apparent. This united energy may be an impelling force in any vocation that requires invention and creation. Together male and female may thus create more effectively. This is accomplished by mutual conservation and appropriation. A transmutation of love's forces is more easily accomplished by man and wife together than by either alone. The alchemy of nature requires duality; the masculine and feminine are the hydrogen and oxygen of human life; the wisdom and love fulfilling the law of parentage; the fatherhood and motherhood not only of the race, but of all creations.

Controlled parenthood is accomplished through the spiritual forces of life, through the knowledge that mind is master and that all functions are subject to mind control. " It is the spirit that quickeneth, the flesh profiteth nothing." By this very quickening of the spirit the flesh becomes redeemed, redeemed from impurity, inharmony and all forms of disease. There is no apartness to spirit and matter. The knowledge that that which gives life to the body, which begets and operates in all and through all, is constant and eternal, thrilling and vivifying all processes, puts new phases on all experiences.

CONSUMMATIONS

or fulfillment of kosmic love in sex union must be impelled from the spiritual or God-life of man. *Bodily union is only symbolic.*

Man has so long bowed at the shrine of materialism that he is often blind to the hidden forces and laws operating in and through the physical. He must remember that there is an impelling, compelling cause back of every effect. All products have a producer; all creations a creator.

In marriage each love consummation must be a renewed realization of the union of souls. Every sexual act should be consciously traced to the spiritual life, and each time it should be a conservation of the brightest and best in united lives.

A soul union satisfies, and all means should be sought that tend to this true consummation.

Religious people have helps in this direction; they are accustomed to consecrating their intellects, their energies, their talents, indeed every faculty to holy purposes. They need also a special consecration of the life that begets life. People who have had no particular religious training usually understand that there is in their nature an intelligence that transcends their own consciousness. If they have never proven the ability to demand aid of this intelligence they may get prompt and satisfactory proof through sexual experience.

Seek perfect understanding; confidence and faith will lead to full expression. Have no secrets. Oftentimes married people carry into their united lives the same secrecy that has been their custom in courtship, each suffering from the degrading thought that pollutes the very fountain of their happiness. The priestly ceremony condones the act, which, in thought, is still held as base and low. The priest of the future, in administering the holy bans of wedlock, will also add a benediction to the sexual life that is the natural sequence of marriage; it will be something as follows.

" Your united life is of the spirit; it is prompted and instigated by love, its derivation is from the source of all love, its expression and symbolism must always represent love. By the law of love I pronounce a benediction upon every function of your life, knowing that it is the natural law of life; love only reigns." (See Supplement *i*.)

So now if you may not have had this benediction you must seek it, not from priest or prelate, but from and through your own intelligence. Whatever your conception of God is you must put the seal of that God upon passion. Replace the ban of condemnation by the blessing of consecration. You must know that the energy that throbs and thrills with a desire to create, is as much God-given as the brain that sends forth thought, or the heart that has holy emotions.

Passion is the insignia of life — of life that begets life and is from the source of all life. It is the kosmic consciousness of man seeking to know the kosmic consciousness of woman. It is creative energy demanding expression. Through knowledge and conscious willing husband and wife may determine the creation. It is in your power to choose to beget a child, a choice that brings its blessing; to choose to create a work of art, to create harmonious conditions in home or society, to create theories of life, of philosophy, or ideals of patriotism. Elect the creation and work for it; think, read and commune upon it; let it be the day and night dream. In close physical embrace, through thought and word unitedly loosen all tension of nerves and muscles; demand the serenity of inaction. Abstract the mind from every part of the body, and seek the deep, deep quiet of the inner life, of yielding your own feelings, your own willing, your own ends and aims. In this quiet and stillness the power of the kosmic intelligence permeates every fiber; then in this calm repose, consciously will that there shall be a procreation of the elected desire. In time local sensations subside naturally, if not unconsciously, and the thrill of ecstasy is in and through body and soul accompanied by the glow of health, the clear vision, the divine consciousness of all life — a blessed holy union.

If a child is to be begotten, the union will be of shorter duration, and in a final ecstatic orgasm the secretions of male and female blend in the wonder of creation; the sperm has been attracted to germ, life to life, and the miracle of a new life is consummated.

Conjugal love demands perfect adjustment, equal giving and receiving. Man is unwilling to indulge in passing gratification that is borne with torture and disgust by the one he loves. The wife no longer imagines she is contributing to her husband's happiness by yielding to an unwelcome embrace. Marriage certificates, wedding rings and ceremonies can not justify it, such an embrace can be called by no milder name than prostitution. (See Supplement *j*.)

LIBERTY AND LAW.

Man is father and creator, he is the progenitor. Woman is mother inceptor; she conceives, broods and nourishes the fructified seed; she nourishes with bodily life and with love. The maternal in woman answers to the paternal in man. Man is ever ready to procreate; woman has periods favorable to conception. In the normal woman, passion indicating the ability to conceive, is as urgent and strong as in man, but ordinarily it is less frequent.

A common sex inversion is want of passion, lack of response on the part of the wife. Irrational as it may seem this is to her a virtue. In times past, when man assumed authority in wedlock and woman submitted, this condition was not heeded; the sex relation was endured by her as a matter of course. Coldness and indifference were no hindrance to the license marriage gave to man's passion.

Innately and inherently woman desires freedom to function as a mother; she prefers to choose important offices; pleasures when compelled are distasteful. Although maternal desires are inherent and instinctive, yet forced maternity is repugnant. Children conceived under adverse conditions are unwelcome. Most women desire motherhood, but with ordinary intelligence they desire to control conditions for motherhood. The usual practice in sexual relations deprives women of any voice in this vital matter. In large families how often it is that none come of design. Children of a chance procreation are the rule.

As the little ones were being dismissed from a school, a philosopher said to a friend, " How many of these eight hundred children do you suppose are accidents?" " Nine out of ten," was the reply. Would he have erred if he had said ninety-nine out of one hundred? The mothers had had no freedom, no voice in their conception. They were not the children of liberty and law; they were begotten in fear, which dwarfs and paralyzes natural instincts, while it stabs at the heart of motherhood.

FALSE IDEAS

We foster and applaud the evidence of the Maternal in a little child, in her play-life with her dolls, but as she approaches womanhood we repress every desire for knowledge of sex life, and plainly leave the inference that nature made a mistake in implanting the natural impulse that is a sign of maternal power. Virtue thus becomes to her a stultification of nature's processes; a killing out of the passion that clamors for a new life.

After years and years of this false training it is no wonder that woman receives even the one dearest to her heart with shrinking and fear. To her the love-embrace shatters standards of morality; these standards, false as they are, have bolted the door against the inherent maternal instinct.

THE OVERCOMING.

Knowledge and patient love can overcome .all inertia and awaken natural impulses.

First bless in the husband the sign of creative energy. Totally erase from your mind any teaching or thought you have had of vulgarity. Remember what I am always glad to repeat, that passion is an evidence of the life that begets life; it is man's surest and closest relation to divine energy — an evidence of his relationship to God-life. So in your mind consecrate and bless this in your husband.

In your daily companionship you rejoice in his manliness, his strength, his tenderness and love; you have for months, perhaps years, lived in the close association of lovers, and now comes the fuller, more complete happiness, for not only are your many interests united, but the one symbol of kosmogenic law and love is yours by right. The joy of blessing and consecration to divine uses, crowds out all fear that has been implanted by ignorance, all traditions of uncleanness, and in the fulness of this joy, natural impulses respond to the controlled impulses of the conjugal embrace. It is love's awakening to a rightful inheritance. It expresses the law of

64

reciprocity and makes it possible, through special appointments and thoughtful preparation, to consecrate the volcanic flame that in man has burned fitfully and irregularly, and in woman has been smothered and perverted. As one correspondent says:

This passion which God has made strongest and upon which he has built the family and the social order, is also the nexus of spirit, soul and body. Every power, every emotion, every resource of the volitional life, the intellectual and spiritual, blend with every thrilling nerve of the physical life in controlled union.

This awakening and consecration has an unrevealed meaning. It gives us a prophecy of progeny that must surpass, in intellect and illumination, even the most brilliant of to-day. It betokens to the man and woman a knowledge of innate powers that may be directed into channels of usefulness or artistic creations.

The poet will sing songs, the artist paint pictures, the orator and divine will build the plastic language in an eloquence that shall call forth a satisfactory response from hungry seeking souls.

Who is the poet whom love has made strong, *strong*, STRONG with all strength? Go shout on the winds that the world is alive, that the Arisen One controls it.

This Arisen One is infinite love discovered in the heart of man. It is the way, the truth and life for him who seeks it. It stills the troubled waters, it calms the rebellious thoughts, it sings songs of joy and always finds the keynote of harmony. The Arisen One is the love power in every heart; to realize it and to have the joyful use of it, is the privilege of every individual in every conceivable relation.

The sexual life is largely the theme in this work because this is more perverted and misunderstood than any other phase of life. But in this, as in all others, the law of love straightens the tangles. It opens the prison door of error and becomes the light to illumine obscure paths. Love is the fire that consumes ignorance, jealousy, hatred and malice. Love sets in motion the vibration of kindliness, tenderness and steadfastness.

The vitalizing, redeeming power of love is effectual in matrimonial life; it is a divine ministration for all inharmony. The love life within manifests in all that makes for peace and power; it is the one potent healing that never fails. It adjusts differences, it reconciles inequalities, it redeems creative impulses, it sanctifies the sex life.

LOVE BUILDS A SYMPHONY OF HARMONY.

In the heart it bursts forth a hallelujah chorus that reaches and strikes a note in every other heart

Love discovers the keynote and the song of life is sung without one discordant note, one jarring tone.

CHAPTER X.

APPROPRIATION AND MASTERY.

By conscious willing desire manifests divinely.

Many writers on sexual science give continence, save for procreation, as the law of life, the end to be gained in sexual relationship; usually they fail to point the means of attainment.

Cowan, Kellogg, Shepherd, Newton and others, teach this theory of continence. They contend eloquently for wiser parenthood, for better children and for conservation; they take you into the domain of stock-raising and animal-breeding, and draw strong inferences for the conduct of human life. They all are, however, far from making it plain how man shall become this perfect animal, and fail to give a method of procedure in following this law of higher breeding.

Works for the young are filled with this idea of continence sustained with the recital of abuses and excesses, the many shoals to be avoided, but they do not make it clear what is to be done to steer the life barque safely in the maelstrom of human passion.

The oriental ascetic and religious recluse counsel the killing out of passion, the complete eradication of what they are pleased to call animal desire. They constantly refer to sexual instinct as the " lower nature," the " lusts of the flesh," " brute passion," " animal life," and are satisfied in forcing vows of chastity and pledges of abstinence from marriage. Do they give a systematic training or scientific treatment for the secret habits, repressed desires, burning passion, which prevail largely among themselves? Do their lives prove that mastery is common among them?

Many religious teachers and philosophers believe that if one studies and searches for the higher life, if he is in tune with the Infinite, if he has spiritual consciousness, the common needs of life and all experiences are in a way self governed; all processes and functions become under control through religion.

It is also customary to advise those who have great evidences of creative energy to divert the mind into active channels, to appropriate this energy in physical exercise or intellectual pursuits. It is supposed that the college student who is a great athlete, and who is able to concentrate upon his studies, is, in a way; using vital force otherwise exhibited in passion.

It may be true that one who evinces great energy in all athletic pursuits, who in university, professional and business life, is employing and concentrating all his faculties, is at the same time the one who most frequently experiences an excess of sexual energy. In some way his training has been at fault. He lacks knowledge. If he desires to master passion, to utilize it as the creative power, or " to kill it out," has there been any systematic method devised or taught for that purpose? Do universities with their rich and varied curricula, do medical colleges with all their research and scientific acumen, include teaching that gives this knowledge? Continence, save for procreation, becomes a byword, unless man has learned the law of transmutation, the alchemy of life that converts the best and sweetest into lofty aims and noble pursuits.

Froebel in his philosophy and theory of education teaches the inherent divinity or God-likeness of the child. He says: " The destiny of man, as a child of God and of nature, is to represent in harmony and unison the spirit of God and nature, the natural and divine, the terrestrial and the celestial, the finite and the Infinite."

Over and over again he insists that the child is not born in sin, but is inherently perfect, and that all training is for the purpose of bringing out this perfection. Nor does he leave this to theory and philosophy. He proceeds to formulate a system of education that shall bring forth this perfection, that shall guide and lead the child to know the unity of all things and his own relation to them.

So with the mature man; he requires training and wise leading from erroneous thinking to thoughts and deeds of righteousness. More especially in his sexual life he must be given the law, and the method of establishing that law in himself, of making it effective in mastery and self control.

Any philosophy or religion that convinces man of spiritual supremacy, that develops him through the heart as well as the intellect, that sees the divine life in all of nature's manifestations, must give an impetus to right thinking and right living.

Through consciousness of the spiritual forces of life, man can affect all bodily activities. There is a life that is not of the body, a kosmogenic force that shows forth in intelligence, and man through his intellect may utilize this force and control physical functions.

To a certain extent every organ of the body is affected by conscious willing. Respiration and inspiration may be increased or decreased through thought power. The organs of depuration are accelerated or weakened by emotion. The absorbents and cells are subject to the stimulating or depressing effect of the mind. Just as surely and certainly the mind may control the activity of creative energy. Systematic thought and training will certainly be rewarded.

The tradition of defilement and debasement connected with manifestations of sex must be removed. The thought of love and power given to sex energy imbues it with new life, with an impelling force that bears fruit in every field of action. This can not be said too often or engraven too deeply upon one's consciousness.

Sex expression is not a demon to be fought and conquered. It is not annihilation and crucifixion that is sought, but redemption and consecration.

Mastery is not negative, is not killing out; it is rather utilizing the greatest force of man's nature — it is obedient service under the law of love.

A visitor at Niagara Falls is awed by the turbulence of the waters in the rapids above the Falls. The foaming, seething mass tosses and tumbles and roars, representing the spirit of unrest, the cry of the human heart battling with error, with disease and passion.

The waters, still foaming and seething, pass over the rocky ledge, tumbling and roaring. Falling among the rocks, there is a wail of lost power, a rebound from destruction, then on and on the waters move swiftly — almost miraculously in a short distance gliding into passivity. What has become of the force, the power, the energy? Lost, lost in negation, worn out in the whirlpool of useless contest, of mighty battling of forces.

Retrace your steps. Here are vast towers and buildings from which is heard the hum of machinery. The rushing flood turned from its natural course is poured deep down upon the great wheels that put in motion the whirring dynamos; every mechanical device, complete in finish and adaptation, works under a perfect law. The impetuous force of the Niagara is utilized and converted into electricity.

Through this subtle, unseen agent, whose power is only known by its results, the belts, hammers and shafts of factories are propelled; every known labor is lightened, and wonder of wonders, miracle of miracles, surrounding cities are illuminated and become an Arabian Night's enchantment.

Niagara, the wonder of the world, is cribbed, curbed and harnessed to lessen the burdens of laborer and artisan, and to dispel the darkness; it becomes a searchlight for remote corners and deep caverns.

Shall not man's genius and power of invention become equally effective in reclaiming and appropriating the Niagara forces of his own nature? Shall passion be allowed to pour over the rocks into the whirlpool of torture, spending itself in the vagaries of vice and lust? No, no! this great kosmogenic force may become the renewal of all life, may give power to every faculty. As the mechanic transforms the force of Niagara, so men and women in knowledge of the law of love, can convert passion into power and efficiency. Passion born of love, guided by love, trained to all of love's behests, becomes the elixir of youth, the germ and sperm of immortality.

TRANSMUTATION.

There are various helps to the transmutation of sex energy — to self mastery. Many, through reason and will, through a life of activity, through special consecrations control the natural forces.

Special laws, founded upon nature's ever-present and potent principle of *activity* and *repose,* govern man's life and he may come into obedience to them; transmutation of sex energy is accomplished by adhering to the following formula: when passion makes its demand, assume any position that secures perfect relaxation. The sitting posture is preferable to reclining; there must be no restraint upon any part of the body; the chair should be straight in the back so the shoulders rest naturally and easily; drop the hands and arms to the side; rest the feet squarely on the floor; *drop* the *chin forward on the breast,* and give up all control of the body (see Supplement *k*). Let go; knees, feet, toes, arms, hands, and finger-tips must become relaxed; eyelids, mouth, indeed every part of the body must let go; throat, jaws and stomach may be last to yield, but repeat to yourself " I give up, I give up."

Breathe quietly and slowly. The expiration is less than the inspiration, indeed, the breath is nearly suspended. Remain in this state of repose fifteen to twenty minutes. When a perfect state of relaxation is secured, quietly will in the inner consciousness that the sexual life shall be appropriated to a renewal of all forces; it obeys the behest; it thrills the nerves and throbs the pulse and awakens energy in every part of the body. You arise buoyant, vigorous and rejuvenated. You have become master of your own life through an alchemic process, a transmutation of creative energy. The wonder is that all local excitation and demand have vanished. At first one should be punctual at a certain time each day, but by a little practice this can be done in any time or place; you will to let go and then you will that the natural inherent creative energy shall wheel into line and serve you. You have harnessed the kosmic force of your life and through systematic thought it obeys you on every occasion. What thus seems simple in practice, is a definite following of law important in results; it is the key to mastery and a revelation of power.

It is a man's privilege to elect what he shall create. He may will through reason and intelligence to appropriate these tremendous forces, surging and throbbing through his being, to high and holy uses.

Set your shoulder joyously to the wheel and make all forces serve you. Over and over demand that creative energy shall be transmuted to build character, to bring health, to produce harmony, to cause effectiveness, to overcome difficulties. Fearlessness and bravery are your adjuvants.

Let the shining light into the soul, that life and all its natural operations are good, and that you are the master of the forces that underlie all functions and processes. Sexual continence may become the source of power.

Enter into the life which is eternal, pass through the door of love out into the great open of deliverance.

IN MARRIED LIFE

sexual control may be more easily attained, more fully realized, and its fulfillment more abundant in every direction than in celibacy. This is according to the law of agreement — strength in union.

Married men and women will find appropriation and mastery through —

Appointments,
Agreement,
Trust and confidence,
A spirit of self control,
Blessing and consecration.

An *appointed time* for love's consummation is an aid to natural fulfillment. The happiest occasions of life are those usually planned for in detail. A journey, a summer's outing, a visit to opera or theater, the result in pleasure and profit is largely according to thoughtfulness and preparation. Even to read a book satisfactorily one secures seclusion and suitable environment.

The occasions are rare when one hears a great orator, listens to a grand concert, or climbs mountain peaks. To these occasions he gives due and thoughtful preparation. He dwells upon the anticipated pleasure. So in conjugal consummations, in life's holiest communion, a day should be set apart for it and the occasion dignified as a sacrament.

For days previous, the two as lovers in altruistic thoughts and deeds, in walks and rides, in enjoyment of music and poetry, in the study of philosophy, in religious unity and fellowship, prepare to make the sexual union one of consecration. At the appointed hour body and soul are cleansed; the physical union is an acknowledgment of the union of spirit; the deep quiet joy in the soul's union is ineffable and transcendant, superseding and supplanting any local thrill or pleasure. (See Supplement *l*.)

While every couple may not have the leisure to regulate their lives on this plan, yet through the same thoughtfulness that is given to most every-day matters, this appointment between two can be made and held as an obligation, as they would hold any engagement for business or pleasure. Shall it be once a week, once a month, once in three months ? Between yourselves come to a certain decision and abide by it. This seems a simple and perhaps an arbitrary matter, but many couples have been saved from misery and unhappiness by following this plan. A regular habit is formed and easy adjustment follows.

The *law of agreement* is an aid to *accomplishment.* The true union is one in which love is the force and spiritual life the law, yet many have attained sexual control without either; still there must be the law of agreement, an understanding by which the two abide. (See Supplement *m.*)

This agreement should include the appointed hour, the method of procedure and the object to be attained.

When two are united on any special plan or object, attainment of that object is more certain. One is a complement of the other; one intuitive, impulsive, swift to come to conclusions; the other logical, working out details and calculating results. It is the masculine and feminine operating under law. In marriage this natural duality has a special opportunity for expression. There must, however, be an alliance of purpose, a perfect agreement.

Trust and confidence must be practiced in thought, speech and action. Lives are already united in purpose; business, pleasures, studies, ambitions and aspirations are mutual and subjects of daily counsel.

The sexual life should be stripped of all secrecy; its laws, its manifestations, its relation to other pleasures of life should receive due attention. In this trust and confidence creative energy will find a natural expression. Out of this life of *agreement* comes naturally and sweetly the desire for offspring. Together there will be plans to beget physical children, children who shall be endowed with a worthy inheritance.

The maternal and paternal, the masculine and feminine seek expression in welcome children, children of light and knowledge.

This natural inherent instinct for reproduction will be satisfied in a rational manner, children will be begotten that will exemplify the parents' desires, and thoughtful preparation for them. The begetting may also be to meet other demands, to fulfill aspirations, to create health and strength, to compose a poem or paint a picture. The two together hold the key that unlocks life's mysteries.

The spirit of self-control is of all the most important. As always lofty desires and holy purposes should rule one's life, so in this most intimate relation this blending of souls in and through body, should be governed by the highest and best at command. Husband and wife together as one should, in their innermost natures, seek for all which tends to best results — desires for truth and aspirations for development.

There must be no prostitution of life's forces.

The spirit of self control is desire or aspiration consciously directed. It is the impelling force, the incentive to action; it is born of intuition or consciousness combined with will and intention; it conserves and directs processes; it transforms the natural to the spiritual.

The means and methods are at one's command. Man, the animal, has power corresponding to all created things; but as man, through his consciousness, he has also knowledge. This knowledge gives him eyes to see and ears to hear that which has been hidden.

It is a realization of the spirit of all power, the force of all force. Man becomes related to kosmic life consciously as well as unconsciously; head and heart combine to discover and develop all forces.

Out of the innermost soul seeking and demanding the best, comes fulfillment. Through realization of the spirit of self control man becomes what he wills to be.

In marriage one is the loving and considerate companion asking and giving according to needs. Every thought, every word, every act is illumined, is an intelligent cooperation with infinite life; most of all, the ever-present creative energy is held in the double leash of love and wisdom to serve and to obey.

One should bless and consecrate passion because it is the insignia of life that creates; some great souls through this blessing and consecration may at once burst the walls of bondage. They get the revelation of power in a flash, and as though born into a new life; all that has seemed low and'carnal becomes transfigured, and in the hour of ecstasy body yields to spirit, matter to mind. Others more slowly work all problems by formula, analyze and reason, and are slow to experience a heart consecration, an exultation of faith.

The wife's love blesses this evidence of power in her husband; it is to her no more a blot and blur upon his manhood. The husband with patience bom of strength, with love guided by wisdom, awaits the natural expression of that which may have been repressed. Through him she develops courage, bravery and confidence; gradually the true life awakens in her, and together they triumph over the traditions.

To know the law and to practice it in transmutation, makes it possible for man and woman at all times to hold the rein of power. In conjugal union the blessing acknowledges the source of passion, the process of obedience to the law of rest and activity trains it into service; the silencing of all contending thought, the releasing of conflicting ideas, leaves the channels free for the influx of kosmic forces, divine love and intelligence.

In all processes of nature there is this action and reaction, an ebb and flow, a giving up to take hold, the swing of the axe to cleave the wood; so man silences thought, stills intellectual processes, that the perfect life, the force that represents the origin of life, may give a new impulse to thought forms.

This exercise of *willing* and *letting* is practiced successfully by individuals, the man or woman alone. In married life the duality of forces, the mingling of masculine and feminine in soul relation, gives an increase of power. The two of one accord have all the coherence and consistency of union. It is the single cord doubled, the two halves united, the negative and positive in a magnet.

In sexual expression that which made special demands becomes diffused, pervading every fiber, every cell. Physical strength is augmented, mental processes vivified, while new truths are revealed. A renewed life and soul ecstasy follow. By a simple natural process creative energy is turned into new channels.

The blindly plodding man united to an intuitive responsive woman, may experience moments of awakening and desire appropriation of sex-life to special purposes. The two, unite reason and logic with perception and insight. They blend the strong colors with soft tones. The unanswered logic and unanswering reason become the minor tone accompanying the penetrating, perceiving refrain, the bass and soprano moving in strength of harmony. This is transmutation of creative life that may become a perfect and continuous ebb and flow, giving health of body, activity of intellect and spiritual enlightenment.

A blessing and consecration of his faculties enables man to use them in an orderly manner. Love for a woman becomes unselfish and blossoms into a holy relation; desire for money ceases to be greed, but obeys the law of demand and supply; emotions become great levers for opening soul perceptions, while feelings dip deep into hidden recesses and reveal the unknown; desire becomes the magician's wand that creates harmonies from discordant notes; ambition converts the machinery of business and politics into parliaments of peace and power.

Creative energy being the most vigorous, and as it were the citadel and insignia of life, in its transformation to a thoughtful purpose gives the fullest evidence of mastery. It is a veritable conversion of all that has seemed debasing and defiling into all that builds character and glorifies life. Jealousy, hatred, condemnation, sarcasm, all inharmonies disappear when sexual energy is trained into pure and useful channels. The demon lust becomes an angel of love, an angel full of power to create a new life, to make a new body, to open the fountains of inspiration and revelation.

Behold! I create a new heaven and a new earth, because the law of love is fulfilled. " The conscious use of this law of love is regeneration."

CHAPTER XI.

PARENTHOOD — ITS PRIVILEGES.

Creation is the law of the universe. By the law of attraction the feminine and masculine in plant, animal or human, fulfills the instinct for perpetuating their kind. Nature in her miracle workings entrances us; we are equally interested whether it requires a day or a year for germination and fructification. In early June a gardener remove? thousands of young elms and maples as weeds, their winged seeds having ripened from the bloom of two months before.

The woods, prairies and farms are full of evidence of propagation, nests of every conceivable variety of insects. The blight on fruit trees, the mold on preserves, and the yeast that lightens bread, are replete with reproduction.

The nuptials of birds are an unceasing delight; the morning matins ringing out the joy and blessing of united loves that consummate the wedded life.

It is a universal or kosmic love that is as inherent in all the world's products as life itself; from atom that unites with atom, from molecule to man, in all love calls and love replies, each by a special intelligence inherent in its kind — and so, the miracle of the perpetuity of life is the result.

In the human there is the same kosmic love or attraction as in the animal, while added to this is emotional or romantic love, and transcending all a spiritual or soul love. Thus man both by nature and development is equipped for a higher parenthood. In his dual nature he has the universal attraction, and through a racial evolution and through successive ages of transformation, has come to have a love that in courtship is called romantic love, and in a real spiritual or soul union after marriage, conjugal love. This soul union, not so rare as some would lead us to think, gives an ideal parenthood — father and mother fulfilling the great heart-desire to perpetuate the race. They are subject to the law of kosmic attraction, to the power of romantic love which, contrary to Finck, does continue in wedded life, and to the greater, far greater, attraction of conscious soul life.

In no department of life does man " know that he knows " more than in this soul union. Herein he transcends all life in the universe; in this knowledge man realizes the privileges and joys of parenthood. Desiring to beget children, this conception of soul life is a new and vital incentive to preparation. Parents know that the child will inherit from them a likeness in flesh and bone, in stature and figure, in color of hair and eyes. The Mongolian will impart special race characteristics, the African others quite as distinct. They know further that intellect and morals of parents, appetites and habits give tendencies to offspring, while later they come to realize that their spiritual life impresses the deeper life of the child.

Concluding that man's origin is divine, that in God he lives and moves and has his being now and forever, parents have it in their power to make children conscious of a life that is not of the flesh, a vivifying process of soul that transcends all other knowledge. In this soul consciousness creative powers take on new meanings, which project in prophetic vision the possibilities for the offspring. The child will no more be subject to a chance inheritance, but will possess characteristics that are an evidence of thoughtful preparation and training.

Parenthood is a privilege because it fulfills a natural inherent desire. It is always accompanied by mother's love for the child, followed by the joy and blessings of that love.

For many reasons a woman may shrink from motherhood and carry in her heart for months a rebellious attitude. She may already have many children, the hand of poverty may seem heavy, selfish pleasure and sensuous life may make a chance procreation repugnant; during the long nine months that the baby life is nourished in the womb it is branded as an intruder, its nourishment is not vitalized by affection. But once the mother has it in her arms, lo, the transformation! Deep down in her heart through all these months the kosmogenic love must have builded better than she knew. Social claims, poverty, sickness, many children, all are as naught to the joy of clasping the soul of her soul, the body of her body to her breast! The helpless life appeals to the maternal in her not in vain. With passionate kisses, with expressions of endearment, with tenderest care and vigilant attention, she proves that the "mother love is the holiest of all love," a divine solvent. Does the warm heart welcome remove any taint that her rebellion might have caused? Has it power to erase in all coming years the stains that prenatal disinheritance may have produced?

Parenthood is a privilege, for it is an opportunity to appropriate in a natural manner highest and best qualities. Remove the race tradition of sex degradation, the fulfillment of marriage in sex union becomes a holy sacrament and children will be begotten who will show forth all the highest qualities of both father and mother. The closing century has been noted for advancement in arts and crafts, all that relates to material comfort; all in the domain of artistic productions and of luxurious taste, has been the result of man's creative genius. Another century will, no doubt, show equal advancement in sociological conditions and spiritual development. In no way will this advancement be made any more certain than a wise application of all knowledge to the begetting of offspring.

For years men have watched with approval and applause the improvement of breeding stock. An old gentleman in western Illinois, among the first to import Flemish horses, devoted a whole life to improving horses, cattle, sheep and buffaloes. Every large city has its society for improvement and culture of cats. Is it not time that men and women devote their attention to raising the standard of human beings?

One of the privileges of parenthood is to give the child an inheritance of body, soul and spirit harmonious, whose endowments surpass its progenitors. He should have a body so perfect that he is not conscious of any part or function of that body, an intellect unhampered by doubts and fears, always ready for duty, with a spiritual nature of innate illumination. His procreation has been the result of the union of souls living in the realization of kosmic forces, and whose every thought is prompted by love.

The last and greatest privilege of parenthood is to love. Family life gives a symbol of the power and coherency of love. Love comes from God and in its expression, use and development, carries us back to God. We may pervert and misuse love, but stripping it of selfishness, obliterating the idea of ownership in children, the father-love and mother-love represent Divine love. The father-love in wisdom provides and protects the offspring, while mother-love nourishes and broods it — one a complement of the other; they thus express the qualities and nature of the Infinite in themselves, it is God in manifestation.

This parental love develops forbearance, patience, justice, self-denial, altruism, and all qualities that represent the true life. Man's tendency and desire to love is inherent; he asks no return, no reward.

How common the spectacle of parents devoting their lives, all their energies and accumulations day in and day out, year in and year out, to the necessities and comforts of children. They are not mere drudges for them; love thoughts go into every stroke of the hammer, every garment that is made, every bit of food that is prepared, and this love is the highest expression of the God nature within man, and through this love, this devotion, the soul gets glimpses of its divine powers.

Emotions have their redeeming quality; they not only bind us, link and link, to those we love, but they reveal to the soul its own powers and capabilities. Love children not less, but put a different quality in the affection, be persistent in the thought of what you are to the child, how you can direct and enrich his life, at the same time thinking little of what he is to bring to you. Love him for the privilege of loving.

Through the great mother-heart eternally ascending!

CHAPTER XII.

A NEW LIFE.

Conception is love's fruition. The male sperm has been attracted to the female germ in conjugal ecstasy, and the miracle of creation is performed. Is this an incident, an accident, a result of marital felicity, or is it a fulfillment of a plan and thoughtful preparations? (See Supplement *i.)*

Is the joy of creating so great that the created is forgotten? Have children no claims on fathers and mothers? May not parentage be so honored that its fulfillment will demand clear thinking, wise planning and soul purifying?

Fathers, mothers, for a day lay aside your toys, your dream of life; put yourselves in rapport with the kosmic plan, and realize the soul stirring grandeur of creating. The oak drops an acorn but never ceases to be majestic; the lion fecundates and the baby lion gambols in the lair. The oak and the lion reproduce unconsciously; man adds consciousness to the oak and lion nature, and it is his privilege to control his creations. He begets a life in the knowledge of the begetting; he is not drunk with passion, he is not stupefied with lust, but rather his soul is illumined by love, and the union of the masculine and feminine is a love union, conscious fulfilling of the law. Man rises in the dignity of manhood, woman responds in the sweetness and clear perception of womanhood, and the twain become one in flesh and spirit of a child, an immortal life to pass through the gateway of mortality. What deep significance is the conception of a human being, what vital import to beget life! Every other experience pales in comparison with parenthood.

And yet men and women go on absorbed in schemes for wealth, for position, for fame; or they are occupied in petty details of living, the making both ends meet, the drudgery of housekeeping, when lo, almost as a surprise, the baby comes, yet its divine innocence brings its blessing. Yes, even if unwelcomed in its conception, a burden and sorrow in the fecundating months, when it opens its eyes to this strange world, parents joy in giving it its introduction and take pleasure in its unfoldment. It is a sacred gift from the heart of God and mutely appeals for love from those who conceived it. In this appeal it reaches out and touches the innermost life of man and woman, it knows not good and evil, it is the innocence of divinity and the kosmic love of its life binds it to the universal of every other life. Unwelcome children thus by the law of the universe bring their joy and blessing, they fulfill the law of conjugal union, the law of fecundation in all nature, but how much greater the joy, how much fuller the blessing when man's consciousness is projected into the act of begetting; when conception is not merely a mating impulse common to all animals, but is recognized consciously as the supreme gift to man, as a copartnership with God. Through reason man and woman are led to choose time and occasion for the privilege of parenthood and through unfoldment of spiritual powers they elect that the highest and best, qualities and faculties of their combined natures shall be projected into the characteristics of the begotten. Their progeny have all the enduring and finer qualities given by open- eyed discretion.

There is no reason why every woman should not have knowledge that gives her the control of procreation and with the tact that she uses about ordinary matters she can have the cooperation of her husband.

Be not too insistent in overcoming minor matters in the choice of occasion. Do not be deterred on account of sentient pleasures; do not wait for a given amount of wealth, for a home paid for; a child adds but little to expense.

Often it is the experience of those who voluntarily put off child bearing a few years, that at last they come to be denied the privilege and the heart's desire remains unfulfilled. Beware of exaggerating difficulties and rejoice in the power to procreate. Remember that motherhood is a holy gift, a fulfillment of creative power, and to each it should be welcomed as a heart joy, and right understanding; nothing brings one closer to the heart of the Infinite.

One day, in talking of an author, I said: " Who is this man that gives us such strong food for thought, whose utterances respond so earnestly in the hearts of men?" Well, first he is not a child of chance; his advent into the world was desired and designed; a joyous childhood was followed by a blooming youth, and his manhood radiates the satisfaction of his life — a full fruition of maternal love and paternal wisdom. There never has been an echo in the child's heart of a lustful begetting, for the fruitful union was a blessing and a consecration.

Parents have it in their power to conceive children superior to themselves. For months they have sought active unfoldment of their own powers, through congenial society, intellectual pursuits, the harmonies of music; most of all through daily religion and meditation they have experienced a conscious spiritual awakening.

The controlled conservation of creative energy has also given an impetus to all faculties and function; this conservation has awakened force and dormant powers in body and soul; but more than all else in preparation for parenthood it is the nexus of vitality for the physical, mental and spiritual life of the child. He is the product of creative energy and this should contain the stored-up essence of life.

A man wishes his mare to foal, and desiring best results does not take her to a stallion that has recently mated; he has long since learned that even horse sense must not be dissipated in excesses.

The woman who finds pleasure in breeding famous cats, knows that the Thomas must not be a night prowler responding to an alley Maria. So human beings, who no more are animal-men, but have passed to the higher evolution of being, God-men, learn from inference and comparison, from reason, and, too, through the kosmic intuition to conserve deific essences, and as they have transmuted them into character and efficiency in themselves, they now transmit them into the soul qualities of the begotten.

Long enough we have gazed on the dark picture of chance procreation, the unregenerate rabble of poverty and vice, the nerveless deformities of drunkenness and debauchery, the vacillating weaklings of opulence. They have no rightful man-inheritance and their God-inheritance is so clouded and bedimmed by the distorted and unnatural life of parents that only a God can discover it. It is well that departments of stirpiculture and home science are being added to colleges, that mothers' congresses, women's clubs and church societies have in their all-embracing work special home features. (See Supplement *n.*)

What schools can be wise enough, what training sufficiently inclusive to overcome the tendencies of erroneous begetting? Let the inception be a child of light and the offspring will not be warped by common evil tendencies. His feet run in light of a divine projection, his human attributes are illuminated by love, for he is a child of light and love. For such a child

PRENATAL INFLUENCES

and prenatal culture must be more negative than positive. The product of conception is an individualized entity, a God-human, like unto father and mother, but more like unto a god, and as the oak wots not of the seedling's growth, so parents in knowledge avoid influencing the mind and character of the unborn.

The truest prenatal culture is to give the babe freedom from any thought save that of nourishing love, a love that sees in the child divine perfection, the image and likeness of God. His major tendencies are given in the procreation, and no hampering thought must seek to warp these. He is an individual, a spark from the bosom of kosmic love, and according to the law of diversity will surprise the world with his characteristics. He is a divine expression of the love that created him, and let him bear the scepter of his kingship. The child in its prenatal life requires freedom from any anxious or disturbing thought; indeed facts prove that it is detrimental to attempt to mold special characteristics, as to make of him an artist or musician; very largely those attempts are failures. Fear is always a disturbance in both the physical and mental realm. A mother's anxiety for herself or her child plants fear germs in her own body, and by the law of telepathy or suggestion the same seeds of inharmony are conveyed to the child. That he is not as sensitive to maternal impressions and conditions as many authors have taught, is probably largely owing to the attitude of the mother's mind.

The anticipated mother-marks are seldom found on new-born infants, and no doubt prenatal influences on the mind have been largely exaggerated. The child that turns out to be a clown perhaps was nourished as a musician or artist, the girl consecrated in utero to foreign missions may find her greatest joy in the frivolities of life; the boy, whose mother s prayers desired a bishop's gown, may satisfy his ambition in running a trust or being a railroad magnate.

While I would beware of making special demands for the unborn child, I would have the mother earnestly seek the highest and best for herself. Enter the gateways of knowledge, and absorb that which interests to the fullest extent, but most of all in silent communings realize the power of spirit, for in this knowledge is the one indissoluble cord of unity between yourself and child. Your love becomes an inclusive love and does not picture for the child a certain form of nose, a definite color of hair, and no, no, a thousand times no, does not discriminate the sex.

Probably sex is determined when conception takes place, therefore, a contrary telepathic influence by parents may produce deformity of body or mind.

When a mother says, " If my baby is not a girl I will not own it, I will have no love for it," she may lay the seeds of vacillating effeminacy in a stout manly form, or she may give him a lifelong desire to be a woman, to possess the intuition and perception of womanhood. Or the blue-eyed baby girl chooses tops and marbles for amusement and at maturity resenting petticoats, aspires to manly attire and occupations.   (See Supplement o.)

To sum up the relation of parent to child during the months of its fetal development, the main thought is self culture. At all periods of one's life the highest aim is spiritual unfoldment — a realization of oneness with kosmic forces; this knowledge at this time frees one from a sensuous connection with the child. While your heart throbs with life and love not before known, do not seek to direct that other life by suggestion, leave it a free life to develop according to its own individuality.

I would honor motherhood and give it the high place of song and story. It should be something more than sentiment; it should be held a privilege that demands special preparation and the best conditions in fulfillment.

A girl graduates from college or university; she is well read in all the classics of literature; she knows Latin and Greek; government and economics are familiar themes; physical sciences are open books, while music and art are the refining polish of the jewel. At this time devoted mothers and idolizing fathers are seeking a suitable and desirable man to be the lifelong companion of this brilliant accomplished young lady. Has she ever had a hint that the maternal in her would some day find expression? Has the inclusive curriculum of her college had courses of study upon wifehood, motherhood and homemaking? She is the belle of her town or her set, the queen of society, with perfect pose and poise. Del Sarte culture has left an impress upon every movement and gesture; the dressmakers' art sets off her form in elegant fabrics and colors that enhance her charms; the beauty artist has perfected the picture, but she stands before the bridal altar, her heart stilled in stony fear at the prospect of untried and untaught experiences. The majesty of womanhood and the glory of motherhood declare that this utter ignorance shall no more reign, but that knowledge shall set a jewel in the crown of parenthood. The importance of the function, the good of future generations demand that this be made a systematic department in the training of youth. A man and woman about to marry must present some certificate of qualification for marriage. The progress of the world requires a better race of children, and this demand can be fulfilled only in educated parenthood. Mothers' congresses and woman's clubs will have failed in their mission until they see to it that every girl that is led to the altar of matrimony has the acquirements, physical and mental, for maternity.

Progress demands a qualified motherhood.

Men seek homemakers and housekeepers, they establish wives in the house as a fine setting to the establishment or as an economic investment; in either case the question is seldom raised as to her knowledge of the function, that, by the law of perpetuation, shall bring a blessing or a curse, the preparation for maternity.

When the baby comes each woman learns by dear experience what should have been given her as a right, knowledge that would have saved suffering and possibly life itself. Love is no more blind to the needs of life; it does not sit around in dark corners expecting a fairy's wand to illuminate the way, but it demands for all relations in life the illumination of knowledge.

> I would sing of the coming woman —
> Moulder of a new race;
> Made perfect by her recognition
> Of the goodness and purity of nature's laws;
> Of the woman who prides herself
> Of every particle of her delicious and sublime body,
> The habitation and sanctuary of the Eternal Spirit.

as well as prenatal influence, has a very important place in all late works on parenthood. Facts and figures bolster up theories of inherited disease, crimes and criminal tendencies.

One fact is seldom accentuated, that health and strength are more frequently perpetuated than disease and weakness. Consumptive women and scrofulous men have had children of more than ordinary strength and endurance. Where do they get their vitality and what the source of their strength ?

All cases of inherited weakness can be matched by those who are possessors of health and robustness despite parental weakness. What is the law, and what are the conditions? The law is of man's creation, an endowment of race thought. It is, however, his privilege to free himself from any limitation that may have been builded for him. He may loose the chains and be free from ancestral inheritance.

Seeming hereditary conditions are best overcome by acknowledging one's original source and by realizing that there is a life within a life that transcends mortal existence. The very acknowledgment is the power of overcoming conditions.

The old catechism that taught the child that God made him may not be an unreasonable truth; for out of being is all existence, from primal cause is all effect. The possibility of the human mind becoming conscious of this fact, of putting the human life in harmony with divine life, of knowing the supremacy of spiritual law gives man his rightful inheritance. He is no more subject to the weakness and frailties of his ancestors, but knowing his birthright and becoming at one with his source, he is put in possession of a body that functions perfectly, of a mind that has no ancestral warp, and of a spirit illumined for life's purposes. This is the birthright of every man, woman and child, and he requires no wills, no testators, no legal enactments to become possessor of it; it is his for the claiming. The process is so simple, so direct, so effectual that the marvel is that all philosophers and thinkers have not known it, and that many people do naturally stumble upon it.   (See Supplement *p.)*

The ability lies in the law of *willing* and *letting* the law so ever present in all of nature s manifestations.   (See Chapter XVIII.)

Therefore, to free one's self from any hereditary taint, one is to swing into the law that enables one to feel the power and presence of the All-life, to put himself into communion with the Presence that is a divine beneficence for those who seek.

Know that inheritance is of God the kosmogenic life.

CHAPTER XIII.

LOVES FULFILLMENT.

The living mother-flesh folds round in darkness, the mother's life is an unspoken prayer, her body a temple of the Holy One.
Sweet love, only love —

The fructified ovum has received the blessing of love — it now must be nourished and sustained in love — all love. If fathers and mothers could realize this, and know that nature's plans are perfect for inception, growth and maturity of fetal life, no further word need be added; the law of life would be fulfilled.

" Thou shalt bring forth in joy " must be shouted into the ears and engraven on the hearts of prospective mothers and thus remove the curse of sorrow that has hitherto shadowed maternity.

Pregnancy is love manifested through nature's law.

Medical science devotes volumes to the symptoms of pregnancy and accentuates the abnormal until it is accepted as the normal. At the inception of a new life this natural state of the mother is treated as a disease and doctors are consulted; neighbor women welcome this as an opportunity to rehearse experiences of suffering, giving to the mother a picture of anguish and distress entirely contrary to the rightful inheritance of health. All the teaching of the past has tended to produce an expectancy of suffering; the heart is filled with forebodings and the mind quickly transmutes these into physical inharmony.

Every one knows the effect of a sudden fright; perspiration starts, the blood recedes from the face, the feet and hands are chilled, the centers of physical activity are congested and disease follows; a continued state of melancholy may produce cancer; jealousy and distrust bear fruit in tumors and abscesses.

A pregnant woman is under the influence of a racial fear; it gnaws at her vitals, it tugs at her heart-strings, it disturbs chemical action, it closes pores, and vitiates the absorbents; it poisons all life's forces. Could we but remove this one persistent, ever present cause of suffering in the expectant mother, we should transform the nine months of anguish to days and nights of joy.

Thousands upon thousands have been blessed by following the teachings of TOKOLOGY. Women are taught freedom of bodily attire, exercises to give strength to muscles, outdoor life for vigor and endurance, simple but nourishing food, indeed in every way to live close to the heart of nature; at the same time it is advised that the mind be completely engrossed in some congenial occupation.

The glad tidings have gone all over the world that woman need not suffer in pregnancy or go down to death in giving birth to children.

THE LOVER'S WORLD removes the terrors of motherhood by teaching its joys. A perfect confidence and trust in God-life, kosmogenic forces, dispels every vestige of fear, of anxiety in the heart of an expectant mother.

Dear mother heart, whoever you are, whatsoever the condition under which fecundation has taken place, let me come close and speak words of comfort and hope.

Your husband, in his eagerness to procure for you material comfort, does not divine the restless nervous dread that clouds your life; you are far from family and friends to whom you would naturally go for sympathy; you already feel burdened with many little ones clamoring for mother's ready help; or in the vicissitude of life you are all alone; no human heart to give you that which you crave.

I need not picture it, I need not recount sickness, poverty, drunkenness or even desertion, any of the causes that have bereft you of what seems your rightful support. I only know that to you a child is given, in your body is performed the miracle of creation. It is flesh of your flesh, bone of your bone, and listen — as your own life is life of the *all* life — so this baby life, no matter how unfortunately begotten, is also life of all life. More than by flesh, more than by blood coursing from your veins to his throbbing heart, does this all life, this kosmic force of nature bind you together.   (See Supplement *q.)*

You may not know a mother's counsel, a husband's love, but in the recesses of your own heart you may know this life of life that is health and peace. The one life, the divine life, trusted implicitly, will manifest in perfection. Cast out your fears, remove your anxieties, and deep down in your heart trust this life. As the bird is unconsciously led to build its nest in safety, as all animals know instinctively how and where to bring forth their young, so you, in fidelity to the brooding care of the All Life, can not err.

Cut loose from all traditions, know positively that God made no mistake in making mothers, and trust yourself implicitly to the plan. In this trust intelligent life permeates every cell, performs every function in harmony; blood courses through the vessels, leaving atoms of nutriment with bone, nerve and muscle; the lungs vibrate with rhythmic motion, sending the vitalizing air into every working cell; the processes of digestion, absorption and excretion are faultless. Thus from day to day all vital action is perfect, all functions obey their law. Through conscious thought you trust to nature's plan, and the unconscious or perfect life is carried on according to kosmic law; every atom, cell and organ functioning in an orderly way. Thus by a simple law of nature you build the body into health and harmony.

You choose or will that there is nothing to fear, no bondage to traditions, and through the law of life the kosmic forces obey your demand; make over and over again the strong assertion that " I have no unnatural appetite, no morbid sensations; good, and good only, rules my life. I am bound only by the law of love." You will come to know that the physical life does not need coddling, that every function in freedom is performed without interference on your part. The normal stomach makes no report of its action, the healthy heart has no telephone to your consciousness. All involuntary bodily processes are carried on by the law of mind, kosmic mind. One's life may ever be in harmony with this kosmic force, but at no time more certainly than during gestation. New relations and new activities give new strength and increase both bodily and mental vigor. In a normal pregnancy there is unusual buoyancy and elasticity.

Lucretia Mott testified that child-bearing was with her the most productive time for work, mental and physical. "The impulse on the part of women, to modify sexual differences, springs from profound changes slowly but surely operating in social economy rather than from restless ambitions; and that this impulse being involved as a factor of the future progress of the race, is in entire harmony with the evolution of sociology as well as with nature and life."

Women, who forget themselves, who devote their thought to some special line as art, literature or philanthropy, testify to wonderful creative ability during gestation. In its soul growth and expression the fetal life seems to reach out, and in its activity impels activity in the mother. Any work of absorbing interest that diverts the mind from self-pity and self-watchfulness, aids in letting nature's forces act in a harmonious and healthful manner.

Be thoroughly absorbed in some one thing, concentrate upon it, be eager, be alert, be thorough. If your home demands your attention put your loving interest in it. Do not give it grudgingly, but bless every kind of labor. There is no menial service. Put your love life into every bit of food you cook, every stroke of broom and brush and it ceases to be drudgery.

Perchance you make some change in home decorations; you are led to the garden, to the cultivation of flowers and vegetables, to care of poultry, to the raising of bees or possibly to the creation of a picture, a poem or a book.

Church work, club life, missionary work, the poor family needing aid; all or any of these may be a delightful diversion.

Are you a writer, a preacher, an artist, a teacher? Your chosen calling need not be abandoned because of new conditions. Your own health and that of the child demand consecration to work — congenial work, if possible; but that which has seemed unpleasant may be blessed and bring its fruition. Always and always seek to know the One-life, the blessing it yields, and then in its manifestation appropriate the renewed energy and strength to daily doings.

A consecrated busy life gives no room or place for inharmony of body or mind. No matter what your education, what your environment, let your heart go out to the larger life of the world. Find joy in little things, but let your faculties and aspirations be given to some special need or purpose.

The details of nest building may delight your heart and absorb you, but if this accentuates your sentient life, if it causes you to be on the hunt for feelings, then seek something outside for appropriation of energies; if you are living close to the heart of the All-life you will be led to do that which will be of the greatest value to yourself and to others. Devote yourself to that something. Your devotion and consecration to any special purpose is not only valuable to yourself, but leaves the child unhampered in its own individual development. You break the telepathic connection that weaves the worries of your life into the pliant baby life. He can then express his own characteristics without the formative influence of your thoughts; becomes the One-life in manifestation.

Thus know that thou shalt bring forth in joy. Day by day weave into thy life songs of gladness, ords of truth and deeds of kindness. Think pure thoughts, speak words of wisdom, and perform the works of love, always true to the highest conception of the law, the law that operates in perfection for him that has a heart attuned to its infinite possibilities.

The secret place of the Most High is in each heart, and by the letting go of material unrealities, one comes into a realization of power which gives health and strength, which lightens the darkened way and guides in tortuous paths.

I sing the song of Divine Motherhood.
I sing the song of the mother-state chosen.
I sing the song of the mother coming —

Strong, proud, free-limbed, easy-stepping;
Knowing her dignity; unashamed; serene;
Healthy; vibrant with energy and fresh air.
Walking, elastic, a hidden joy deep in the eyes;
Of her great body exultant, with a fierce mother exultation; —

Walking, elastic, holding the gods by the hand,
Walking, elastic, herself worshipping.

Chapter XIV

A MOTHER'S MELODY.

And Mary kept these things and pondered them in her heart.

I am a mother! Long, long has maternal desire filled my life, long has my heart yearned to clasp a life of my life in close embrace. Now I look out upon joyous happy children and know that the wish for motherhood is gratified. The lives of my husband and my own now blend in a united life, the sacrament of love. This joy is too sacred for words, too holy for alien sharing. Joy insuperable!

For long life has been rich. I, through love of friends, through devotion of husband, have felt the throb and thrill of a life divine. The unity of life has been experienced in all, but the conception of life in my body is a new awakening. Buds are radiant with colors, flowers rare with fragrance and brilliant of hue, birds sing their sweetest songs, skies reflect the deepest blue; all, all celebrating the joy of my heart. Child of love, no taint of fear, no trace of sorrow, shall ever mar thy life ! Only divine perfection shall manifest in thee!

Daily, hourly new joys are mine. Silently I view the placid waters; in them is imaged peace for thy heart, the green path in the woods gives the joy of solitude — alone, and not alone; for thy life and love reveal the All-love; I breathe the fresh air, I scale the heights, I drink of pure living waters, I greet a friend, all with the new joy; my bounding heart and beaming face, my buoyant step, all plainly tell the tale; all life is harmony, all nature one grand symphony.

I still this ecstasy and rest in the thought of cooling waters, the still night, the moonlight glow, the hush and silence of nature, the bursting seed in the dark mold, the chrysalis in its silken tomb, the silent incubation of the egg beneath the feathered breast, the hushed life of plant and tree in the embrace of winter, and my life becomes an unspoken prayer. My body is a holy temple. In an attitude of sleep, with curved limbs, hands and feet scarcely formed, the little body is enfolded safely, sweetly in the living couch of flesh. It may not be defiled, for it the sun shines, the fresh breath of the morning is inhaled; the pliant walls of its dwelling are given fullest freedom; the arteries and veins in recurring streams convey pure nutrition, and day by day cells are builded from atoms, conveyed in the red river of life — a beautiful, perfect form.

For this gift of God I fill the happy fleeting moments with the joys of life. On wheel, in carriage, by the footpath, I seek the storehouses of nature, plant, animal and rock — all yield their treasure and contribute to my joy. Art emporiums, concert halls and the eloquence of enthusiasm are my delight. The soul's emotion expressed by poet, orator, artist, appeals to the deep emotions of my life and His love is perfected in me. I sing the songs, I paint the pictures, I repeat the eloquent story to the expanding heart of the little one beneath my breast.

Last night my husband and I took a long stroll in the moonlight, through an unfrequented path by the lake. Our hearts were stilled, for with a new consciousness we seemed blessed by the presence of our child. The pressure of feet upon leafy mold, the quiet rustle of leaves scarcely stirred by the gentle breeze, the glint of stars in the far-off heavens, the wash of the waves in rhythmic beat; indeed all nature echoes our joy. In tender embrace we rest on the green bank and watch the perfect reflection of moon and stars in the water. The seeming in the placid lake is a reproduction so complete that eyes fail to discover the line where the real sky terminates and the mirrored sky begins. My husband was saying, " Is not this picture, this reflection, an emblem of our joy? The joy of the perfected life in our lives is so complete that we can not draw the line between what is human and divine — indeed, this is the divine in the human."

At this the throbbing fetal life in unmistakable signs gave a response in awakening activity. It was as though the soul was quickened by our benediction and out of its own realization answered in consciousness of its joy.

For hours we sat in silent meditation, and, as streams their channels deeper make so we more fully realized that all life is one though many in manifestation. The unity of life and love expressed in quiet nature found sweet response in our hearts; the still waters; the unseen flowers; the bird protecting with outspread wings her young; the squirrel snuggling the infant life in an adjacent tree; the bee, after a day idled with provident care, hushed in its house of stored treasure; the flickering, subdued lights at long distance sending penetrating rays from homes where the hurry and bustle of life had ceased, where hearts were resting from the daily conflict between seen and unseen forces. All blended in a refrain of joy. To every house we sent a thought of rest and peace. Listen, O man, for the keynote, and woman, if thou wilt, every chord of thy life will answer in harmony — listen in the stillness of soul to know this key.

Thus in sweet converse we retrace our steps, while the third, the life of our life in quickened heart-beats, took up the refrain of joy never to cease. The ecstasy of living, the refreshment from the universal source, seemed to preclude the necessity of sleep, for had we not been renewed from Infinite Life?

My daily duties have a new joy. The house becomes the home of the new life; the pictures, the furniture, the fabric and color of hangings, all are arranged and adjusted to suit the occasion. The nest takes on an air of coziness, of comfort and protection; warm colors, soft materials, dainty *bibelots,* all speak the approaching event. Necessary cares and duties of the household are no more a drudgery; the joy of my heart enters into every detail.

A keener insight detects the food required by members of the household. The viands are not only wholesome, supplying physical wants, but contribute to an aesthetic sense; as the eye is gratified by landscape or picture, as the ear revels in harmonies of music, so the sense of taste in a like manner is gratified by the delicacies of the table. The simplicity of well-chosen food served daintily and artistically gives delight to all. The blessing of my life is impressed upon every preparation; my love and joy are woven into a web of happiness for all.

In the divinity that fills my life there comes no thought of pain and suffering — no self-demanding attentions; no slavery to inconsequential details; only love and the joy of loving. This love builds about me a wall of defense. No one can move me with recitals of suffering, for the knowledge that perfect love only is manifesting in me precludes the injurious effect of any sad or painful experience. On the contrary, the joy of my life produces a contagion of joy that repeats itself in the hearts of friends. I have no regrets for the past, no foreboding future, only the joy of the present. The *now* of each day, of each moment, sings a glad song of fruition. Every hour my heart realizes and reflects a benediction. Alike in the busy day and the quiet of night, joy uplifts my heart and permeates the new life with harmony; its heart answering to my heart in throbs of ecstasy.

SONG OF THE LAYETTE.

I linger over this snowy pile
Of dainty muslin, linen and lace,
Imagining all the while
How they will look round a baby face.

Tiniest garments of fabric fine,
Royal with costly embroidery,
Fill my heart with a spell divine,
Only the earnest of that to be.

God is love; and my cup of bliss
He has filled to the very brim.

All the glory of motherhood
Has already enriched my soul,
Stirred my pulse and warmed my blood
Even before I have reached the goal.

— Ruth G. I. Havens.

In these dainty garments of linen and lace I stitch the love thoughts that shall forever shield my darling, a selfless love that knows that my strong attachment is not one of emotion only, not one born of ownership, but a deeper love that knowing the apartness of every soul, still knows the one golden cord of unity. I can have no fear, no anxiety, for he is a child of life and love, and I trust the innate intelligence of that love to weave the web of his baby life in beauty, in harmony, in perfection.

How wonderfully sweet are these days of preparation. The layette is like a rose in full bloom. In its simplicity, in its daintiness and perfect adaptation to its needs and in its purity it symbols the beauty and perfection of infant life. It tells the ever-new story of brooding care, of thoughtful attention, of a mother's devotion. In these garments are woven the enduring thoughts of love, and as they are laid carefully away the present hour is full of present joy. It is not all in imagination and anticipation; the physical relation, so close for many months, is proof that this our child is part of our life.

Child of my heart, a mother's deepest desire enfolds thee in the protection of divine love that is both a promise and fulfillment. I give myself to thee.

I am filled with wonder and joy.

I will keep my body pure, very pure.

To-day my husband put in my hands a cluster of lilies of the valley. All day, as an undertone, I had an unexpressed wish for a symbol of his devotion; ever attentive — almost too solicitous for my comfort, and yet as a fuller joy I wished for this symbol to prove that he too knows the happiness of parenthood.

Ah, there is only one love, but many in manifestation. One life in these pure lilies, but many on each stalk to prove its presence; my husband with a tenderness born of strength, with a reverence for the life within my life, gives this simple token, a benediction from a holy presence. To-night we sing together the songs we love — the songs that gladden our hearts and reveal the power of spirit.

TWO LOVERS.

Two lovers by a moss-grown spring;
    They leaned soft cheeks together there,
    Mingled the dark and sunny hair,
And heard the wooing thrushes sing.
0 budding time! O love's blest prime.

Two wedded from the portal stept:
    The bells made happy carolings,
    The air was soft as fanning wings.
White petals on the pathway slept.
O pure-eyed bride! O tender pride!

Two faces o'er a cradle bent:
    Two hands above the head were locked,.
    Those press'd each other while they rocked,
Those watch'd a life that love had sent.
O solemn hour! O hidden pow'r!

Two parents by the ev'ning fire:
    The red light fell about their knees
    On heads that rose by slow degrees,
Like buds upon the lily spire.
O patient life! O tender strife !

The two still sat together there:
    The red light shone about their knees,
    But all the heads by slow degrees
Had gone and left that lonely pair.
O voyage fast! O vanished past!

The red light shone upon the floor.
    And made the space between them wide;
    They drew their chairs up side by side.

Their pale cheeks joined and said:
"Once more, once more,
O memories! O past that is! "

— *George Eliot.*

How can love be fulfilled except in parenthood; what means the lover's love except to express the kosmic force that ever seeks to perpetuate life? And so comes this holy experience to man and woman, it is as it were a breath of the Infinite and with it comes the awakening and growth of soul. As air in motion stirs and sweeps through all created forms, so this new love stirs and sifts the impulses of life.

Man, in his strength and wisdom, adds power to this through tenderness. The new life calls out sacred responses; books, pictures and songs, heart's-ease.

Together we know the joy of parenthood, together we are led from day to day, a child, *our* child is leading us in the path of devotion, consecration and illumination. Through the love of the child we know the love of divine wisdom. In the exultation of song, in fragrance of flowers, in the hush and stillness of nature's miracle workings, in the everyday busy doings, in faces and forms of friends, we thrill with the joy of Infinite life.

I take a last look at the Layette —it lacks nothing for completeness.

I hear the pull of the thread through the cloth!
I see the sewing pinned to the knee!
I hear the double-quick of the heart!
Lay your ear to the world; do you not hear the mother-pulse beating, beating —
With strong and steady pulsations beating under the world?
Do you not see the women — the women — with bent heads hiding the glow in
     the cheek —
Do you not see the pricked fingers and the prayer in the heart ?
Lay your ear to the world —

To-day I complete an essay on Froebel's Law of Unity. In this is summed up the teaching of this philosopher, whose works have been

104

an inspiration through all these months, and in which I have found a solution for many of life's problems.

Deeply, sweetly I rejoice in the love that has come into my life; as health and joy have filled the feeting months, so must the fuller joy of the child presence be a fuller happiness. In calm peace and trust I await the hour.

There is no voice in Heaven more high than this,
So clear and deep, that calls thy soul to be
A mother here of Godlike symmetry,
Sacred, with infinite exalting bliss.
Since Eve first breathed above the First-born's kiss,
Touching the earth's enduring ecstasy,
No thing of Love hath seemed more sweet to Thee,
Than this of life in life and soul, I wis.
The shadowing heights of God seem near and still;
The mystery that holds His changing sway
Is thine, as Thou art watching, day by day:
And night by silent night, beneath His will,
This growing soul, this life that knows no ill,
This answering of all thine heart did pray.

CHAPTER XV.

LOVE'S MANIFESTATION.

The fulfillment of nature and the prophecy of God is Man.

For nine months the soul has been building a body, and truly one may say that when a child comes into the home, a soul, a spiritual being is born.

> 'Tis of the soul the body form doth take.
> For soul is form and doth the body make.

The born child is the spiritual life in manifestation. Through all the joyous months it has been committed to the life that gave it, to the perfect intelligence functioning through material atoms. Its birth is no infringement upon the perfect plan. Creative life brings forth an immortal being in joy and gladness.

Fathers, mothers and friends must penetrate deeply into the secrets of life. All must know that the process of birth is fruition in life. As fecundation and germination have progressed in fulness of health, according to natural law, so also does the child pass from its physical confinement into the freedom of active life, giving no conscious pangs. This is the possible experience of every mother; she may train her thought forces so that all of nature's processes shall function in an orderly manner and without suffering. Experience of the many has been so widely astray from nature that woman must be insistent in overcoming this racial tradition, this " sorrow curse" of Scripture. No more shall it be said, " Like as a woman with child . . . is in pain, and cryeth out in her pangs."

That childbirth may be a joyful, painless experience, one must have:

Bodily freedom,

Desire for offspring,

Conservation of sexual energy,

Confidence in the One-life.

Physical freedom is the natural outgrowth of a spirit set free. A woman conscious of the spiritual life, her soul attuned to infinite harmony, as a consequence claims free development of every part of the body. She expresses life and power from vital organs, through pliant muscles, even to the finger tips. She enhances this expression by an active life, by climbing stairs and hills, by games and gymnastics. Lack of bodily freedom disturbs the functions of life. The restraint of bands and stays upon the yielding pliant portions of the body prevents natural processes; they also picture a false artistic development; at all times they restrict and pervert physical functions; but when it comes to the office of motherhood they attack the citadel of life — endangering the lives of two. The new life, so closely united with hers, is not only an occasion for bodily enlargement, but is an impetus for general activity. Every nerve throbs, every artery and vein speeds the life's blood on its mission of nourishment with increased power. Put the body in tune with this activity, give it more sunshine, more air, greater freedom; so apparel it that it shall have no restraint.

Greek gowns, the modified Japanese kimona, and various styles of wrappers are adapted to house wear, while the street or outing costumes should be devised to give freedom of the body, individual needs and taste devising and governing the special style. Thus appareled, rides, walks, the visit to friends, the search for nature's treasures, the tourist excursion, each fills the life with its special pleasure without the annoyance of unsuitable garments. The expectant mother thus expresses the freedom of her individual life, which in turn gives her grace, strength and pliability.

The *desire for offspring* is innate in woman. It is seldom that she would by choice pass her entire life childless. Indeed to most women it is a great sorrow not to have this heart's desire realized. In ordinary sexual life women have no control of the fecundating power; conception is an incident, it takes place at inopportune times and without preparation. It lacks all the joy and stimulus of free choice. Men often regard the sex relation as a means to work off superfluous energy. With a want of consideration that in any other relation would seem brutal, he permits a selfish gratification to bring about undesired results, undesired probably by himself as well as by his wife.

Forced maternity brings a long train of ills. It is so unnatural that one recoils at its contemplation. It perverts all the best qualities of men and women. The lack of choice, of time and occasion for fecundation naturally brings about a revolt in the maternal instinct. This revolt is a frequent cause of suffering in childbirth, it bears a close relation to fear; the two travel together in the work of disintegration.

Fear is deadlier than all disease-producing germs.

Job uttered a tremendous truth, and the world has been slow to apply it: " For the thing which I greatly feared is come upon me, and that which I was afraid of is come unto me."

The body functions according to conscious thought. How is it that one man's meat becomes another's poison? It is the fear thought put into it. Some people can not eat potatoes, others rule out butter, others the luscious strawberry; while for others the nutriment of an egg is a poison.

These are familiar illustrations of the power of fear. Through some unreasonable notion certain food good in itself is condemned and robbed of its nutriment. It lacks the blessing of confidence.

Man fears drafts, damp air, night air; he flees to the mountains and seashore; if he does not leave his fear behind he finds neither health nor pleasure.

Each within himself has the power to build a thought wall of resistance, and doing this he is equally robust on the mountain's top, in the valley or by the seashore.

Woman in child-bearing is under the influence of a racial fear; it has come down through the ages that she must bring forth in sorrow, and this word *sorrow* has been amplified by the synonyms, suffering, pain, anguish, agony. This belief of agony is engraven into every thought-fiber of woman's nature.

Among early races she was man's equal in strength and development. In many countries in pursuits that require endurance women work side by side with men. In China and India they may be seen carrying the hod or working upon the road. In Germany and even in our own country, they labor in garden and field, tilling the soil and performing heavy manual labor.   (See Supplement *r*.)

Weakness of women is no more natural than the same quality in men. In conditions where they have strength and robustness child-bearing is natural and free from suffering.

Man stands for wisdom, intelligence and reason; woman for love, consciousness and intuition. When love is known as being as great in power as wisdom, when intuition reveals that which reason conceals, there will be no sense of superiority or inferiority. Feminine qualities will not be represented by disease, and intuition will cease sensing morbid feelings, but rather will know the All-life that is vitalizing and manifesting in every function of body.

Through ignorance woman is dominated by the idea that morbid conditions attending maternity are natural, that weakness and pain are an original inheritance. All this has produced a *fear* that holds the thought of the race in thralldom and robs child-bearing of naturalness and joy.

To overcome this fear woman must know that there is One life, this life is love and intelligence manifesting through law. In animal, bird and plant life, this manifests in perfection. They take no thought wherewithal they shall be fed, no anxiety how royally they shall be arrayed.

Man has departed from this perfection, but through power of thought may retrace his steps: by right thinking claim his own.

Fear thoughts are overcome through confidence in kosmic force, the intelligence, the mind that makes no mistake, that operates according to law; that performs all functions in a natural way. Some people readily accept this fact and soon get power; while some natures who have builded strong thought-walls of limitations, who are bound by traditions, who are overconfident in self, learn this simple natural way with great difficulty; ruling their own lives they take the combatant's way of doing it; they are at war with conditions, with environments; they live in a constant state of antagonism. One must fall in with the natural ebb and flow of life; must become perfectly non-resistant, silencing all thought, stilling all fear and putting away all worries. To do this effectually seek repose of body, lying or sitting, and be very still, hush every thought, saying, " Peace, peace; I am at peace, I trust the source of life." Avoid going to sleep; revel in the consciousness of peace.

Gradually, gently, the fear-thoughts vanish, and from the kosmic processes of life the sense of safety and confidence flows. The influx brings vigor and victory. In a way it is a mastery, a mastery by the conscious recognition of innate powers — rather a letting of forces work in a natural way. Practice this several times a day until it becomes a natural habit.

You thus put yourself in harmony with law — in tune with the infinite of your own life — which, by your letting, operates to fulfill the demands of life; it creates health germs that resist all contagions. It is a simple law of faith that has a logical foundation; a law known by many sages and interpreted in various ways; in our own times this law has been given simply and observed consistently by the Friends. One prominent among them said: "To the Christ, who was never crucified; to the Christ, who was never slain; to the Christ, who can not die, I commend you with my soul."

It is knowing the Christ which abideth in each that brings peace, that banishes fear and is man's salvation, a salvation for body as well as for soul, not for a future, but for the now, for every moment and every occasion.

Woman learns that there is a deeper life than the body — that there are unseen forces more real than matter, forces that may be brought into joyful service.

Thus the pregnant woman banishes fear of the throes of travail; she puts herself in tune with nature's processes; the joy of maternity is not lessened by physical anguish. (See Supplement *s.)*

But for her, O the rest, the rest and the peace — now it is all over — no desire to move, only to lie and rest for joy.

CHAPTER XVI.

THE LOVERS' HOME.

The true home is the abode and paradise of love.
Except love build the home, they who build it labor in vain.

A home, however small, with however few members, is a cooperative community. If this cooperation is an outgrowth of love, is instigated by altruism, it surely has a permanent foundation.

In the most literal sense a home is the nest for nestlings, it is a wise preparation on the part of parents for the care of offspring. In a broader sense, it is the retreat or rendezvous of the family; the place in which to welcome friends and strangers. It is a center for the development of the refinements. It is not secluded and walled in for the family — a man's castle — but rather ar place of joy from which is extended to friend and stranger a warm welcome.

There are many houses but few homes.

Homemaking is more than housekeeping. The latter is the business of the home, the former is the ethics. In both business and ethics, husband and wife should cooperate.

The husband usually provides the maintenance, while the wife transacts the business and is purveyor and executor.

United love and natural interest demand union of thought and plans in building a home and carrying on the details.

In general woman is the homemaker; the affairs of the home are her affairs, but all regulations should be sufficiently elastic and should be so directed that the taste and wishes of the husband are consulted and respected.

Some men consider that their part of homemaking ends with the funds furnished, but the working plan demands their vital and enthusiastic interest.

There should be no domination.

Love makes it all cooperative.

A home founded on love is original.

Some people sacrifice comfort and pleasure by a slavish conformity to fashion, by imitating their neighbors. As each plant blooms in a color and form of its own, as no two lives are alike, so no two homes are alike — each expresses its own individuality. One does not buy a certain carpet or a certain style of china because it is like Mrs. Smith's or Mrs. Brown's ; one does not have polished floors or antique furniture simply because it is in the fashion.

The home, like one's clothes, represents character. It is indicative of standards, of the knowledge of life, of culture. Whether a palace or a cottage this home is one in which friends will always feel a welcome; the very atmosphere is pervaded with the characteristics of the occupants.

Eighty per cent of American women are their own homemakers; they live in rooms, flats, cottages, farm houses. The woman who :can do her own work and be master of it, is, as a. ,rule,. more. independent than the one who must have assistance. The woman of the future will have training in all branches of household economics; she will know the best ways of cooking, of laundrywork, of general housework; she will understand the business part of housekeeping —the requirements in every department, purchasing of supplies, the· kinds and quality of food, the employment and oversight of ·help, the preparation for teas, receptions and all special functions. In the well-ordered household nothing is drudgery. The woman will have learned economy, judgment, alertness, as well as a neatness,. all of which she applies to household arts.

She is not only a good cook, a **good provider,** but her heart, filled with cheer, is ever ready to extend this cheer to a guest. She knows that it is not the fine house, the many rooms that constitute a home, but the wise adaptation of what she has. Her living-roorn may be dining-room, sitting-room and sleeping-room, in turn, but with; judgment the quick changes afford no annoyance.

Those of us who remember log-cabin days recall the many purposes to which the one large room was devoted. The great fireplace with the hanging crane was a symbol of good cheer; the one room was used as bedroom, sitting-room, dining-room and kitchen. Social Iife in America ever finds soil for free growth and full expression, but never has there been fuller growth and freer expression than in pioneer days.

What welcome on special festive occasions when friends and neighbors were invited ! All superfluous furniture set outside, making room for games, dances, charades ! Were there ever floors more resplendent in whiteness, or food more appetizing? Aunt Peggy's biscuits that seemed more like young loaves of bread, mether's doughnuts and mince pies ! then the apples and cider, the walnuts and butternuts, all furnished cheer and refreshment.

In these later days tent-life in a camp approaches in a degree the social abandonment of the pioneer days. People who break away from conventionalities, who are not bound to finger-bowls and napkins, can, in a small measure, reproduce the experience, the deep- hearted fellowship that prevailed among early settlers.

Those who realize the unity of all life, who understand the law of giving and receiving, get great joy from the abandon of free life in tents, rustic cottages by lake and in the woods; the blue sky, the singing birds, the wild animals, the many-hued flowers, all combine to reveal the divine life in nature. Men and women can, through this simple living, realize, per-- haps more than in any other way, the spiritual power that is in all and through all.

May not the life of the cabin or tent be a lesson to all homemakers? Can not the free joy that pervades these simple homes be reproduced in village or city? Shall we not cease to be governed by false standards ? If each family had its own rules for living, its own ideals, the homemakers might easily lighten their labors; they could thus secure to themselves time for devotion to music, art, literature and pleasures. •

Every woman should know the best ways of doing things, especially in cooking. Household magazines, home journals and cook books, are full of practical and useful hints. There is no excuse for ignorance as to best methods of preparing all kinds of dishes. It is not essential in culinary arts to make application of ideas that tend to complicity, that require a needless amount of labor. A woman desiring to make the most perfect home and the best use of herself in the preparation of food, will study economy of time as well as economy of funds. She will learn that bread with proper yeast may be made by molding once only, when she may put it in the pans for baking; perhaps it will take three hours for it to rise, in which time she is free to do other duties about the house, or, if there are needs, be absent from home.

She will learn, too, in the preparation of certain foods, to cook more than is necessary for one meal. (See Supplement *t*.)

Housekeeping is becoming a profession, and those who engage in it are educated for it. One who is to follow this as a business will not fail to prepare herself for it; she will know that strength and good intent are not sufficient qualifications to fulfill the office of housekeeper. She must be purveyor, chemist, artist and decorator; she must understand furnishing a home as 'well as arrangements for festive occasions.

All these qualifications are essential for a woman who is her own housekeeper, but she must also add many more. She must not only be the perfect housekeeper, cooking, adjusting and arranging for all occasions, but must be comrade for her husband and children, and ever the agreeable hostess. It is well that universities, colleges and schools are incorporating in their courses of study household economics; every girl is given an opportunity to fit herself for housekeeping. This knowledge will aways serve her well. She may not become a homemaker herself, but as it has been a means of her development so it adds to her accomplishments for usefulness in whatever profession or industry she may engage. (See Supplement *t2*.)

A woman who is master of her work is inventive and creative; she is on the alert for all improvements. The present century, no doubt, will give us much advancement in all branches of housekeeping.

The tendency to cooperation will probably bring great changes in homemaking; comparatively few women in cities do their own baking, so in the future probably it will not be considered an essential to good homemaking for every woman to be her own cook. . No doubt, especially in city life, cooperative laundries and kitchens will supply the needs of families much better and more economically than they can do it for themselves. When this is accomplished, woman will have more freedom to be the comrade of her husband and children. She will have time for pleasures which will in turn be dispensed to others and will thus become a better homemaker.

The good New England country and Southern hospitality now exists in memory, but that memory should inspire women to become free from the daily routine of labor, that their lives may blossom out into greater perfection.

All of life should be a joy, for out of joy is the true art of living.

ETHICS OF HOME AND FAMILY.

Love in a home originates its own ethics; it abolishes the mine and thine possessions; it develops a contagion of harmony that dispels sarcasm, jealousy and anger. The wife is not a scold or the husband a faultfinder.

A six-year-old boy was asked by a new cook what his father liked best to eat. " I think he likes mostly what mamma has not got," he replied. This boy revealed volumes of the family ethics. Every word and act is a revelation of the heart's intent. Love's power and efficiency is evinced in companionship, comradeship, and cooperation.

Father, mother, children, the guest within the gate, each fills his place, performs his duties and contributes to the joys of home; all in harmony and adaptation. A hand does not do the work of the foot; nor the foot that of the hand, yet each acts in perfect accord. (See Supplement *u.*)

Strong natures with great executive ability find difficulty in doing their part in a home without dominating in it. A man who considers the home his establishment, who places the woman at the head of his table for ornament as he wears a diamond stud in his shirt bosom, or places a piece of statuary in his library, may think it his prerogative to order all the details of the home, the furnishings, the picture hanging, the menus; he arranges entertainments, and dictates the garments of his wife. The woman may meekly acquiesce in all this, for is not submission the part of love? (See Supplement *u2.*)

A woman of a dominating character begins housekeeping in her home. She has received this as the price of marriage and immediately takes command. She buys, furnishes, regulates; this is her province and she brooks no interference; she will not listen to suggestion or criticism; she inaugurates a prison discipline; plans that she makes must be executed; food that she serves must be eaten; when she rings the bell it is time to get up.

Love fulfilling the law will lead to adjustment; tastes will be consulted, wishes respected, and all work together in union.

COMRADESHIP.

Come, let us live with our children.

Comradeship is a word that fits the home. Husband and wife are comrades in every sense of the word. They join in life's activities and are happy in all beginnings and all completions.

As children enter the home they extend this comradeship.

The heart and essence of all child-culture is to live the life of the child. You need not go back to the past and make a memory picture of your own lives.

Many see in their children only a new edition of themselves, expecting in them like experiences and demanding for them the same training.

If they have been brought up in the hard school of force — a word followed by a blow — this has resulted in such a remarkable product that it must be repeated in the children. Through the law of unity and diversity each child is unlike every other — a new book to be read, a new life to unfold.

The *lover's* child is full of surprises. No program can be outlined for the day's lesson. From day to day its desires and activities are evidence of the soul growth — of its blossoming. Parents take a sensuous delight in this unfolding, at the same time are alive to its deeper meaning, to the opening of the soul flower. They not only assuage its griefs and allay its pain, but rejoice in its joys.

Many parents are ready to meet a child on its own ground if he is in trouble; if he has a pain in his head or a hurt in his finger; but, alas; have no fellowship in his joys; this is only child's play to them.

As a boy comrade plans for a fellow, so you, as parents, are full of schemes for the child; there is no disposition to be free from the annoying activity and persistence of childhood, but many plans of comradeship, plans into which you enter with the zest of childhood. Perhaps it is a springtime tramp in the woods. Have you not a childish eagerness for pussy willows, the first hepaticas, the spring beauties and the fragrant arbutus ? Are you not watching for the robin and the oriole ?

Then hand in hand you accompany him to lake or river. What fascinations in the sandy beach, the toy boats, the wading in shallow water; the plunge and swim in deep water. As years go on you visit machine shop and foundry, you are an invited guest at soap and candy factories, repeating at home with skill and delight the

118

processes you have witnessed. In all this you learn the happiness of becoming a child.

Many parents have, in their association with their children, only a vocabulary of " Don'ts." Fathers especially are inclined to feel their parental authority and exercise it in constant restrictions and a perpetual " do not." " Now, did I not tell you to shut that door ? " " Have I not told you over and over again to bring some water ? " " Will you never learn to sit up straight at the table ? " " How many times do I have to tell you not to play with John Smith? "

So, from morning until night, with no plan of work or recreation that would make these " do nots " unnecessary.

Naturally, a child is full of joy, and often he is himself sufficiently inventive to find his own amusement. Should he lack in resources the parents' stronghold is to have something in reserve that will not only give joy but will bring out the faculties of the child.

You should enter into the games and plays that he has himself invented and institute new ones.

Make up a train of cars with the furniture, you sometimes being the engine and sometimes the child. Play it is a freight or passenger train, in any case there are times when the engine has to stand still and wait for the filling up of the train.

The butterfly game of the kindergarten is also a favorite one, alternating action and repose.

Nature in all her dealings gives us the succession of night and day, of active life and slumber. The child's power of self-control is developed by giving him games where he must be still. We talk a great deal about directing the activity of the child, but we must also direct the opposite, making stillness and repose a motive power. In the home games incorporate this action and repose.

Many children can never stand still; they can not sit still at the table; they can not walk but must always run, tiptoeing around with hands and arms flying in the air. This is an evidence of undirected activity, of a mind that has never learned to keep still.

One morning in visiting a kindergarten, the children had had an active game which wound up with the flying of a whole flock of birds. After this the leader struck the piano; they all took their seats and laid their heads down upon their arms, representing the birds going to their night rest.

As she played softly each child became very still; you would have thought every one was fast asleep. They were kept in that position about ten minutes. One mother, who was visiting that day, said that it was worth everything to see her little Mary enter into the life of this game and more than all to be able to join in the stillness. " I have never seen her in her little life still that long when she was awake." Those who are familiar with the kindergarten methods will observe that many of the games represent activity and repose, and thus it should be with the entire life of the child.

Comradeship should always be the keynote. It is a comradeship with freedom. A small child should be able to amuse itself and be alone and yet have a feeling that the parent is his comrade. Of course the fathers and mothers have a life of their own to live; they are not to sacrifice that to the child; neither are they to sacrifice the child to their own life; through wisdom and love one strikes a happy medium and learns to deal justly. Of course one's own true life influences the child more than anything else. Live the life that you desire your child to live, a life of joy and trust. Such a life reflects in his pliable nature in happy days and restful nights.

Show forth the best in yourself and this best is reflected in the child; what has seemed to be a great problem in government becomes comparatively easy because through sympathy and comradeship with the child its needs and wishes are forestalled. You do not wait until it cries for things; his life is so filled that he has no time or desire to do this. Many plans have already been instituted for his occupation which give him freedom and independence. In the summer he has a place upon the porch that he may call his own, or a sand pile protected by boards. In the winter a large box just high enough to keep him from falling over may furnish him an independent play room, or some corner of the room can be fenced off for him. In these he has a few playthings which give him joy and supply his desire for activity. He soon learns that this is his province, that this territory belongs to him, and by a little tact he becomes happy in his possession. The mother is thus left independent possibly for hours while the child is learning through its own little devices; by the employment of some such measure as this you have saved yourself saying a thousand times a day, John, don t touch that." " Leave that alone." " Put that back." " Now come here to me." " You know you are not to have that, for it is papa's." You have command of your own time for whatever purpose you desire, knowing at the same time that the little one is safe and happy.

It is impossible in the scope of this work to go into details, but every parent is advised to further inform himself upon kindergarten methods of training. The founder of these methods, Froebel, constantly reiterated the idea of bringing out the good of the child by appropriating all of his active and creative faculties, also demonstrating that play was a true and natural form of development. He also made it very plain that the mother was the one who should wisely direct these plays, but of course he never intended that the father should be released from these pleasures and privileges.

We know from the trend of education in this line that the fathers are to take a great interest, even an equal interest in child culture. Some fathers plan their business so that they shall be absent from home only during the hours that the children are at school, and while they are at home they are comrades of the children, joining them in their plays, games, excursions, manual work, and childish devices. This is a privilege and joy of fatherhood.

A child brought up in a home of love and freedom is a law unto itself and this is true obedience. He has freedom to live his individual life, and parents who have not put upon him the searchlight of suspicion seldom find aught to restrain in him. The motive back of all of his actions is understood. Time and again perhaps, if the parents search themselves, they will find that what they condemn in the child is the result of some thought of their own. So in the training of children, first search your own hearts. When a child is irritable, fretful, or what you call contrary, look inward and see if you have not been indulging in some condemnation or criticism of either friends or neighbors. See that you have not been harboring unkind thoughts in some direction, or rebelling against some situation of your own.

Not long since I saw a letter from a lady who said that she had everything to make a happy home, a kind husband, plenty of means, plenty of leisure, but her children were so cross and irritable that she daily wished to go away from them. She was tied to what seemed most disagreeable to her. If she had given a little thought to the mental side of this picture, she would have seen that she made her own discon- tent. By acknowledging her blessings, a kind husband, the pleasant home and the dear children and reflecting upon the fact that there are thousands of women who are heart hungry for the maternal life, her heart would have been satisfied.

This woman's children were cross, irritable and disobedient because she was not their comrade; she was not living their life. She had no sympathy with their joys and no knowledge of their real needs.

Hold the attitude of trust and confidence toward the child. Believe in him and he will reward you for this belief.

HOME ACTIVITIES.

As children advance in years parents must not expect the school, though well established, to do all for either boy or girl. The home may be considered the rendezvous for child life; it is the one center of its existence, but unless it furnishes means to direct and appropriate its energies, it will not hold him. Both girls and boys will seek the street, the down-town diversions with influences and companionship that become a great factor in molding the pliant life. The hours should be filled with activities that are both absorbing and instructive. Employments, games and recreations that utilize energies and engage an undivided interest should be adjusted to needs.

A child should be both busy and happy, work should not be done as drudgery, but should be so directed that it gives pleasure and joy. It may give happiness to the child and at the same time is of educational value in the development of the pliant nature.

I would make a special plea that the responsibilities of housekeeping be divided among both girls and boys of the adolescent period. In most families where children are permitted to do household service, they are put at the drudgery; the boy to build fires and bring in wood and water. In cities where water and fuel is automatically supplied, be is released from these, while the girl washes the dishes day after day, day after day, and perhaps mops and scrubs. The mother or some elder sister does the cooking, baking and all manner of things requiring thoughtful care. At this period creative and inventive faculties are especially active. An outlet must be provided for them. Nothing gives a better outlet to a certain degree than the rightly ordered home. Long before this time both boy and girl are adepts at making beds, washing dishes, sweeping, cleaning windows, etc. It is now time that they are instructed that they can make out the bill of fare, do the marketing, get the entire meal and be responsible for it. It may seem easier for a mother to do this than to give instruction to either son or daughter, but if she could realize what it does in the evolvement of power she would be as patient and persevering in it and as exultant in the performance as she was in teaching the infant to walk. When they make bread and cake or griddle cakes, give them a good receipt and let them be responsible for the results. In school work they are accustomed to attention, and if you are particular with your instructions they will listen and will be happy in carrying them out perfectly.

To keep up interest in housework, give different parts of the work each week to different children. One week one is responsible for the care of the sitting-* room, the bedrooms, porches, lamps, etc.; the next week he takes the dining-room, setting the table, washing dishes and cleaning the silver, while the next he is the cook. It is much easier and gives greater zest if the cook makes his plan for the entire week at one time. Sitting down with mother he devises each meal, making memorandum of things to be procured for each. With a little practice, a boy or girl, of twelve even, can be entrusted with the entire preparation of meals, and can be taught to do it well. If he is fortunate to attend a school where cooking is part of the training, the home practice becomes a splendid supplement to school instruction.

At all events the home presents a ready means for appropriating child activity. It is not that the mother is relieved from incessant work, though this is well; it is not that it is more economical than employing a maid; it is not that every boy and girl is in preparation for household service; no, not any of these. It is that we have the child with a tremendous storehouse of power, tremendous energy demanding any and all means for expenditure and appropriation. Some time we may have a system of education better adapted to direct this energy. Now we have the appliances in the home; as a matter of economics, as well as justice to the child, these means should be utilized. Every time a child makes a loaf of bread, plans and gets a dinner, he has developed power to do other and greater things. He has had a lesson in attention, concentration, alertness and adjustment that can hardly be given so thoroughly and practically in another way. For the sake of the boy and girl analyze this a little.

Suppose he prepares what seems a simple break- fast: oatmeal, an omelet, griddle cakes and cof?ee. Given an untrained hand, a man or woman who has never cooked a meal, the mistakes he makes in preparation and execution are both laughable and pitiable; while with training the oatmeal is not stringy 0r scorched, but rolls out of the kettle, the grains entire, well cooked, retaining the characteristic sweet flavor; the omelet light and friable, evincing skill and delicacy of touch; the griddle cakes uniform in size and color, light and appetizing, are of themselves a satisfactory achievement, while the coffee of amber, the unmistak^ able aroma pervading the house, proves the " piece de resistance." With what nicety of adjustment the cook places stove cover and asbestos under the boiling oatmeal, so that it will steam done and not adhere to the kettle; how swift the workings of the mind and what knowledge of chemistry to make and bake an omelet, while the cakes require unceasing care and attention.

Shall we scan the movements of the cook more closely? She has prepared her batter for cakes. She has taken one pint of milk, one pint of flour, one egg, two teaspoons of baking powder; these are thoroughly beaten together and are better for standing awhile. While waiting for the griddle to heat, the omelet is prepared; beating the yolks of four eggs, adding a little salt and two tablespoons boiling water, folding in the whites that have been beaten separately. These are placed in a small, hot skillet, well greased, and then covered, leaving them to cook slowly.

She looks at her coffee, almost boiling! Puts some cakes on the griddle, then with a knife-blade raises the edge of the omelet to see if the heat is just right, turns the cakes and again looks at the coffee. She removes the cakes, looks at the omelet, lowers the heat under the coffee, puts more cakes on, and by this time the omelet must be raised so as to cook through, turns the cakes, takes off the coffee, another look at the omelet. Removing the cakes, slows the fire under the omelet, and when it is done to a turn folds it on a platter for the table. If more than three in the family, another omelet must be prepared and still the cakes go on. The coffee taken to the table, then the omelet and a plate of cakes and now more put on the griddle. No hurry and no flurry in all this. It is a simple plain breakfast, one that women get over and over again, with perhaps a child pleading for attention, milk to be cared for, dinner pails to be filled, etc. But if one boy or girl puts this breakfast on the table, perfect in combination and cooking, we will exempt him from the other pleasures; he has had no time for by-play, and has a valuable lesson in alertness.

It is serious attention and concentration, at the same time it is a development of that other faculty, the opposite of concentration, the faculty of going quickly from one thing to another, for the want of a better term we call it alertness, a faculty required in every business and profession in life.

The concentration is on the whole, the breakfast is the result, but the process requires a live, quick faculty of going from one thing to another — alertness. Standing around and watching mother do this one thousand times does not accomplish the good for the child that one performance develops for her or him. It is an appropriation of natural, inherent, creative energy; it is constructive art in domestic lines; and while the child builds, it builds him, builds for him character through the application of force, through the training of powers.

Ethics and comradeship are both cultivated by a social habit at mealtime; memory gems are recalled; conundrums given; lecture or sermon reviewed; the day's incidents recounted; current events summarized. Thus shop talk and comments on food are discouraged. Food discussions, the quality, the preparation, likes and dislikes, are not in good form at the table. An occasional expression of satisfaction or pleasure at some special preparation — a new dish or an old-timer revived — may be pleasant as well as encouraging to the cook. General conversation about food leads to likes and dislikes, and credits power to food that is in mind only. True etiquette avoids discussions and dissensions at the table; the hour is filled with pleasantries, stories, jokes and incidents.

The meal over, the work presents a splendid opportunity for cooperative comradeship. The mother directs the part of each, while she cares for food and plans for the next meal.

One cleans and brushes the table, another one washes the dishes, one wipes; if the family is large another washes the cooking utensils and tidies the kitchen. In fifteen or twenty minutes the work is done and all are ready to join in the evening's pleasures or pursuits.

The early hours of the evening naturally belong to the children, and should be dedicated to them. Games, music, etc., in which they can take a part may give pleasure to all. (See Supplement *v.)*

In another chapter mention has been made of the excursion, a visit to another city or country, original dramas, etc. Children delight in the thrilling and stir- ring events of life, they have a thirst for the heroic and this thirst must be quenched at home or it will seek satisfaction in more enticing haunts. Parents should be on the alert to take advantage of current events, making suitable application, both for amusement and development.

How well I recall an event at a summer school. A boy taking little interest in the excursions, the manual training, the sketching parties, had intimated several times that the lack of book work and study drill was proof that it was not a school.

He had, however, become proficient in rowing and swimming.

One night there was a tremendous thunderstorm, and the rushing waters from the hills down through a ravine brought sand and gravel that formed a small island along the shore.

The superintendent of the school at once interested the pupils in the new possession. A flag was put upon it, a name was given it, improvements were begun; then the question arose to whom did it belong — to the owner of the shore land, to the government, or to the first discoverer?

The boy mentioned became intensely interested. He was encouraged to get up a mock trial to have these three sides represented. He did so, and no event of that stirring eventful summer was so interesting to old and young as that mock trial. He had a judge, lawyers on both sides, and the United States District Attorney. A jury was impaneled; witnesses were called and testified, then the lawyers made their pleas. This young man represented the owner's interest, and the speech he made, full of argument and eloquence, would have done honor to a man of experience. He ' was wholly and thoroughly awake. When the jury brought in a verdict that it was all a dream, that there had been no storm, there was no island, etc., and the judge pronounced it a joke, the lad was almost sick with disappointment.

The next day those who had his interest at heart rehearsed the whole business with him and showed him that although a mock trial, it was no more so than many trials that were managed by the most honored men, even the verdict was as just as many verdicts. The days devoted to that land question and to that trial contributed to that lad's development more than any one month of schooling he had ever had. His perceptions were quickened, his judgment aroused, while he realized the nice adjustment of the scales of justice. He was called out in his social nature from habits of reticence and self-abstraction.

A school or a family may never have an occasion like this, but every school and every family will have events that may be made as valuable in the soul's evolvement. Sometimes what seems of very slight significance may be construed to mean as much to the child as this trial did to the lad. At all events the occasions should be frequent in which children and parents unite in recreation and amusement.

Thus through comradeship, through home activities, pleasures and amusements, true home or family ethics are established. They are founded on unity or kosmic love which compels manifestations that are full of life and love. The home is thus builded that is more than a shield and protection to its inmates, that is not merely a castle, but is a radiating center upon which the hearth-fire burns that imparts glow and warmth to all who perchance may enter, and from which a flame may kindle the fire in other hearts on other hearths.

Home is founded in the hearts of men and women; the love that builds a home is inherent and can not be forced.

CHAPTER XVII.

HEALING POWER OF LOVE.

The mine knows nought of emeralds within its rocks; the sea is ignorant of gems within its caverns, of corals in jagged reefs; these are as buried treasures, yet they are all there.

The admission to one's self that man is God's own likeness, sets one free to master this infinite idea.

Man is an intelligence that inheres in kosmic mind. Science has striven in vain to separate him from God. After ages of weary wandering through materialism, pantheism, and through a belief in a personal God, man at last sees that to understand life he must change his idea of God. God is life, love and intelligence acting by law through and in matter. This intelligence transcends human intellect; by results, by manifold operations in nature we know that it is primal cause.

Each man has his own conception of this cause, and measure of its immanence; hence come the varied theories of existence and philosophies of life.

Throughout this work the operations of nature and the relations of human life have been spoken of as wrought upon and instigated by love. To understand another's philosophy there must be a common meeting ground; so you are led through the Lover's World to the world of love.

The human heart responds most readily to the great kosmic force of life by reiterating, " God is love." In quick heart-beats, the eager, hungry soul, having once known the tenderness and faithfulness of maternal love, longs for and accepts the brooding warmth of divine love. The man or woman who has had the soul stirred in ecstasy by romantic love, comes to know that back of all human experience, all pleasure and pain, all joy and sorrow, is an omnipresent and omniscient power that projects itself in his consciousness as love. It is that love at the center, radiating to the circumference, that awakens

129

a sense of the divine in man, that makes him realize that he is man spelled, as William Blake says, with a capital M. He is man with powers hidden like the emerald in the rock, or the gem in coral reef. He is man with the strength of beast, the flight of birds, the magnitude of mountains, the mobility of waters. He is all this because of love, mighty love that is born of his life heaving at the heart of things alway.

Whenever the love principle is infused into the life of man, so that he has a sense of his kinship with divine love, the seed of health is planted in his body, and if cultivated with the dew and shine of that love it will yield a harvest in health and strength.

Compare this love potion with all the powders, pills and chemicals of the pharmacopoeia! Its application is universal, its supply inexhaustible.

How luxurious to rest in the bounty of love! There is no pain of body, no inharmony of mind that may not be healed by the realization of the all power of love. As a cultivated vegetation is destructive to weeds and brambles, so the sweet influence of love destroys the flush of fever, the darting pain, weakness of body and wanderings of mind. As a lighted lamp dispels darkness, so does love root out the seeds of disease.

The man who is healed by faith is healed through love of God; love shows forth in perfection; he images in his own mind the All love, the divine unity, setting in action the vibrations of love, perfect love.

" The healing power descending from within, calming the enfevered mind, spreading peace among the grieving nerves, Lo! the eternal Saviour, the sought after of all the world, dwelling hidden (to be disclosed) within each; O joy insuperable."

" As the body in air, so the soul sustains itself in love."

To heal thyself, to heal another, be at peace; fear not, rest in love, thou shalt conquer all ills. Drop anxieties, cease the hurrying to and fro of thought, simply rest in the source of perfect love. In silence and stillness find the love life —abide in it, live in it; then with a certainty realize that every life rests in the same love life; be conscious of the golden chord of unity.

Sweetly declare that life, health and strength are all products of love; joy, happiness, satisfaction are the fruits of love. Believe that you have planted the seed and know that it will draw to itself sustenance and nourishment.

To become conscious of this love makes one a god of health. You live it, radiate it and transmit it. You can not withhold it, for by its virtue it permeates all with whom it comes in contact. This is the great healing agent of human ills.

When you have the healing power of love you carry your medicine chest always with you. You may label the vials health, harmony, strength, endurance, but all these are only names of the one great elixir, bountiful in supply, universal in application. Cease giving power to any material remedy, to any mechanical device, and with child-like confidence trust the spirit of love within yourself. The secret is in the ability to close the door to intrusive thoughts, to fear, to selfish needs, to what others think. Quietly, surely realize the center of life, the Christ love, and in that state of exaltation is the power to heal.

Do not attempt healing on the intellectual basis; to will a friend into health may be possible, to hypnotize him, that is to enter the domain of his mind and change the character of his thought so that he believes he is well, may give relief, but the love healing, the Christ power is realizing one's own love center and the connection existing between that and the one who is ill. You stand for the manifestation of love; the result is the glow of health, the elasticity of youth, the life of vigor.

Love healing is more than adjustment; it is a re-creation; kosmogenic love is both inventive and creative. It impels thought, it loosens the mold of materialism and underneath, it discovers the rootlets of life, which, when nourished by daily shine and shower of love, develop into a perfected tree. Intellectually one accepts the fact that there is the one source of life and intelligence, a grain of faith — just a little at first, enough to experiment — then a willingness to *let* these kosmic forces shine in and through every part the physical being. This is the process of healing.

The process is not unlike lighting a darkened room; one can not, by any means, take the darkness out, but by a touch of the curtain you let the light in. When the room is dark it seems full of furniture; one stumbles over stools, rockers and tables, but a little light, a very little light, clears the way so one can walk or run without hindrance.

So in mind culture, raise the curtain of doubt, banish belief in physical forces and processes, of power in restoratives and medicaments, and let into the soul the light of love. Forget the past and have no thought of the morrow;

brush aside every intrusive thought; simply become an empty vessel; the curtain is now raised and the light of love reveals infinite resources and impels them into action. Kosmic love is always at command, it is a living fountain, a running stream; drink from it, dip in it, lave in it, trust it, yea be one with it, for it is life of your life, strength of your strength.

Sit in the middle of the stream and realize the present, tangible, quickening, creating power of love. Feel its thrill and potency in every fibre and cell.

> God is love, that love surrounds me,
> In that love I safely dwell;
> It is above, beneath, within me,
> That love is mine and all is well.

The wheel of life has love at the center. It is the pivot of all existence. The circumference or felloe of the wheel is life's expression and consciousness; the spokes are thoughts and feelings, the means of communication between center and circumference, between the inner and outer; these may be transmitted in stagecoach sluggishness or in lightning celerity. Love is the propelling power that gives strength for weakness, joy for sorrow, illumination for darkness.

Teach thy ears to bring thee, and thy tongue to speak, labor, and spend all thou hast for love — faint not; be faithful.

Cast at last, thy mortal self upon it, and let it be consumed; and behold! presently the little spark shall become a hearth fire of creation, and Thou shalt endue another garment — woven of the sun and stars.

CHAPTER XVIII.

MIND-CURE OR RIGHT THINKING.

MAN IS MORE THAN BODY.

In the light of psychological truth it may be as immoral for a man to be ill as to commit a crime. Living in the truth of his being he can not do either.

It is no new thing to recognize the power of mind over body. Physicians and people have been quick to attribute ailments to the action of thought, to thinking. " O he *thinks* he is affected by climate, she *thinks* she can not walk a block, she can not do a little housework! If she was a poor man's wife and had to do her own work she would have no dyspepsia, no uterine diseases."

You can go into any clinic and, after the examination of certain patients, the professor gives a knowing wink to the students — " Now, gentlemen, what is your treatment? " " Placebo! " is the reply. What is placebo? an inert substance like sugar of milk or cornstarch, and is prescribed because it has no power and the case is supposed to need no remedy. The disease is of the imagination.

Most famous doctors have had their bread pills and starch powders for certain cases. They would lose their patients and the fee if they were frank enough to say: *"Only your mind is diseased. A dose of right thinking* will make you well."

In these latter days certain religious sects and philosophers have arisen who declare that all diseases are of the mind's creation; that man naturally has a body of perfection and harmony, but through ignorance of this perfection and by perverted thoughts he has brought direful diseases upon himself. Their essential idea is that all power is in mind, that conditions of health and disease arise in mind, and that in mind only is healing.

It is held that climate, food, impure air, overwork, none of these at all enter into the causes of disease; rather this is of man's own creation, — he is a victim of wrong thinking — he has, like the prodigal son, left his father's house; the mind is filled with doubt, fear, anxiety, jealousy, hatred; these are outpictured in his physical life; he is out of harmony with the source of being; thus man makes his own bed of pain and digs his own grave.

There are many sects and cults who disseminate ideas similar to the above; their theories demand attention, while the healings and conversions must command respect. The blind are made to see, the deaf to hear, the lame to walk, and those bound to the sordid details of life are set free and filled with lofty aspirations. Students are sifting the theories and gathering facts, hoping to find the truth that is logical and practical, and yet so simple that every one may grasp the essentials and make for himself a new heaven and a new earth. One needs to realize that none has given the final word or reached the ultimate in a perfected life.

MIND CURE,

stripped of its superstition and its verbiage, may be both a science and a religion.

A science because it teaches the direct relation of cause and effect, — finds in mind the cause and in body the effect.

As the science of numbers is based upon a principle, a law unerring and exact, so the science of life is based upon a principle equally exact.

All unfoldment of life must be according to law; it is man's prerogative to understand and apply the law. It is a religion because the element of faith is required to apply the principles; this is the bridge between man as human and man as divine; it is the seeing and

134

knowing that illuminates reason and logic.

Heretofore many great souls have taught that material life is only the shadow, while the spiritual is the substance. Innumerable volumes have been written to prove that the physical body is an illusion; that matter has no power; that the senses are not to be trusted; emotions are to be killed out; ambition and desire destroyed, thus annihilating the very tools of service.

Many philosophers have had glimpses of truth, but, as we come to look longer and deeper, we find the missing links and develop a science of life that gives healing to mind and body. A brief statement of this is as follows: Spirit is the ego — the cause the divine principle in the world within and without — the absolute and uncreate. Spirit is mind, alike the law of the atom and the universe, the inherent intelligence of all nature.

Soul is spirit in action; soul includes the intellect, consciousness, sensation and emotion.

Body is the soul's expression or manifestation, the register of thought and growth; it is the cipher in an arithmetical calculation and has no power of itself.

Mind cure is a knowledge of one's true self and the becoming that self. It is a harmonious adjustment of spirit, soul and body; it is the soul's acknowledgment of the power of spirit which manifests in and through the body; it is the setting in order of all forces and faculties, obedient to kosmic law

Mind cure is for all, rich and poor, educated and ignorant, the religious and skeptical. The law in its working is no respecter of persons, it rains upon the just and unjust alike, it serves him who seeks and who walks in the path of light faithfully. A knowledge, a realization of one's own divine nature brings the healing; brings harmony out of discord; gives strength for weakness and health for disease.

SALVATION IS FOR BODY AS WELL AS FOR SOUL.

As soul evinces the awakening to spiritual verities, it stamps itself upon every cell and fibre of the body. The body partakes of the awakening and illumination equally with the soul, which proves the unity of life. According to the soul's acknowledgment is the body's expression.

The body becomes a fitting vehicle for the soul's manifestation. It does not hamper and hinder, but is molded by the soul, showing degree of development.

The mechanism of the body evinces an intelligence that transcends human intelligence. Every part is perfectly adapted to function; the ear in all its wonderful details fulfils the office of hearing; the eye is an optical instrument never equalled by man; the hand is a combination of mechanical principles that makes it a machine for the application of all these principles. Man with all his genius and resources has never been able to give the world a hearing instrument to equal the ear, a combination of lenses to compare with the eye. or a mechanical device that has all the qualities of a hand. In all inventions the thought power of the inventor is evidenced in the construction. Every joint, every wheel, every lever, each screw, from the largest to the smallest, has its use. This use is given by the mind power of the inventor; it is intelligence operating through law upon material.

A greater intelligence that never errs operates in all nature. In no place is this more evident than in the human body. The lungs, with rhythmic motion, night and day, without our volition, perform the function of respiration. During a long life the valvular force of the heart propels the blood through arteries and capillaries to carry and fetch the products of nutrition.

The force that operates bodily functions is kosmic mind, the universal intelligence that holds and controls all forces of nature from the constellations in the heavens to the tiniest flower or insect of earth.

Through man's consciousness it is given him to cooperate with this kosmic mind. By thought he can accelerate or decrease the action of organs that seem independent of his control. He can increase the lungs' capacity; he can call the heart's blood to the surface of the body; he can cause the glands of the skin to perspire and accelerate other functions of depurition. All this is accomplished by the action of will.

Healing is both willing and letting; the active and passive mental states combined. Man wills to let the kosmic mind work perfectly and harmoniously, as if he had no conscious intellect. So far as the body is concerned he becomes a perfect animal — *letting* all life processes operate naturally. *One wills to !et go.* He withdraws all interference in the processes that belong to kosmic mind. His is an active ruling out of normal thought; he lets go; it is also an active trust in the great life force. As it were the supernormal consciousness or kosmic intelligence is left free to operate in its own perfect manner. Man has side-tracked his own train of thought, leaving the road clear for the great unlimited express. Then follows the passive state, the state of silence. In this silence one consciously directs the kosmic life in self-healing; in healing another he recognizes in that other the unity of kosmic mind; as it were he establishes a wireless telegraphy from conscious mind to sub-conscious mind in the other and frees it from apparent limitations, reaching out of self to discover the self in a brother. (See Supplement *w.)*

To know kosmic mind seek THE SILENCE. One stills the normal consciousness — the tangled net-work of thoughts, the product of intellect and sentiment, to allow the operation of a deeper consciousness. This deeper consciousness is known as the Infinite " I " of Fichte, the Noumena of Kant, the Unity of Froebel, the Christ of Christians, the Kosmic Consciousness of Carpenter. The last is especially expressive. Kosmic is the whole, the entire, the infinite intelligence; it has no beginning or ending; it is boundless, limitless, pushing, pushing forth in power and efficiency; the normal consciousness is limited, having boundaries to its functions.

There is no definite demarkation between normal and kosmic consciousness, still we classify the operations and functions of each. Normal consciousness reasons, argues and dogmatizes; it devises and plans, setting up a man of straw to see it consumed in a blaze of argument; it has emotions, loves and hates, joys and sorrows; it has sense perceptions, smelling, tasting, hearing; it has feelings — rheumatism declaring a southwest wind, or stinging corns predicting a blizzard. It is swayed by suggestion, the hypnotist nauseates a man with a thought of a fly in his food, the business man operates it with adroit schemes; it is tossed here and there by the silvery tongue of oratory or the chimeras of opera and theater. It is also the realm of romantic love and emotional religion. In general, it is man's outward thought and activities.

The deeper our kosmic consciousness operates without volition or effort; it is distinguished by intuition, and progresses immediately to knowledge without intermediate process. St. Augustine says : " There in the depths of the soul glows something which is not in space; there a word is heard which has no syllables; thence there breathes a perfume which no breezes waft away. Who shall express God ? . . . Here inheres the sense of the absolute, the unchangeable consciousness of immortality. It is the inspirer of all the eternal verities which appear to the personal mind. Its trans- scendence has sustained man in every age of struggle, and inspired him with invincible courage and abiding confidence in the purpose of existence. It illumines every phase of known consciousness, but transcends them all."

In silence one touches the Absolute, knows the omnipresent, omnipotent principle we call God, feels the throbbing heart of being.

To experience soul silence, the divine perception of things, is the highest attainment of man; to hush the hastening to and fro of confused thought, to gain the sweep and surge of the ocean of kosmic consciousness, is the aim of the adept; it is the finding of the Christ; a touch of the hem of the garment reveals the soul's possibilities.

To attain to silence, one must first desire seriously to realize the operation of the divine in man — the knowable self, and must use every effort for this realization. Second: he must seek this habitually; the entire universe is formed in law and order. As day succeeds night in one constant rhythm, so the communion of kosmic and normal consciousness may be established as the systole and diastole of the divine and human. Appoint a certain hour for this communion and be true to the appointment. There is a philosophy in the Catholic being summoned to recount the symbology of his rosary thrice daily, and in the Mohammedan prostrating his face toward Mecca at the going down of the sun; habit and regularity belong to mind as well as to matter.

At the appointed hour, seek a position of perfect ease; relax all physical tension; the knees, feet, arms, hands to the very finger tips, all must be in a state of repose. Give up; let go; reason and emotion become as nothing. Be very still; ears forget to hear, mind ceases to think; in this nothingness and stillness consciously direct that the deeper self — the kosmic consciousness — shall manifest itself; shall permeate the intellect to awaken it into activity, shall endow the emotional life with perception and wisdom; shall quicken every cell and atom of the body with all life and all health.

Silence is a process of willing and letting.

You let go to be lifted out of conscious self into the realm of divine realization. At first one may get a glimpse only, or a thrill of the kosmic life, may merely hear the rustle of the seamless robe; but that glimpse, that thrill, that rustle, is the most precious experience of life. Through stilling the personal self, the common consciousness, and setting into activity the deeper or kosmic consciousness, the absolute self, a rapport is established between the outer life and the essential self; the fire is lighted upon the altar; always and always the flame may burn.   (See Supplement *x.*)

This is a conversion, a resurrection into a new life. The Self is trained into service and at any moment is at one's command. To the faithful the length of time and frequency of what may be called realization will increase. Until man is developed into one harmonious whole, existence would be impossible if the illumination were continuous; the physical and spiritual, the divine and the human must be adjusted gradually to perfect rhythm.

The habit once established there may be a continuous ebb and flow between the normal and kosmic consciousness. One leads a dual life, one devoted to the details of existence, the hurrying to and fro for seeming necessities; the other in communion with the spirit, the deep, deep self that from the calm of ocean depths moves the surface of the waters with illuminating power; it is the stillness of the soul that redeems life.

> . . . to know,
> Rather consists in opening out a way
> Whence the imprisoned splendor may escape.

Consciousness of the universal source and its wonderful mechanism, but rather sees it as a perfect whole, as a divine gift to be honored, while the exaltation of spirit, the knowing of God, lifts the mind into higher realization. In this state there is little or no consciousness of matter, and the finer forces permeate and build, construct and reconstruct on an orderly plan. Matter ceases its domination, obedient to laws of mind; the clear conception of life brings life, the mental picture of health produces health; the thought seeds of strength and endurance find fruit in agility, power and longevity; the sweet, harmonious heart songs create, evolve and build the love life.

Project the thought through seeming darkness and disorder and dwell upon the perfect life; the picture thus formed becomes the reality. The law compels the light that bursts the bonds of

140

superstition, the power that breaks the chains of ignorance.

One goes beneath the surface to see the cause and relation of things, to see the design and harmony of nature, to follow the thread of development, to know the life that impels all life, and through this process he becomes conscious of the soul's possibilities.

Right thinking gives to each and all the possibilities of health and longevity, the power of efficiency, as well as the soul's illumination of its own greatness.

Right thinking compels both disease and sin to be considered as illusions of normal consciousness, and replaces them with the shining truth of man's wholeness, his *oneness* with kosmic mind. This wholeness is health of body, activity of intellect, and clear vision.

Right thinking, through effective *silence*, is a gospel of health and prosperity, for thus man finds the Kingdom of Heaven in his own soul and realizes the fulfilment of the promise that all things shall be given unto him; *all things* include health, happiness, friends, and the joy of living.

Little by little one realizes the power and domination of spirit, and through this realization, this quickening, all of life's pursuits and life's relations become ways of pleasantness and paths of peace.

CHAPTER XIX.

RECREATION.

Rest is not quitting
This busy career;
Rest is the fitting
Of life to its sphere.

Amusements, recreation, all the so-called pleasures of life are born of the soul's desire for satisfaction.

The world has gone mad seeking pleasure. In this country it has taken a great rebound from the serious and puritanical aspect of life so thoroughly stamped and infused into all relations by the Pilgrim Fathers. In the winter it is theater, opera, concert, reception and ball, and the seeking of a warm climate. In summer the cities are emptied into the country, and the pleasure excursions to lake, mountain and seashore become fashionable *exertions* — full of discomfort, wanting in profit and devoid of satisfaction. What is the result of all this hurrying to and fro for pleasure, this hard work and worry to find happiness ?

Satisfaction comes from the joy of service and from daily and hourly *re*-creation. The man who loves his work, and works for the love of all the details, is filled with the pleasure of it. He needs no quitting, no rest from it, no taking hold of pleasure activities for refreshment.

The woman whose household duties are a service of love, whose every act is an outpicturing of her soul in accomplishment, is blessed each day with the satisfaction of the doing.

If a man's business is a burden, possesses his soul and drives him; then, until he learns the law of mastery, he must seek relaxation in that which changes his thought, in that which compels the strain and stress to quit the hold upon the mind.

The woman, as the presiding genius in a home, fills the many offices of cook, nurse, laundress and seamstress, and if she is working *on her nerve,* as she expresses it, she must by virtue of the very attitude of her mind toward that work seek rest from it. She requires a vacation; she must be amused.

The man seeks his change in billiards, in clubs, in yachts, in games, in church work and philanthropy.

The woman in guilds, in societies, in theater, card playing and social life.

The student loosens the strain from mental application in various kinds of athletics.

All these are amusements. Is an amusement a recreation? In changing the vibration of thought from study, business from household labors, does it give that impetus to one's life that renews it — that stands for strength and activity ?

Love and I create our own world.

One early spring my little six-year-old granddaughter and I spent a few days in our summer camp. We were greatly interested in watching an oriole build her cradle nest. What mechanical skill she evinced! How deftly with bill and claw she wove the threads in and out, in and out, to make her house cozy and secure! How eagerly she used the cords we cut for her! To test her, we placed strings in hiding places, under bushes, under the porch. Quickly she discovered and utilized them.

How does a bird know when to build a nest — how did this one bird find the hidden string? By love, kosmic love, which in bird life is unconscious unity with the source of life.

Through intellectual attainments, through building thought images, man has been separated from and lost this unity. He dwells *apart* in a garden of his own creating; but the joyful tidings may be proclaimed that through the very faculties that now seem to limit him, he may regain this consciousness of unity.

Symbolically he returns to his father's house and becomes reconciled. He finds within what he sought without; he does consciously what the oriole does unconsciously; he and kosmic love create a new world.

He lets go his intellectual grasp of all that which dominated his life, he makes of his mind a blank; the hurrying, crowding thoughts cease their chasing and scurrying, they pass out of existence, they flee before the effective word that has declared the reign of love and law.

The mind thus stilled becomes to know its kinship with the all life, it is awakened to a new sense of the soul's greatness, it is exalted on the throne of dominion and power. This is *re*-creation.

If a game of cards, with its nonsense and nothings, rules out the day's many thinkings and doings, leaving the mind a blank for renewal, who shall say it is not at least a distant relation to *re*-creation? If an actor, through his mimic representation of life, sidetracks the train of business thought, is not the mind left fallow for *re*-creation ?

If the symphonies and harmonies of music, the oneness of infinite tones produced by many instruments, lead the soul to a realization of the oneness of all life, then this is *re*-creation.

If the shine and shimmer of lights, the iridescent glow of color, beauty of form and rhythmic movements of dancers, touch the soul with reverence for the gifts and achievements of the artists, then it is more than a daze and a dream,— it is a *re*-creation.

Dancing as an amusement has within itself the germ and substance of recreation. It combines rhythm of motion with rhythm of music, and is adjustable to the law of action and repose.

It affords comradeship guarded by the etiquette of conventionalities, and gives a natural commingling of the sexes.

Dancing stripped of its excesses, under the influences of church,

144

school, home or club life, becomes an amusement that presents great claims to the thinker and philosopher; for old and young, for learned and ignorant, it is an effective means of self-forgetting. It breaks the bonds and limitations of self-consciousness and opens the doors for command of that which stands for power.   (See Supplement y.)

Dancing need not be ruled from one's life without knowing its philosophy and psychology, because it has been abused and conjoined to gluttony and debauchery, and has been specially classed among worldly pleasures.

George Fox, and his followers, the Quakers, in seeking the inner life, denied to themselves the pleasure of music as well as dancing. Both of these were the tools of the ungodly. They were the magnet and power of the saloon and brothel, and so not understanding that all evil is perversion, they elected to worship God in silence; no sounding of timbals, no exultation of spirit in song and chorus.

To most people the melodies of music strike a chord of harmony aiding them to know God. May not the rhythm of bodily movements awaken the soul to its possibilities and be to it more than an amusement, be veritably a *re*-creation?

The child in the kindergarten spends a happy forenoon with its cheerful leader, producing from forms, colors and gifts and in active play the creations of his imagination. He is in turn the farmer that sows the grain, the miller that grinds it, the express-man and train that transports it, the baker that molds the pliant dough. In myth, song and story he is the millwheel, the water or steam that gives it power, the father and mother dear that provide for his wants. At home, in the afternoon, he reproduces with blocks, with chairs, in company with baby brother the busy doings of the morning. He is so at one with all the activities of the natural awakening, that it goes on with new inventions and new constructions.

So in life's great kindergarten a natural unfoldment of powers renders it possible that all of man's doings and dealings shall be ruled as easily, as happily as the child life under Froebel's masterly direction.

The *re*-creating power is ever present at command. It does not argue, combat or dogmatize, but rather quickly sees and knows.

The busy goings and comings in office and shop; the buzz and whirr of machinery, the noise and bustle of commerce and trade, none of these can close the door to the *re*-created light.

The housekeeper becomes the home maker, for the awakening of kosmic love in her soul gives her lightness of heart, knowledge of needs and strength for execution.

In the hour of stillness she has experienced the *re*-creation that enables her to meet the demands of her home, to carry out the details of life. In listening to this power she recalls John's favorite dishes; she remembers stored fabrics that will make garments for the children, she leads her sons and daughters in ways that are an unfoldment and delight; indeed she becomes a princess in her household, for by re-creation she ruleth her own spirit.

In seeking a change, seek that which transforms, that which *re*-creates and builds anew. Pleasures have their ministrations. One may sense the new life in rambles through wood and field, in scaling mountain heights, in the abandon and freedom of water sports, in social pleasures, in joys of friendship; at the same time in the midst of all activities one may experience a daily, hourly renewal, a bringing forth of vigor and virility.

Running away from work or worry is not adjustment. One should not seek to change environment and circumstances, but to change his attitude toward them, the fitting of life to its sphere.

Herein he finds inward peace that may express itself in outward joy, a satisfaction that is a permanent pleasure, a calmness that is deep and lasting.

Knowledge of spiritual law enables one to *let* the source of life and health build up bodily tissue, stimulate mental faculties and recuperate all functions.

This knowledge leadeth one by the ever present still waters and feedeth him in perennial pastures.

CHAPTER XX.

SLEEP.

GODS DO NOT SLEEP.

Man as an animal requires sleep, much of it. Probably like beasts and birds he requires as many hours in sleep as there is darkness in the day. Man as a spiritually awakened being may free himself from the limitations of sleep.

The race has a strong belief in the requirements of sleep. A recent article on Beauty states that health, beauty, even length of days, depend largely upon refreshing sleep. The society woman who begins her day at four in the afternoon and seeks her bed in the early hours of the following morning, leads not a whit less wholesome life than the farmer's wife who begins her terrible daily drudgery before sunrise, and, without rest or diversion of mind, works hour after hour as unremittingly as though she were running a treadmill through a working day sixteen hours long.

All this, the writer claims, detracts from health and beauty. She continues: " Sleep is innocence and purification. Blessed be he who gave it to the poor sons of men as the sure and faithful companion of life, our daily healer and consoler. Strength, health, beauty and happiness depend upon a full supply of natural sleep."

" To sleep," says Amiel, " is to strain and purify our emotions, to deposit the mud of life, to calm the fever of the soul, to return into the bosom of maternal nature, thence to reissue healed and strong."

Usually physiologists advise eight hours of sleep in well-ventilated rooms, well-aired beds and clothing fresh each night. Most laboring people sleep at least eight hours, but often do not arise refreshed. People may carry their labors into their sleep, the soul never losing consciousness of them.

We have many illustrious examples of people who required very little sleep. Humboldt is said to have slept only two hours a night, traveling, studying, writing, yet he lived to advanced years. Napoleon and Wellington are both cited as being men of remarkable endurance and allowing themselves very little sleep.

It is told of Littré, the author of the great French Dictionary, that he never went to bed for the entire forty-two years he was performing that stupendous task. It was his custom about I at night to lie down in his dressing-gown and sleep from forty to eighty minutes. The following afternoon he would take a bath followed by a walk or gymnastics. His endurance was simply marvelous. As solitary instances these men proved that to them eight hours of sleep was not a necessity and many would like to know how to overcome this necessity.   (See Supplement z.)

The unconsciousness of sleep is supposed to be the liberation of the soul, and the rest it thus obtains is freedom from the process of adjusting soul and body. Soul activity through the physical body seems to weary of the constant friction between the two, and departs into realms or conditions that are more harmonious; visits friends either in or out of the body, and does this more freely according to one's willing. Possibly in an animal man, the soul has no separation from his body, and dead lethargic sleep may only serve to imprison it night as well as day.

The question arises, if people like the examples named are more harmoniously poised, all parts of their nature balanced, is it not important for all to attain the same poise ? May it not be that many cases of insomnia are simply people who do not require sleep — that have this adjustment naturally and can work or study many more hours than is customary.   (See Supplement a a.)

If one is unable to sleep he should seek rest and recuperation through the recreating process. He must learn to connect his human with his divine nature, and through this will get far more satisfactory refreshment than through ordinary sleep.

One should not carry the day's doings to bed with him; he should, like the child, forget his plays and toys, banish from the mind all schemes and chimeras, all griefs and sorrows, and, with some strong positive thought, connect his life with divine life; he thus, as it were, puts his soul in condition to get the best repose.

One can consciously direct the soul during sleep to seek such conditions as shall lead to its evolvement, and gradually it will return the fruits of research to waking state. It seeks resources in the world of spirits or by coming into rapport with other souls that are still in the flesh. Some obtain through this means positive facts and solution of problems. One can also send it on missions of special service. The more one learns to control and concentrate the mind in his waking hours, the more power he has over his faculties in the sleeping state. It is only a thin veil between consciousness and unconsciousness — the veil that shuts off memory while other faculties are operative.

I recall that at one time I had a friend, who was watching night after night by the bedside of her father who was very ill. One wakeful night, when my thoughts were unusually wandering — playing tag with each other — I called a halt. I said: " Enough of this, go off now and be of some use; go to Mary and help her take care of her father." Two days after this I had a letter from my friend saying: " You seemed with me hours last night. You were so tangible that I told father Alice seems here — he was quieted by your presence and I was strengthened and rested." When I awakened I had taken a longer sleep than usual and was more than ordinarily refreshed. I had no consciousness of the visit that I had imposed upon myself.

If one's occupation requires many hours he can train himself out of the sleep habit, or at least be able to lessen the hours; he does this by developing his spiritual powers; by realizing that mind, not matter, is rather the force of being; he thus passes out of the animal to the spiritual life, and by harmonious adjustment is able to use his mind or body to an unlimited degree. It might be dangerous to attempt a prolonged wakeful period if one is living a sensuous life, and has not felt the quickening power of spirit.

An amusement that is a veritable recreation, that gives adjustment to the entire man, takes the place of sleep. Those who use stimulants that produce wakefulness are working on borrowed capital, and nature will demand payment with interest.

Most people can, on going to sleep, set an hour for waking. The soul is more obedient to attend to requests than is usually known. Call yourself by name and state the hour you wish to arise; you are to say: "John, waken me at 6 — remember, not a moment later, and be sure that I am refreshed." You will seldom be denied a response, and thus from obedience in one thing you can proceed to greater accomplishments. Sluggards have no place in this busy world, and when we can learn that we are not opposing nature by taking less sleep, we will feel free to make the demand.

The *Dream state* may be a half animal sleep, caused by stimulants, narcotics, indigestion or what is called nervous exhaustion. The stupefied brain wanders fitfully from the objective life to one of imagination, and the dream life is full of detached incidents, a patch-quilt mimicry of life, often accompanied by tossing and incoherent speech.

Many claim that dreams are impressions from other souls or entities who may be in the body or not; that they may converse intelligently with living or departed friends, and receive information which is brought into the waking state.

Some people attribute all dreams to hovering spirits, who impress their thoughts upon the sleeper or actually converse with him, and often get great satisfaction from even this vague method of commumcation.

Another dream state is where the higher or kosmic consciousness of the Self becomes cognizant of the universe of things; it follows the pageant of history, the panorama of the living, the thought world of philosophy and religion. It becomes acquainted with rulers and the schemes and intrigues of dynasties. These different dream states are held of great value by some people, who listen to the warnings, the prophecies and comfort they bring.

The young shall dream dreams and the old men see visions. Who shall say that they do not or may not, to some extent at least, become a valuable factor in raising the mists and giving a clearer vision of life's realities ?

One thing is true, that any dream state can be cultivated. This is done by relating the dreams, by commanding the memory to retain them and by an effort to utilize them in answering questions and solving problems.

A continual practice increases the frequency of dreams. A singular fact in connection with them is that symbology is intimately connected with the sleep vision, and to give value must have an interpretation; another singular fact is that every expounder of dreams gives his own interpretation; besides each individual has different meanings for different symbols. Compare dream books and writers upon symbology and you can verify this.

A dream-wedding portends a funeral, a birth, glad news; a serpent, a new birth, an enemy, a disappointment; a young babe is trouble, inspiration, a new beau, a friendly visit, a scandal; a garden is prosperity, callers, letters, new friends, sickness; vermin, enemies, slander, money, short journey.

One through successive years finds a dream of washing (laundry) portends a move from one house to another. If the water is clear, the clothes white, the move will be pleasant and satisfactory; if the suds are dirty, the clean, soiled and colored clothing mixed in the tub, the change will be attended with no end of trouble. To another, experience proves that this dream means the transaction of important business; to another the loss of a friend; to another a journey. So on through every conceivable dream, each thing or circumstance, according to the author or dreamer, means every possible state of human consciousness. When dreams thus present different meanings to the dreamer, can any one hope to reduce their symbology to a perfect system? It is probable that their meanings vary according to varying human consciousness, and their reliability must necessarily depend upon proof obtained through experience of that consciousness.

A friend of mine lost a son, a beautiful young man, in the Ashtabula railroad disaster years ago. During the same night she awakened from a frightful dream, having seen his beautiful body consumed in the burning wreck of the train. She awakened her husband, who quieted her fears by telling her that she often had dreams that proved meaningless. She went to sleep to repeat the identical vision and awoke sobbing: " It is true, it is true, Myron is burned." Again her husband soothed her, and again she repeated the sad story in dreamland.

The last time she refused to sleep, but arose, calmly put her house in order and prepared breakfast; her husband went early to his office, where he found a dispatch verifying the dream; Myron was dead and his body burned in the disaster.

Few people live who do not some time in their lives have dreams that come true, especially dreams of death. On the other hand the same people have many, many dreams that, so far as they can ascertain, bear no relation to actual experience. The proven dream is remembered, the fleeting one forgotten.

In brief, one may consider that dreams are unreliable and not to be depended upon for a guide to daily action, nor may one claim to propound living truth by the fortuitous symbology of dreamland. One should rather seek a conscious state of vision in which the human consciousness blends so harmoniously with divine wisdom that one perceives the clear statement of truth. This is an awakening, an illumination that requires no symbology.

The messages, wireless, are conveyed from the heart of the Infinite to the divine in man, and reveal to finite mind unheard of powers and capabilities. The journey is neither long nor difficult, but requires the application of principle and faithfulness. This is possession of the Holy Grail celebrated in story, the sacred passover, the divine principle recognized and appropriated in the human heart. It is the finding and consciousness of the Christ within, which becomes manifested without. It is this vision of Universal life that all seek and all may find and is rest and peace; health of body, strength of intellect and consciousness of the light, that lighteth every man.

> Dreams in their development have breath.
> And tears, and tortures, and the touch of joy.
> They leave a weight upon our waking toils,
> They do divide our being; they become
> A portion of ourselves as of our time.
> And look like heralds of eternity.
>
> — *Byron.*

CHAPTER XXI.

DRESS.

All the harmonies
Of form, of feature and of soul displayed
In one bright creature.

A new life and new ideals require freedom in dress; require personal study, so that one's attire becomes as a part of herself; an expression of individuality. The whole tendency of the times is toward this. Those of us who have gray hairs can remember that when a fashion was started in Paris for any one thing, it became the fashion of the entire world. If it was the edict to wear bustles, every woman on all occasions, under a party gown, street attire, or house dress, wore a bustle. If leghorn hats of any one particular shape were worn, they were universally adopted. Going to church or theater, seeing one hat, you would be sure to know the style of all; possibly a little variation in the colors of ribbon or floral decoration. Feathers were worn in the winter and flowers in summer; you could always draw the line between the seasons by the trimmings upon the bonnet. So too if trains were decreed, the ball dress, the garden dress, the mountain dress, it was all one and the same; all had to have the elongated dust collector because Dame Fashion said so.

Now every woman has a wide choice in her apparel. While she may, in a way, be devoted to what is called conventional dress, yet in that there is such a choice of fabric, style and adaptation, that she necessarily puts her own character into her wardrobe. A student of dress can go to the closet and say what kind of a woman wears these clothes; her shoes and her gloves even reveal characteristics.

Dress should not only express individuality, but should give freedom of bodily action and should be adapted to occasions. This requires a special study. A woman need not have her thoughts so devoted to it that it takes her mind from duties or from interest in any of the great movements of life; but a sufficient amount of study making it a real evolvement of one's own mind and an evidence of personal characteristics, becomes a satisfaction to herself and friends. A garment thus formulated, when once completed requires no more thought. It seems not only a part of one's self, but is rather more than that. She has studied fabric, color, tone, style and adaptation. All of these thoughts are woven together into the one garment, and if her ideas are carried out by herself or the modiste, it may be said that the garment is a triumph of art; the art is as much in the fact that it is an expression of her own ideas and specific in its construction as any other work of her creation. Through design, color, material and ornament, it transmits her emotions and perceptions to the understanding of the beholder; it causes in others similar emotions and perceptions to her own. Dress thus is more than clothing or vesture, it is an art.

A student of dress gathers her ideas largely from representation of art in galleries and books. She studies fashion plates for hints in adaptation. The time will come, no doubt, when fashion plates will cease to be the grotesque representations they now are, but will fill the demand that sensible women are making for clothing adapted to various occasions — clothing that permits the fulfilment of life's demands.

Already there are evolved dainty and suitable walking dresses, sensible outing costumes, while we now and then get a hint of the house garment.

The business woman of the day has made a demand that has been answered in what you might call " Utility Gowns "; combining in every way service and usefulness, the accessories for ornament and decoration only are avoided.

If the woman of leisure sees fit to wear a skirt that is a hindrance to her freedom and becomes a burden because it must be cared for, requiring hands that should be used for other purposes, the business woman is independent enough to make her skirts less cumbersome, and has too much respect for herself to become, in any sense, a street scavenger. Her limited purse compels her to buy material that is durable and serviceable, while her continuous association with many people requires that her garments should be unobtrusive. The tailor-made suit having a short skirt has fulfilled these requirements.

THE OUTING COSTUME

to fulfil its purpose should be made of light and durable material, and shorter in the skirt than the one of which we have been speaking. Those who have gone into camp or climbed mountains know what solid comfort there is in divesting one's self of the skirt entirely and simply wearing bloomers.

The central thought is not for appearance, not what some one else thinks, but what benefit is to be derived from the excursion or from camp life. So one fashions her garments to conform to this thought. She builds into her clothes the independence that the life is to give. From time to time women have adopted special styles for outing costumes, and then again they have lapsed into an ordinary traveling dress for any occasion. But the new woman who stands side by side with men in vocations, in investigations, in athletics, has garments so fashioned that they shall not be a hindrance. She is bright enough to adjust her clothing to these conditions and uses her ingenuity to adapt them to special occasions.

HOUSE DRESSES

of women who perform the labors of home are entirely wanting in purpose and adaptation.

Women have their tea gowns, their lounging robes, their chamber robes, but for housework they put on cast-away garments that are too shabby for intended purposes. They have nothing suitable for their labors. If any thought has been given, it has probably been that of economy, on the ground that they might better wear out what has become unfit for other occasions than to make a garment especially for work.

It seems extremely grotesque to see a woman hurriedly getting breakfast, wearing tight-fitting corsets and dress with a long train. When she mops or dusts a floor does she do it with mop, broom or duster, or with her trailing skirts?

Eighty per cent of American women are their own homemakers; we wonder that more of them are not bright enough to choose garments especially suited for their work.

It is always best that a house dress should be of wash fabric, short in the skirt, and have elbow sleeves, while a finish of ruffle or lace about the neck gives a neat appearance. The skirt and waist should be made together; either an ordinary round waist with belt, or else a mother hubbard that can be belted in. Avoid using cheap material; the making really is more than the price of goods; so get good gingham, percale or print. One doing her own work with all the modern appliances, say in an apartment house, and who is especially neat, may find it desirable and economical to wear white goods. There are fabrics like crepes and dimities that can be washed which do not require ironing; if one can attire herself in a neat dress of white, with lace or ribbon at the throat, she is ready for anything else that may come into her life.

There is no excuse for wearing dirty, ragged and dowdy-looking clothes because a woman does her own work; she shows that she is master of conditions by neatness of attire, by wearing a dress that is so much a part of herself that it is becoming and at the same time so well adapted to her work that it is no hindrance. The short skirt, the free waist, the elbow sleeves, the low neck, are all in themselves artistic; they are a gain toward converting what has seemed a drudgery into pleasure.

Suitable attire is one factor toward making housework a joy and a most important one.

DRESS ADAPTED TO PREGNANCY

should be light, loose and comfortable, offering no restriction to any part of the body.

Bands and belts can not be worn loose enough to prevent restriction of the body, which above the hips at the *supposed belt line* is more pliable than any other part. Nature forgot to make a belt line and seemed not to foresee the stricture and stress that would be put upon the waist, otherwise she would have extended to this part a bony protection. Through respect for the maternal in her soul, and through knowledge of artistic models, woman will adjust her clothing at all times to preserve the perfection of the human form, in which perfection there will be freedom, for the performance of special functions. All the organs will retain their natural position, while there will be no hindrance to free development during the bearing of children. Gowns designed for fleshy women are suitable and artistic for maternity gowns, while Greek costumes and Empire dresses always give hints for styles adapted to pregnancy.

Already no doubt a lady has adopted union underwear and skirts made from princess patterns. She may find difficulties in modeling the outer dress so that it shall fulfil above conditions. This is more especially the case while separate skirts and waists are in vogue; she can obviate this difficulty though by making for the dress a princess lining, and in the two side seams putting lacings which will allow ad-justment to the increase of size. Over this princess lining she can dra-pe a gown of any fashion; a tea gown, or a skirt and waist or skirt and jacket as in later styles. She will only need to buy a pattern of a princess dress, giving waist measure, natural size, and then buy the eyelets by the strip and have them stitched to the side seams. Thus with lacings the garment is adjusted to increasing size.

ARTISTIC DRESS

is drapery rather than clothing; it is the setting of the picture and enhances, by its perfect adaptation, beauty of form and grace of movement; at least it is never a hindrance to beauty or grace.

In the picture of Elizabeth of Roumania (Carmen Sylva) we have a combination of grace, beauty, elegance and stateliness; her rich costume adds to her natural poise and dignity, while the artistic lines of the drapery give a queenly grace to her form. It bespeaks the right to command. Such a gown is a true queen's gown, and would give no offense to fashion or conventional dress in 1800, 1900 or 2000. It has so many points of adaptation, is so in harmony with the character and position of the beloved queen, that it can not go out of fashion.

Queen Alexandra's robe as Doctor of Music, in its attractive features gives hints for a study robe, wrapper and cloak. For the latter it should be made of velvet, broadcloth or drap d'été. These two types give examples whose station frees them from any conventional necessity   (see Supplement *b b*).

Queens fashion their own robes; so, as one reigns in her own realm, becomes master of all mind forces, she will naturally create for herself queenly robes: It has been said that taste is the only morality — that is, taste in the broad sense — the choice of things: By what one likes is he judged. His choice in reading, in amusements, in music, in dress, in companions; all these are signs of character. From these you read his judgment, wisdom, his attainments. In the same sense one clothes himself in make-shifts, in the dictates of

160

CARMEN SYLVA.

fashion or according to one's own taste. Taste for suitable and appropriate clothing is morality; taste for jargons and nondescripts represents notions of many people in composite expression.

Thus what we like determines what we are. In our dress the sign is always out. If we wear a coat of many colors, cut in many pieces, artistic lines broken by belts and cords, bonnet, gloves and shoes inharmonious and a misfit, the mind is unsettled; one has no individual taste; the wearer represents the " they say " of many people. One soon tires of such garments and rejoices in a change of fashion.

Does a woman choose soft, clinging fabrics in neutral tints and preserve the art-line in the outer garments? Does she wear a hat that is less prominent than the head and face it adorns? Do the gloves, buckles and jewelry match the suit? Then you know her feet are on solid rock and her character a harmonious union of love and intelligence, of intuition and judgment; she has the morality of clear vision. Her dress is the sign, the poster, that attracts those who need her counsel, who are willing to sit at her feet and learn wisdom.

An artistic gown frees one from the bondage of fashion. You wear a certain cut of sleeve because you choose to do it, a bonnet, a ribbon, a buckle that belongs to you — the inner *you* — born of original thought, and so long as they last there is no purloining quality reflected in your soul, for you have not even stolen the ideas that produced them; they are created out of the whole cloth of your own character. Out of it is born the beauty, art and character of clothing that represents soul loveliness, for love demands that all the equipments of life shall represent love. Like the bride's trousseau, every garment must be a speech of joy; all the robes, robes of peace.

If one is clothed in her right mind, her dress is fashioned by it; in the fabric is woven the golden cord of unity — the one cord that is found in every garment of all the people, and by this cord she knows her relationship to every man and woman; the relationship of absolute or kosmic love.

ARTISTIC DRESS FOR MEN.

Dress to be artistic allows freedom and suppleness; it conceals and discloses the form at one and the same time, but avoids the appearance of stiffness and constriction.

Man's attire usually gives freedom of movement but lacks artistic appearance; the mobility of the body is concealed by unyielding material and inartistic lines in vesture.

Man's ordinary dress is a utility dress; an insignia for business. The cut of his coat and the fabric unitedly speak in plain words that he is ready for action. He has eliminated every ruffle, every fold, every ornament, indeed everything that gives a hint of leisure or of taste, and as an expression of individuality, he has very little choice.

In man's attire it will take a strong character or an association of strong characters to break the bondage of the conventional. The dress of men gives them freedom of bodily movement, and they are beguiled into the delusion that they are free to dress as they please. Let a man wear a long robe, a shawl or a military cape on the street, when not in fashion, and a rabble of boys will soon prove how little free choice he has in matters of dress.

Fifty years ago shawls heavy and warm were the universal outside wrap for men as well as women. Let a tall man wear one down the principal street to-day and he would attract quite as much attention as Mary Walker in male attire. Man must wear some form of starched bosom and collar, woolen coat pantaloons and vest; the varying cut of these give him small opportunity for change or adaptation to individual taste and character. One man in the great city of Chicago, a University Professor, has the independence to contribute to his own comfort by avoiding the stiffened shirt and collar and in their place adopting those made of soft white silk. Would he have the independence to wear outside garments equally as comfortable and artistic away from college halls?

The evening dress, full dress of men, so long in vogue, is a great travesty on the independence and freedom of Western manhood. Men appear in this straight, rigid, cutaway coat, displaying a square field of glazing, glassy whiteness; as artist, orator or professor, they have only environment and personal presence to distinguish them from the man who serves them their supper. As a help to break down class distinctions we may tolerate it, but as an expression of individual life and character, it is a failure.

Men have a right to have their apparel give some hint of soul development, some little suspicion that dress in its symbolism has a deeper significance than simply a covering and protection. Color, fabric style of drapery, gems and precious stones should all be at their service to express their lives, their ambitions and aspirations. In the evolution of the race both men and women will express character, emotions and development in the garments they wear.

Men of the Orient, when clad in their native costumes, often give a hint of what may be accomplished in the application of art to man's attire. Our standards are so conventional that we are apt to see the picturesque or grotesque in what is really artistic. The long Persian robe of soft fabrics and blended tones in color, and loose Turkish trousers, is the dress of men of leisure, the student and the merchant wherever the Mohammedan faith has penetrated. Should one of their people visit England or America he may wear a stiff derby hat, a Prince Albert or cutaway coat, and unyielding neck and foot wear of the West, but on his return to his own country he is soon rehabilitated in the native attire that is more comfortable and more artistic in outline. The doti and oppurna of the Brahmin, consisting of two strips of fine white India lawn or muslin, are made at each wearing into an upper and lower garment; are put on so deftly, are so spotlessly clean, that though his brown shoulders and legs may be bare he seems to radiate purity and the power of a peaceful mind. His white turban, made up of many yards of the same white muslin, only accentuates the symbol.

The white coat, the sash and peculiar turban of the Parsee remind one always of the fundamental principle in his religion, right thought, right speech, right action.

The Japanese, quick and responsive in mind, pliant and peaceful by nature, in their kimonos of soft silk and many hues represent their natural characteristics far better than by the adoption of foreign fashions.

The man of the future who creates or molds the fashion will be a student of the science and art of dress. He will be an ethnologist, gleaning hints of fabrics, of color, of shape from every nation. He will find that the composite production will represent the composite characteristic of the people who have arisen from and show forth the combined qualities of the ages.

Dress is vesture; in the web and woof of the garments is woven the strands of thought that have builded individual characteristics.

These strands are silken and golden, strong and flexible, indicating the soul's power and place. Thus it is inferred that it is not trivial to give attention to the purchase and making of one's garments, for in this attention one symbolizes the accumulated wisdom of his life. In his dress he creates a picture that renders his soul an open book to friends and associates — a self-creation of the Self.

CHAPTER XXII.

BEAUTY AND ITS POWER.

Grace was in all her steps, heaven in her eye,
  In every gesture dignity and love.
If eyes were made for seeing, then beauty is its own excuse for being.

" Beauty is a Multitude in Unity" is the old definition given by the Roman School, and Coleridge says: " There is no doubt that such is the principle of beauty."

The definition would seem more like a familiar acquaintance if we would reverse the words and say "unity in multitude."

Beauty is more than grace of form, more than manner, more than the art of culture — it is a combination of many (multitude) faculties and graces to make a harmonious whole. " The perfection of outward loveliness is the soul shining through its crystalline covering."

That " beauty is more than skin deep" is a trite saying; faultless attire, the tonsorial art and cosmetics on a face in repose may delude the beholder, but soon the scornful glance, the dissatisfied expression reveal the unbeautiful spirit, the combative and critical composition of the mind.

" Every trait of beauty may be traced to some virtue; to innocence, candor, generosity, heroism!"

All states of mind, all emotions make pictures on the face. Jealousy and pride turn up the nose. Anger pouts the lips; avarice and secretiveness squint the eyes; melancholy and doubt give a falling of lip muscles, a " down in the mouth" expression; candor, frankness and ingenuousness open wide the eyes, the open eyes of childhood; cheerfulness and content give placid features.

Straight up and down lines, deeply furrowed in the brow, indicate sternness and sharp, abrupt manner. Faint crisscross lines about the mouth and brow show a nature constantly irritated by small worries.

Spiritual development or consciousness gives a clear, liquid expression to the eyes, revealing through them the soul's illumination; the man who sees God, who has the inner light, shows this light forth to the beholder.

Standards of beauty are changing. Once a pale, delicate, willowy woman was the type for feminine loveliness, and men scorned for themselves the appellation beautiful; a beautiful man was a type of effeminacy; if he were an Apollo in form and figure, a god in facial expression, he might be called handsome, but to be *beautiful* was an insult. Now a beautiful woman must possess strength, color and robustness. The standard has progressed with ideas, and lo! a man as well as a woman may be beautiful. He is learning to cultivate and utilize the feminine qualities of soul, and expresses them in features, in movements, in thought, in action.

Woman is developing intellect and physique, but this is not at the expense of intuition and perception; she shows forth strength and wisdom in all activities, while her keen insight and quick judgment were never more reliable. So to the word beauty is given a larger significance; it is truly a *unity in multitude* expressing and representing a diversity of gifts, a combination of the best soul qualities — it is a composite picture of all these qualities in activity.

Standards of beauty vary in different countries and among different people of the same country. " These standards are indicative of the thought and progress of the people. The high cheek-bone, war paint and feathers give virtue to the warlike and combative spirit of the nation. Large waists and fleshy women, types of beauty in Japan, represent a joyous free life, while small and deformed waists of Western nations typify constraint and conformity to custom. A child sees beauty in the grotesque Dutch dolls and brownies, a child-man or woman in deformed feet and misshappen bodies.

The art sense must be awakened to see the beautiful in the true. The boy or girl in school is given models of beauty in the Greek Slave, Venus de Milo, the Winged Victory; tbe student of art selects living models that have beauty of face and natural development of bodies and feet; the woman of fashion makes a scrapbook of her monthly magazines, pasting over the distorted figures elegant half-tones of madonnas, photogravures of statuary, and models from the works of famous artists.

These are types, an imitation of which repeats their grace and loveliness, for women learn that :

" The first in beauty first in might, and at her feet are laid the scepters of earth."

FACE REFLECTS THE SOUL.

As a girl grows to womanhood she molds her face from within. The happy or unhappy mind is recorded.

A woman's face in early youth, smooth, fair and beautiful, year by year becomes the index of her mind. What one reads in the features, surely reflects the soul of the individual.

ALL LINES ARE EARNED.

Time, the inexorable master, does the chiseling on each countenance. But the soul of every person is back of the graver's hand, and old Father Time, if inflexible, is just to each and all. Time never graves a line not earned.

Wrinkles are the outward and visible manifestations of the inward and invisible spirit. It is the " I told you so" of months and months thinking. No living woman ever breathed who has not legitimately earned each line, each depression, ridge, or crow's foot, which mars and destroys her beautiful face. The mental state of each, the attitude of her spirit toward the world, is reflected in the expression of the face. Sit down before a mirror suddenly and without feigning an expression, without assuming " company manners," what do you see ? The reflection and serenity of content, or the crisscross lines of worry and discontent? What kind of a face are you making?

Do you see with amazement significant droop of lips and furrows between the eyes? You have earned those hateful little wrinkles. They record fits of temper, pettishness, unrest, a slave to trifles.

Health and beauty are synonymous. There can be no perfect physical beauty without health. If you are ill, bend your every effort toward getting well. Health of mind gives wholeness of body, and both unite to produce beauty.

Lines and wrinkles are evidence of dead tissue; cells have been killed by poisonous thoughts and leave unfilled graves. Sour words, crabbed looks, grumbling, fault-finding dig these graves. The face of the scold of past generations was a well-filled cemetery. I remember when teaching in the country I boarded with a woman only forty years of age. I was about sixteen. Her housekeeping was immaculate, her cooking famous in her world, but from morning until night it was scold, scold; her face and neck and hands were covered with the tell-tale wrinkles. I prayed that I might never live to be as old as she, for I recoiled at wrinkles that I supposed were merely the imprint of time.

I saw her again when she was seventy; she had learned that non-resistance was a better attitude of mind, and really from a habit of serenity had, after all these years, removed the old-age verdict from her face.

Wrinkles must be removed from the soul; when one lives in the love world the furrows will leave the face.

Massage and skin foods have their value. Muscles may be developed and tissues nourished, but all combined skill of science and beauty professionals can not permanently remove wrinkles until the mind is straightened out, until one has found in non-resistance the true law of life and understands that love does not tolerate wrinkles in the face or in the mind. If you are worried or vexed, if you give way to the soul-demoralizing and beauty-killing forces, envy, hate and intolerance, these will destroy your face and leave great tell-tale marks which all who run may read. What sort of a face are you molding? What lines are you carving? For it is you, the inner *you*, who are accountable for each one.

Beauty that is the outpicturing of a lovely character has for its foundation that which is more permanent than paste or colors.

AVOID THE WORRY HABIT.

Keep a record for a month and see if you have not worried over many things that never happened, or at least that turned out all right. Look in the mirror when you worry and see its effect. Worry is not a good beauty powder. The bright, clear eyes have become dull, the laughing mouth droops, the brow of which you are justly proud is corrugated and knotted. No wonder you turn away disgusted with the picture. The same face picture and figure portrait is forbidding to your friends. When you are joyous and lighthearted you spread a contagion of joy and well may the mirror reveal to yourself the satisfaction of the picture. A looking-glass tells no falsehoods. The face as well as the body is the reflection of the mind.

Physiognomy becomes a science when we know that it is absolutely impossible for a sweet, patient, gentle woman to create a crop of wrinkles.

Trustfulness, forbearance, confidence in the Self, knowledge of one's own divine nature, harmony between the inner and outer, produce the god-like expression. The mind, steadied for all occasions that has not become driftwood for the river of events, keeps its serenity and reveals its poise in lines of beauty.

As Holmes says: " Beauty is divinity taking outline and color."

MIND AFFECTS THE BODY.

One author writes: " The prevailing state of mind or character of thought shapes the body and features. It makes us ugly or pleasing, attractive or repulsive. Thoughts shape our gestures, our mannerisms, our walk. The least movement of a muscle has a mood of mind, a thought behind it. A mind always determined has always a determined walk. A mind always weak, vacillating and uncertain makes a shuffling, shambling, uncertain gait. The spirit of determination braces every muscle. A persistent, joyful spirit fills every nerve with strength." Rather, it is more true to say that a peaceful mind and joyful spirit crowds out all thought of nerves and muscles. It is as though they were not. The squirrel in his grace and agility makes no record of his physical development. He has never learned the location of the biceps or spinal cord. In the joy of a game of golf or tennis youth and maiden forget the mechanics of muscles and the function of nerves. Perfect health blots out all consciousness of body, leaving it to express in freedom.

Real beauty, the immortal bloom of youth, must be a trinity comprising wholeness of body, a harmonious mind and a joyous spirit.

The perfected man, the perfected woman, compels beauty of form and feature, compels an expression of loveliness that is truly beautiful.

To gain beauty, seek this perfection. Dig out the rootlets of greed, avarice, envy and strife; in their place sow seeds of kindliness, trust and altruism, all gathered from the garden of love; water these with patience and forbearance, strengthen with justice and mercy, watch over them with faith and hope, when lo! The harvest will be beauty — beauty of person and beauty of character — all the flowers of the garden have combined to produce this wonderful creation. This is not for a day, not for a year, but its most charming property is that it is immortal. It is so engraven in the heart that it can not perish, but abideth forever.

Sermons and sermons are preached upon love and character, books are written upon justice and right living, poetry is full of ideals, and yet man goes about making up an ugly face for his neighbors to behold, and woman photographs her unrest on her features.

May not I present each reader with a package of beauty seeds, bearing the stamp of genuineness, that will germinate, bloom and fructify ? This genuineness is within; it is knowledge and expression of kosmic love, of the love life that is limitless and boundless. Consciously it may be set into operation to build and mold character, cell by cell to renew and perfect body, and thus shine forth in beauty. Science reveals this force of all force, and faith, the spiritual perception, builds it into manifestation; the sign of beauty follows the building.

Man at home in his own garden, by conscious thought develops the love seed already planted by the Master hand. It is one of the discoveries of the age that he can put himself in harmony with this seed life, this love life, and through the union develop Beauty spelled with a capital B. From the human man — the sense-man — he becomes the god-man with godlike powers. The Apollos and Minervas in his soul show forth in bodily movements and facial expressions.

Each man and woman has a *right to beauty*. Hitherto it has been supposed to have been parceled out and given to a favored few; it has also been thought an accompaniment of vanity and hence only coveted and sought by the vain. With the knowledge that beauty symbolizes the perfect character, the picture of the thought life, there comes the conviction that by rights it belongs to all.

The beautiful are queenly in grace, are royal in deportment. They are not arrogant or presuming, only confident in their own powers and virtues. They wear the bodily beauty cloak harmonizing with soul qualities; as one chooses colors to bring out hues of complexion or gloves to accentuate shapely hands they clothe themselves in loveliness, for it is the bloom of loveliness.

Beauty gives power to both men and women it is a sign of accomplishment and an aid to success.

The man who would be successful in business has a handsome office, marble floors, plate glass, fine furniture. His garments are equally elegant, silk hat, broadcloth coat, clean-shaven face — all these are stock in trade. The woman in business or social life patronizes the hair-dresser and manicurist; her collar is the whitest, her gloves faultless, her shoes a perfect fit; from head to foot, from bonnet to boot, she has prepared herself to win. Her whole vesture is a poem in form and color; her gloves match her bonnet, her bonnet her dress, and the cloak accentuates the harmony of the whole.

If man's garments in their care and adjustment are good business investment, if woman's clothing enhances her power to charm and please, how much more may the face and form made beautiful through soul development give power.

Beauty as well as good bearing is a letter of credit. Indescribable wealth is packed into a fine, beautiful personality; such a person carries success and can not be refused. Both men and women who outpicture in face and body, graciousness, love for all creatures and a sympathetic heart, are successful in dealing with their fellows. The soul's victory revealed in the features is an unmistakable prophecy of success.

In every motion of the body, every expression of the face, the soul radiates its potency. Sousa as a band leader may have studied dramatic effects and the poetry of motion, but this gives him power over his artists and charms his audience. He wields his baton with a skill born of harmonious conceptions.

BEAUTY GIVES SATISFACTION.

In the highest sense beauty is the emblem of love, and love vaunteth not itself, is not puffed up, but filleth the mind with peace.

Love unites with wisdom to produce the perfect man, the soul's nuptials have been completed, and the joy of fulfilment is deep, calm, serene — is satisfaction. One may wear vestures that are beautiful, may use all the beauty arts to produce bodily perfection, but for a beauty that has permanency and power, that is not dependent upon clothes, station or garnishment, he must go down into the recesses of his soul and seek that union with absolute being, with kosmogenic love and life. In this union he will realize the quickening of the all-power, the all-life. It will result in a flame, of beauty that shall kindle a kindred flame in the hearts of neighbors and companions, a living flame that none shall extinguish. It shall spread by self-contagion until every baby girl and baby boy, every youth and maiden, every man and woman, shall be possessed with it, shall feel its fire in his heart, shall realize and emanate the Christ beauty in his life.

> For of the soul the body form doth take;
> For soul is form and doth the body make.
> — *Spencer.*

To be beautiful one must love beauty and desire it. To behold and admire it in another is not sufficient; each one must hold sincerely the picture for himself. " I have the shine and glint of stars, I have the radiance and perfume of flowers, I have the glow of youth, the serenity of mature years, because my body pictures forth its own loveliness."

All souls are free to express themselves in health, harmony and beauty, and I claim this freedom. In all my life I manifest beauty.

CHAPTER XXIII.

COURTESY LOVE'S LANGUAGE.

What care I for robe or stole?
It is the soul, it is the soul;
What for crown, or what for crest?
It is the heart within the breast;
It is the faith, it is the hope,
It is the struggle up the slope,
It is the brain and eye to see,
One God, and one humanity.

Sincerity is the basis of all true courtesy. Deference to age, attention to parents, politeness to friends, etiquette between lovers, all must be the soul's outpicturing of inherent love. Hearty handshakes, a joyous greeting, the timely assistance, all these are the utterance of the abundance of vital love overflowing in the heart. It should be no pretence, but a genuine expression of joy and good will.

The soul's gladness, like the rays of sunlight, goes out to meet the gladness of all hearts.

Emerson says: " The maxim of courts is, that manner is power; a calm and resolute bearing, a polished speech, an embellishment of trifles, and the art of concealing all uncomfortable feeling are the arts of a courtier."

The finished, finely dressed, polished gentleman may be only a counterfeit. His dress, his speech, his conduct are perfect; he is trained in the schools. The true man, the lover man is just as polite, just as polished; his is the spontaneous outpicturing of his soul.

Possibly the cultivation of the counterfeit, symbolizing as it does the real, may in some way develop the genuine in life. The fingering of the keyboard is not music; but adhering to technique, to the mechanics of expression, may awaken unsuspected talent and introduce the soul to unusual harmonies. But certain it is that one whose life is impelled by love, by justice, can not be far amiss in conduct. Every movement of body, every word, every gesture of hand, even his attire, all are the speech of love — are the language conveying love's messages to associates.

This is no varnished politeness; love impelling, he chooses the words of comfort and joy, and does the deeds of altruism.

The soul demands a practice of sincerity to produce a habit of courtesy. As one must have a daily look at the sun in order to gaze long at it with comfort, so must one practice the saintly character.

The real power of manners lies in their being genuine. The smile must be a heart smile and not that of one seeking a favor. The man's home-coming after a day of business becomes the joy of his life. His eyes gleam, his body sways, gleefully he rubs his hands, the home-content speaks from his soul. Does the same gleam, the same bodily movement, accompany him in his down-town relations? Are joy, content, energy such a habit of his soul, so genuine that he meets men in business with pleasure and expresses the religion of character in every-day affairs ?

Manners are the ensigns of character, the flags that take your ship into port. The man of you speaks through your manners.

The lover as girl or boy, as woman or man, must know that the forms of politeness express love; they arise from the real, the true of the heart and are genuine in proportion as they express the real and the true. Form in etiquette is an attempt to organize the love life according to rule; the inherent quality of love is elastic and the parliamentary rulings must be correspondingly elastic. Each situation, each relation to others, makes a new rule or an exception to a general rule. Like Wagner's compositions, ignoring all common laws of harmony, but in all and through all finding and disclosing the keynote. Boys and girls in natural association find this keynote of harmony.

From my study window I see a small fraction of the army of youth going to and from school. Girls and boys from twelve to eighteen, in grammar grades and high school. Their arms are loaded with books; their dress smart and modish. They group in twos and threes and sets. They seem full of fun, news and confidence. Boys keep with boys and girls with girls.

From babyhood the thought of romantic love is engraven upon the child's mind. By all sorts of bantering and inuendoes the boy is made to feel that every girl he speaks to or walks with must of course be a sweetheart. This prevents a natural, free association. It restricts him to class comradeship, an occasional word or interview provoked by a desire for lesson helps and more frequently to the exchange of notes and small gifts. Under this restraint he is a brave, manly fellow that can choose girl associates freely.

To the boy whose love is not quarantined, companionship with the girl is natural and healthful. In grammar and high school she has stood side by side with him, indeed often distancing him in special studies; in athletics, lawn tennis, cycling, she is his equal. She proves that a girl is as good as a boy. She is the new woman in embryo. The idea of superiority slowly but surely has been erased from the boy's mind. He is not living in an age when the lady class are angels and the working women serfs or slaves. Wise parents have ceased claiming bravery and leaderships for sons only; they sacrifice equally for the education and equipment of daughters. They give to boys music and accomplishments that conduce to refinement; to girls, manual training and athletics that give power and robustness; the result is that boys and girls learn early to get their bearings.

A boy learns that gallantry is not based upon superior powers, but rather is the natural outcome of justice; that politeness is not a symbol of strength, but is an outpouring of the love that is inherent in every soul. Arrogating no privileges to himself he meets a girl companion on a footing of justice and equality; she responds with frankness and freedom that can not be misunderstood.

The old-fashioned obsequious gallantry is out of place. Man is no longer a buyer of feeble minds or weak bodies; in his associates he looks for and expects equality. As a boy, in the classroom, he recognizes the ability and proficiency of the girl, so in all life's walks, in courtship, in engagement, in marriage his manners, his every relation is based upon a similar recognition; he is not looking for an ivy to tenderly twine around his majesty the oak, but rather gallantly nods a greeting to another tree, different in quality and characteristics but equal despite the differences.

Genuine courtesy evinces a largeness of heart, a desire to share the joys of life, a relinquishment of the *my* and *thy* theory; if discomforts are parceled out, a willingness to be the first to accept them; the first to be deprived of a seat in a car, attention at a hotel, a berth in a steamer, a short allowance of food. One does not crowd for the best place in a park, the best seat at a concert, the best pew in church! He knows there is always a place for him, and the quiet, no hurry, no flurry spirit, always and always with a thought of others, proves a gain rather than a loss. One ceases to rush into a train as if he were afraid he would get no seat — if any one has to stand, it is his privilege; should the gates be closed and he is forced to take a later train, some good comes of it; he meets a friend, transacts some business he had long wished to, or meets with some pleasant circumstance that is more than compensation for what seemed a deprivation.

Man's life is not made up of patches and pieces. What has seemed a crazy-quilt, through the etiquette of love becomes a harmonious unity in form and color.

Courtesy is equal in power to beauty — indeed forms of beauty can scarcely be separated from forms of behavior; both are the speech of the soul, are love's language pictured on face and figure

and portrayed in demeanor. The courtesy that wins a lady's heart —
that guides the association of lovers — is the language of love.

One's introduction is not merely through a mutual acquaintance,
but more surely through the responses of soul to soul. The soul
speech must not be hampered by the clumsy use of tools; the pliant
features, the mobile body are soldiers under command; they obey
the heart captain. The young man scarcely need wait for an invitation
to call; he has already the request in a glance of the eye, the tone of
the voice. The acquaintance easily proceeds on the basis of mutual
understanding. The visits, the invitations, the gifts, the comings and
goings are responses to love, are symbols of the heart's devotion. The
symbol may be the crown of prince or cross of priest, but it must
truly represent the heart of royalty and allegiance. Effectiveness of
manners is in proportion to genuineness.

Antoinette Brown Blackwell says:

" In its palmiest days knight errantry was embodied religion and
poetry — chivalry somewhat fantastic in kind. It held brilliant
tournaments, wielding sword and lance skilfully in single combat and
in war; its exciting pastimes, bloodshed and the defeat of
antagonists; its sweetest rewards, the smiles, the admiration, the
gratitude of the women championed by those plumed heroes back in
the eleventh and twelfth centuries.

" Chivalry, from those days to these, has been steadily changing in
non-essentials, and somewhat in motive, but always it has
proclaimed a steadfast championship of womanhood. In different
times and countries it blossomed into many varieties of curious
manifestations, but it has so steadily maintained loyalty to women
that this central idea — the protection of one sex by the other — is
fairly entitled to be called ' the survival of the fittest. '

" In those days the wedding ring — the golden symbol of
masculine chivalry — truly meant something; it remains a poetic
survival; it even glitters still on some of the whitest hands —
presumably most brightly on those of the more docile anti-

suffragists.

" Our own country has never been so careful of its women as England, but it has old-fashioned chivalry; enough to see to it that women are not weighed down by the cares of the General Government nor with any of those troublesome public affairs which it lays so heavily upon the shoulders of its male citizens."

Woman reveals herself as man's counterpart; she leads through her heart, he through his head, both coming to the same adjustment, the same conclusion, and both reaching the same goal.

In matters of etiquette there is special deference given to woman because of this leading, because the spiritual and intuitional are recognized as higher faculties of the soul and speak as it were from the heart of all life. In this knowledge man's heart responds to her heart and her wishes become a law that leads both into paths of right thinking and doing.

The evening call can never be an intrusion, the invitation to park, concert or excursion will always be welcome, and the hours spent together will become hours of genuine *re*-creation. He may wear faultless attire, his hair may never be ruffled, his boots polished and his nails manicured — whatever his outward appearance his motto must be genuineness, for of this the true man is made. Genuine courtesy, a sincere virtue born of one's knowledge of his real self, the real that is within, makes him know the genuine coin, to respond to the real in character.

The real king wears no crown, the true nobles have no titles, genuine courtesy has no forms, sincere virtue recks not of moral rules, genius ignores canons, love knows only its object. The real is tolerant and inclusive.

THE CHAPERON.

Whitman says: " She has no reason to fear and she does not fear." The freedom given to girls and women in this country is born of the chivalry of American manhood, and a magnetism of innate equality of the sexes.

The chaperon is a product of ownership and serfdom; a free manhood demands a free womanhood.

Self-government is the true government. Men and women who have learned this are above the law. Courts, judges, juries and legislatures are not requirements. The policeman and chaperon alike may look for other vocations.

Goldsmith says: " That virtue which requires to be ever guarded is scarcely worth the sentinel." An American girl in her confident manner, her knowledge of life, is her own apron. In some languages the identical word is used for chaperon and apron; both signify protection. A maiden in a foreign land in her shyness and servility must often be upon the defensive, asserting her virtue by resenting assaults upon it; must prove whether it is marketable or not. To save her this indignity she is provided with a chaperon.

The intellectual culture of the American girl, her broad view of life, her experience from early associations, all give her the power of being her own mistress, of being affable, agreeable, sociable, companionable and yet to carry herself independently; she would protect herself even if American manhood were less chivalrous.

In foreign lands she may flirt, seem saucy and impertinent, but she ever knows how to defend herself. Her confidence in manhood rules out any double standard. Indeed home and school life furnish her equal advantages in every way; she is equipped for life as the boy is equipped, and this very equipment is her best chaperon. It is a chaperon for daily association and protects from a hasty and unsuitable marriage.

In material life an independent purse is a protection; this may be supplied by her own earnings, by an allowance or by inheritance. In sociological evolution the woman of the future may be supported so as to give motherhood freedom commensurate with its obligations and racial influence. To-day we are in the transition stage and a girl seeks financial independence through many professions and industries, She enjoys the proceeds of her labors; sets up an establishment, has a home of her own, adopts children, gives a quiet home to mother, entertains guests, all of this out of her own pocketbook; she supplies her own pin money, sub. scribes for the magazines of her choice, selects her garments and house furnishings, purchases her own theater and concert tickets, and proudly goes to lectures and places of amusement without a male escort or a female attendant. Possessing a pocketbook supplied with her own earnings she is free from the necessity of a chaperon. She is the new girl waiting for the new man, who through the development of intuition and spiritual unfoldment, is well on the road to be the companion, comrade and husband of the new woman.

"Woman no longer acts the part of a mere appendage to man, sup-pressing her own individuality. This is no better for her than for the male. He loses his self-conceit, and still is no less a man. Whitman, in his " A Woman Waits for Me," gives a picture of a woman who is in no way feeble-minded. A woman who can swim, row, ride, wrestle, shoot, run, strike, retreat, defend herself. She is both strong-minded and strong-bodied.

In her strength and freedom she seeks and demands the freedom that her own pocketbook gives. So long as money is a symbol of success, so long as it stands for power, in the hands of woman it is not only evidence of her independence, but gives her the right of choice in matrimonial affairs. She ceases to be in the market for marriage, flaunting in colors and manners special characteristics; by virtue of her independence, she knows that the *awaiting* man on meeting her will recognize the soul of a mate. He bows in reverence at the shrine of womanhood, but not as a possessor or usurper. She has no necessities that her own purse can not supply, and is saved the humiliation of bartering her talents, accomplishments or beauty for support either in or out of a home. This is economic freedom and is the invincible protection that is the right of every girl. In her educational and financial independence a young lady is her own chaperon, her self- constituted bodyguard.

In the growth and development of spiritual knowledge will be added the protection of an ever present intuition; as she knows the inner law, as Her soul is filled and thrilled with infinite life, as she realizes from day to day the quickening of kosmic love, her resources for self-protection become inexhaustible; she is a law unto herself. Resolute, invincible, courageous, she dwells in that truth which maketh free. Her resources are equal to every demand, and life's experiences become a series of conquests; her strength is the strength of the Spirit, her might the might of infinity. For her, bravery means that her inmost soul speaks to her will, and her will shines in her deeds; also that her inmost soul breathes purity to her will and purity lusters every act.

Thus sweetness of soul, loveliness of character and purity of life become one's stronghold in protection. Abiding in spiritual verities, through all experiences she is guided and guarded. The flashing inspiration of her heart is a true and reliable chaperon.

Love is the everlasting worker of miracles. When all seems hopeless, and the soul is descending upon the road that has no turning, let it be awakened to love, and immediately all the forces of the spiritual world converge upon it to lift it to God. Love is the savior, love is the perpetual wonder of life.

Living jewels dropped unstained from heaven.
—*Pollok.*

CHAPTER XXIV.

THE LOVER'S CHILD

Come, let us live with the children.

To know the golden thread of unity interlinking parent and child, and to follow this out in its varied manifestations, creates a bond of harmony. Parents must first find the center of their own lives, must realize the poise and peace of the true life; this in itself gives sight and sense of the child-nature; it is really the connecting link in the chain of all life; it is a storehouse of perception, judgment and wisdom from which to draw upon all occasions.

This is not an exhaustive treatise; the psychology of the child is not attempted, neither does the scope of the work allow extensive details in meeting its physical demands. The theories presented and illustrations given are intended for simple helps to parents and an incentive for them to seek larger knowledge.

No work can give every possible relation between parent and child. Circumstances are likely to arise that never before occurred. The details given in the following pages are hints of the workings of the law; are evidences of the outpicturing of a godlike life in the lover's world.

Love will always find the best way of doing things. It is not a small matter for a mother of several children to know the best way of making bread; this best way includes the economy of time, of fuel, and the preserving of the nutrient qualities of the hour. It embraces knowledge of chemical action, brands of flour, the products of corn, rye, oats, wheat; and also the most wholesome and best relished forms of bread.

In the clothing of the body, at any time, knowledge of fabrics, of adaptation to use or adornment, is capital invested. So, too, in all that pertains to the child, one seeks the simplest and best way to clothe a child, first for its sake and, second, for one's own sake. One knows the best manner of giving baths, of preparation of food, of planning its amusement. One seeks to give the child suitable conditions for sleep, and also for that deeper inner rest that all require. All this in accomplishment is a joy, a real satisfaction. The profession of motherhood does not tolerate guesswork; best ways help to create brightness and joy; love seeks the harmonious adjustment to environment and occasion.

The one unchangeable motto of the Parsees, symbolized by a triple cord, is right thought, right word, right deed. A spiritually illumined soul thinks only right thoughts, speaks the shining words of love, and fulfils the law in every deed. It is a joyful outflow of a perfect heart. No service is burdensome, no work is drudgery, for, as perfection is expressed in tiniest leaf and tendril of vine, so each act of life is essential to the completed whole. The lightest word may result in the most significant lesson, may be the point of decision in a wavering life. Let each day and the most trivial details of the day be filled with joy of life, with the love of being.

> The moon and stars are commonplace things,
> And the flowers that bloom, and the bird that sings,
> And God who studies each separate soul,
> Out of commonplace lives makes a beautiful whole.

THE NEW-BORN CHILD.

Love's requirements for the infant, who has had natural conditions in fetal life, are notably simple.

Love reverses the customs that have become complex and chaotic, and returns us to arcadian simplicity. The directions are so few and so easy of application that, in absence of a nurse, they may readily be followed by the father or a friend. Indeed, many a woman under natural conditions has had the ability and the joy of giving the first necessary attentions to her own baby.

When the child is first received from its mother it is wrapped in a soft flannel, which has already been prepared for it; the nurse takes it and rubs it all over thoroughly with sweet oil, using either her hand or a piece of old soft flannel. She should take special pains to oil thoroughly the head, axilla and groin; after this she wraps him up closely and warmly and lays him down in a quiet place to rest. He will probably sleep all the way from three to ten hours. This first rest before bathing and dressing is not only natural but quite essential — it gives an opportunity for adjustment to new conditions. The child is kept warm and quiet, the oil softens the sebaceous secretion on the skin, all the functions become active; following this rest attentions will be grateful.

When he awakens, the nurse, provided with her basket of necessities, takes him up in her lap and proceeds to cleanse the surface. She may use warm water and castile soap, but it often proves better to rub the surface again with the oil, using a soft flannel cloth. This method usually removes all of the cheesy matter, called *vernix caseosa,* that usually is found upon the skin of a new-born babe. Many rely entirely upon the ausweitet-oil bath, rubbing well with a clean cloth before dressing. The cleanliness of the child is perfect, while it is far more simple than soap and water bathing. Sometimes this *vernix caseosa* is difficult to remove from the scalp and the groin; if so, and the oil does not take it off, use the yolk of an egg, rubbing the entire body; this forms an emulsion which cleanses quickly and thoroughly and leaves the skin sweet and smooth.

The navel is dressed with absorbent cotton, without any unguent or other preparation. Take a piece about the size of the palm of the hand and lay one-half of it on the abdomen, under the cord, then

188

wrap the other half over the cord, laying the whole mass upward and toward the right axilla; usually this dressing requires no change or attention until the cord sloughs off.

It is all held in place by a band of knitted fabric, which is fastened smoothly about the entire body. This bandage, as simple as it is, can be dispensed with as soon as the healing of the navel has taken place, which may or may not require a dressing for a few days after the removal of the cord. This latter dressing should be simple cerate or vaseline on a piece of old soft linen or absorbent cotton.

The first clothes should be very simple — really there need be only two slips, one of half wool and the other made of muslin. By having one inside the other, they can both be put on together, bringing them over the feet first, thus avoiding the troublesome process of putting on many garments. Place a linen diaper, folded square, under the child and within the skirt; this will not require pinning or it may be simply fastened loosely around the hips; a smaller fold of old linen or absorbent cotton may be placed loosely under the child, which can be changed often without removing the first. A very young baby, if kept quiet, will not soil its clothes, and there are good reasons for not pinning on the diaper in the usual way, which will be explained hereafter. First discharges are usually copious and of a dark color. This is a natural secretion and soon changes in character   (see Supplement *c c).*

The skirt can be wrapped about the feet or an extra piece of flannel may be used for this purpose. Many mothers now make the first set of clothing sufficiently short to avoid the second set that is usually made when the child is six months old. After a few months, dresses may be made with yoke and waist, and for needs an extra skirt added. If for any reason it is desired to cover the child more than he is covered with skirts, loose diaper-drawers may be worn. Always let the clothing be light, loose and easily adjusted, avoiding bands. Remember that the clothes are for the child, not the child for the clothes.

Whenever the child is awake his feet should be uncovered, often allowing them freedom of activity. Nothing assures perfect circulation and warmth as well as this. Feet and legs gain as much by exposure and free use as the hands; this exposure and freedom contribute to real growth. The feet may also be put in cool water frequently, and in warm weather placed in contact with the earth several hours each day. All this aids in equalizing circulation as well as giving power of resistance. If you adhere to custom in putting on socks, or shoes and stockings, remove them often, always when the nap is taken. Only recently I heard of a child of eighteen months who had never worn either foot or head covering. When he was eighteen months of age his parents went to the seaside to reside. For the entire season he wore overalls only, and spent his waking time in the warm, shifting sand and the splashing water. The child was unusually robust, healthy and, at the same time, precocious in intellect. Of course this is an extreme case and many things may have contributed to robustness. It is given here to help parents think out the problem of freedom to think how to let the child live near to nature's heart. More children are killed by coddling than by exposure, more by overdoing than by not doing. It is a wise mother that knows when and where to take her hands off and give the baby its development according to kosmogenic law — its natural life.

FOOD.

Long ago nature solved the question of nutriment for a new-born baby.

> The starting beverage meets
> The thirsty lip;
> 'Tis joy to yield it, and
> 'Tis joy to sip.

When the infant evinces an inclination for food, it should be put to the breast. It will at once find what it requires. It needs nothing but the natural secretion — no panacea, no catnip tea, cracker tea, sweetened water, nothing but the fluid always ready and adapted to its wants. Early establish a habit of regularity in nursing. Two hours at first, then as long naps are taken, three hours, and, by the time the child is five or six months old, four times a day, it having learned to sleep all night without food. Do not imagine a child is hungry because he is restless and uneasy or simply because he demands his food. Children are often too warm, or uneasy from other causes; therefore, quiet him by other means than by giving him food that he does not need. To be sure children have thrived nursed any time and all the time. I have seen a baby given the breast six times in one-half hour. It is a bad habit for the child and inconvenient for the mother. One can not begin too early in the matter of controlling the appetite and freedom from the sense of hunger. Think this out, mothers. You will find that you not only establish a regular habit that is of untold advantage to yourself, but the baby has early learned a valuable lesson in adjustment to life's conditions. *Seeming wants are not necessities*. It is not merely that the digestive organs are better prepared to receive and appropriate food, but it has a deeper psychological significance in character building.

Avoid resorting to artificial food. It seems almost as though the young mother of to-day is hypnotized by the enticing food advertisements and by the " traditions of the elders," so that it is rare to find a child sufficiently fed from the natural supply.

Free yourself from the thoughts and opinions of others and give your child this proof of a mother's love. It is your strongest bond and, though a sensuous delight, can be so utilized by thought direction as to give to your babe bountifully from your storehouse of love and wisdom. Even an infant is not fed by " bread (milk) alone." By the attitude of the mother's mind he may be awakened and quickened in soul development, and no occasion is more suitable for this process than when taking his nourishment. As you have sought best prenatal conditions to give foundation to character and beauty of soul, so, still, while in the impressionable stage of the first year you can convey to him, in thought, your highest aspirations. Good, and good only, rules his life, for out of the *all-good,* you help him to the knowledge of his oneness with all life, his unity with the God-life of the universe. You undo the traditions of natural depravity and put the seal of God upon his soul. In thought and intent you do this always, but the time for giving nutriment to the body is symbolical and affords an especial opportunity to meet the soul's demands. So as we see inner meanings in all phases of life, we find a stronger ground for a mother's feeding her own child than can be revealed by the microscope or chemical analysis. The artificial food may contain all required elements for nutriment, but it is devoid, first, of the life of the mother's milk, and, second, it breaks the sweet bond of mother fellowship. Dr. Wood-Allen says: " The mother who nurses her child herself, most perfectly comprehends the divinity of motherhood."

If for any reason artificial food must be resorted to, goat's or cow's milk furnishes the most complete substitute. For a young child, use the top from milk that has stood five or six hours, adding an equal quantity of water. Reduce it less and less and by the time he is four months old give the milk full strength. After this a gruel from wheat, oats or barley may be added. The next best substitute is a good condensed milk or cream. Failing to secure either good cow's milk or good condensed milk, then come the artificial foods. In adopting any of these care must be used in preparation and keeping the bottles in order. It is well to have two bottles. The one not in use should be rinsed thoroughly and laid without the nipple in an earthen vessel containing a solution of common soda, one teaspoonful to a quart of water.

A child, if strong, may be weaned any time after he is ten months old, or this may be delayed until he is a year old. Let this be done gradually; omit nursing at first once a day, then twice, substituting other food. In this way the little one is weaned almost if not quite unconsciously. One will find most suitable nourishment in barley, wheat or oatmeal, bread and milk, fresh fruits, avoiding the starchy foods and mixed diet until the teeth are well developed (See Supplement *d d*).

BATHING.

The child's bath is rightly an important matter; the skin, aside from a covering, performs many functions. It breathes, it absorbs nutriment and throws off waste. It may be said that in the skin is an incessant process of birth and life, and besides forms a connection between all functions. It acts as a living battery, between cells and tissue, bone and muscle, nerves and blood-vessels; between organs of sense and automatic functions, it is the sounding-board of natural processes.

This living battery has a right to demand care and usage that will protect it in service. This care is summed up in cleanliness and exposure. The child's natural love for water teaches a truth in regard to its requirements. It never tires of the dip and splash, whether in a small bowl or on the ocean shore. Wet and dripping garments afford no discomfort, every feature of the face and every movement of the body reveals its joy. It is an all-over happiness. The purity of child-innocence becomes one with the purity of water. In the process many hues and shades may have been mixed, but the product is pure joy and life to the child.

All bathing should be in accordance with the natural instinct for water. Ordinarily the temperature should be about the same as that of the room, ranging to that of the body. The most ordinary form of a small child's bath is in a pan or small tub, which may be set upon a table for convenience. This may be taken every day, while added to this, he will rejoice and grow in frequent exposure of the skin and the application of sponge and towel. We cover and coddle the skin too much; we invade natural rights when we hinder the processes of growth and the free interchange of life's forces in the integument. Irritability with some children seems a part of their clothing and may be removed with them.

During a journey I became interested in a roly-poly baby of four months, who seemed in continual pain. The young mother vainly endeavored to quiet it. Taking it from her I found it burdened with long heavy clothing; a band, two flannel skirts and a cotton one, all pinned tightly. I loosened the garments, rubbed its skin and gave the limbs an opportunity for action. It repaid the attention with crows and smiles, while the tired mother took a nap. Upon awakening she felt that she was troubling a stranger and insisted upon taking her baby. She soon again imprisoned the child in his garments and he evinced his resentment by renewing his cries. She nursed him several times within an hour, walked up and down the car and resorted to every means but the freedom he demanded. After a while I kindly explained to her that the baby's cry was resentment to unnatural conditions; the heat of the day and the new experience of traveling may have added to his discomfort, but, as he was quiet when I freed his body from clothing, it should prove to her that here lay the difficulty. She consented to remove one flannel skirt and the band, and the little fellow soon rewarded her by quiet slumbers (see Supplement *e e*).

The body is not the child. It is a spiritual being — a soul in the largest sense of the word; the object of every care given to the body is to let this soul unfold. It is soul life first, and though the body is more than raiment, its power is as nothing compared to the spirit. When a child creeps and crawls, wriggles and giggles, runs and leaps, it is not body — but the ever-awakening spirit. So his dress and environments should not impede these activities,— should, on the contrary, encourage them; a baby jumper, a walking chair, creeping trousers, are all aids to the accomplishment of this end; most of all, the night and morning frolic in nature's own costume is a means of growth. One child, a year and a half old, subject to cold feet, was each evening undressed and took a run and a romp in full undress. His parents were surprised to find that in this naked frolic his feet soon became warm, and he showed no remonstrance to cold, but, on the contrary, a perfect delight in the freedom.

Mothers, revel in the joy of a baby, but also learn to remove all hindrances to his development. Rules, plans and order, in the nursery, are only helps to unfoldment. A stake for a rosebush does not interfere with its comely natural growth; it may be removed when the bush is strong enough to stand alone. So with the child; hours for sleep, times for feeding, certain kinds of food, special massage or gymnastics should be considered as aids to soul growth, all details of its material life are simply accessories to this growth.

Remember, too, that love is awake to the needs of the child, building its nest, selecting its food and fulfilling all requirements. In all, love is the directing power. A child of love blooms in the law of love.

CHAPTER XXV.

DON'T WORRY

Why shadow the beauty of sea or of land
   With a doubt or a fear ?
God holds all the swift-rolling world in his hand,
And sees -what no man can as yet understand,
   That out of life here,
   With its smile and its tear.
Comes forth into light, from Eternity planned,
   The soul of good cheer.
Don't worry —
   The end shall appear.

                — Elizabeth Porter Gould.

Every mother should belong to a Don't Worry Club, even though she is compelled to organize one herself. Her husband should also be a prominent member, while the grandfathers, grandmothers, cousins, aunts and all other relatives and friends must be induced to cooperate in this association.

The principles of a Don't Worry Club are faith, hope and trust. A whole family, true to these principles will perform what seem to be miracles for a child.

Fear is the most deadly germ of all the category; one has said that there is nothing to fear but fear. A mother's anxiety is a virulent poison.

Confidence in the child's inherent right to health is the best doctor to employ. This confidence creates health germs, abundant and powerful, that make a wall of resistance to bacteria and fear germs.

The germ theory is good, only we must remember that health germs are more numerous than disease germs; the cultivated health bacilli should so fill the body, so permeate it that there is no room for the lodgment of those that bring disorder and death.

The air we breathe, the water we drink, the food we eat, are alive with germs, each having a living family with family traits and likenesses, with their ancestors and descendants.

Chyle and chyme could not be converted into nutriment if they had no bacteria; saliva and gastric juice would cease to be solvents if they contained no living germs; blood would have no life and cease obedience to the commands of the heart's valvular action if the microscope revealed no micro-organisms. Myriads of living creatures are hurrying and scurrying through bones, nerves, muscles, symbolizing the mental activities of man. They are born of divine intelligence, and if we do not set a steel trap of fear to disorganize their life, we can trust them to so hold the bulwarks and citadel of life that no enemy by any means can storm the fort or creep insidiously into any crack or corner.

Whenever the world sounds a prophecy of an epidemic, set up the power of resistance in yourself and your children, by continuous and unyielding thoughts of the perfect life, of the fulness and bounty in the universe, which is yours by claiming. Partake of this bounty; it is tonic, elixir and restorative. It is never failing; every demand creates an abundant supply.

Fathers and mothers, long before they welcome a babe in their house, should evince no sign of the darkening, blighting shadow of fear. The joy and trust in your home so fills it, so pervades it, that fear flees from it as darkness before sunlight. You protect your child by optimistic thoughts of life and health; by positive affirmations in acknowledgment of omnipresent good; by letting him manifest in freedom the divine life that is his birthright. There has been no fear to blight the developing fetus, and should be none as it comes into the larger life.

When a young mother thinks her child is not nourished by her milk; when she is on the alert to protect it from drafts, heat, cold; when her ears hearken for intrusive sounds; when she listens for his breathing in sleep that becomes so perfect its stillness resembles death; when she is ever watching, watching lest some evil happen to him, she casts fear shadows upon his life. She sets in motion vibrations that are likely to produce inharmony in the child — inharmony that shows forth in irritability and disease. By a certain law she brings about the very condition she has feared.

By fear she plants colic germs in the food she eats; poisons the fresh air of the morning; causes cold or heat or any environment to become inimical to the child. Irritability of the mother, as well as disagreements and quarrels in the family, picture themselves in colic, fever and convulsions in the baby. Before attributing physical disturbances in an infant to material causes, reflect if the mental atmosphere is clear; if not, dispel the clouds and mists and behold the quick response. Love and trust replace fear and anxiety. Jest and ridicule of unwise elders yield to joyous interest in the sports and life of the child.

The parents whose lives are perfectly in tune with the infinite life, will rarely find discord in the child. In freedom he lives his life; they avoid that never ceasing watchfulness that causes self-consciousness and creates a demand for undivided attention. A very young child needs hours of stillness in which his soul may begin to expand. Of course he requires sleep, but he also must have the stillness that all souls need for best development. Psychologists are yet to discover whether a child's mind develops most through physical sensations or spiritual perceptions. At all events the opportunity should be given him for the inward awakening.

Mental anxieties have their telepathic, formative influence; they may convert the milky nourishment into poison and are the never-ending, clanking chains to hamper and obstruct his progress during his entire life. He is constantly subjected to suggestions of disease and inharmony. The mother must not partake of luscious fruits lest the babe be warped with colic, and tradition teaches that a like result follows if the sturdy boy feast on green apples or a combination of milk and cherries. He is limited by the " I told you so" of whole generations of grandfathers, grandmothers, of parents, aunties and uncles.

In Kensington Gardens, London, I met a bright Irish nurse whose charge was a three-year-old boy, dressed according to English custom, heavy, thick-soled shoes with short socks that left at least six inches of beautiful, rosy flesh exposed to view. In conversing with her, I said: " I wonder why it is the English mothers do not clothe the legs of the children ?" " Sure ma'am, that is to make them tough." " But why not let them go bare-footed as well — why do they always wear such heavy shoes ?" " The little fate are tinder intirely; they must have the thick soles to keep the fate from the damp ground, and, sure, if they did not they would take their death of cold."

With no more consistency, through the demon of fear, we toughen and tender every vital process of the body. Unconsciously through the potent operations of thought, silent or expressed, we fan the flame of fever, we chill the processes of nutrition, and lure death to do destructive work. The thought of baked knees or frozen feet need not be given a child; the spiritual energy or life should be free to operate in the molecules of his body.

Under the effulgence of parental love that trusts the divinity within the child, he grows and grows. He knows not the dwarfing effect of anxiety and fear, the stultifying language of negations, the poison of overwatchfulness and interference. He pictures forth the love and trust of your own soul, and you learn of him as you have learned of leaf and flower, — the divine love operating in law, unity in diversity.

FREEDOM FOR THE CHILD.

As Froebel has so well demonstrated, a child's natural development is through play. A very young child ordinarily gets the most out of his play by being left much to himself, that is, left to make his own discoveries. Leadership and association are more desirable later. To depend upon his own little world for amusements develops self-reliance, independence and individuality. He is permitted to live his own life. In this way he is not so likely to become bound by habits. Overwatchfulness and anxiety create habits that cause him to demand undue care and attention. His mind is easily impressed and soon he is what may be called self-sensitive, and in the development of sensations easily discriminates between methods of attention and amusement. He may very soon demand that you shall not only rock him to sleep, but rock him all the time he sleeps; not only to nurse when he is hungry, but to worry and fret for food continually. Through the mental attitude toward the child very much of this can be adjusted satisfactorily. Parents have a right to freedom as well as the child; a loving life side by side without any tyranny on the part of either is possible.

Could I make this clear and give an understanding of the principles of life that make this possible, I would ask no greater good for each and every child. It is freedom in love. A love that does not create and foster parental solicitude, but a love founded upon an understanding of and insight into the deeper things of life. Not only do the parents realize the divine life of the child, but they themselves, through an understanding of their relation to the source of all things, come to. have a poise that is self-adjusting to all circumstances; their intuitions and perceptions are the impelling force. This must be no semblance of self-control, no mimic mastery assumed for occasions, but, on the contrary, must be the outpicturing of a genuine experience; the whole character is dominated and adjusted to the divine energy in themselves. This adjustment results in selfless love, a love that blots ownership out of its vocabulary, that permits in the child an independent existence; a divine soul that must not be restrained or hampered by any personal consideration; a love that rejoices in its best good; a love that embraces all children and all humanity. Such a love is, of itself, an inspiration, and intuitively it chooses the direction of the child-life. By and through this impelling force parents act wisely and deal justly at all times. Their own joy and trustfulness reflects in the child, who beams with gladness and happiness. Any system of child-study or psychology that gives to men and women the knowledge of this law gives to them the key to parental excellence.

A knowledge of this divine love renders every child a gift of joy. It is so nourished by it, so enveloped in it, so much an expression of it, that, really and truly, it is an image and likeness of God.

CHAPTER XXVI.

FREEDOM OF CHILDHOOD.

Each soul is a little divinity in itself.

The Lover's child rejoices in two essentials — love and freedom. They are its natural, inherent right. A parental love that is mere sentiment, a love that simply sees in the child an object of personal and sensuous pleasure, is likely to limit its freedom and curtail its activities.

The greater love, the Lover's love, beholds in offspring the germinal, independent soul that through the miracle of creation comes into the world for unfoldment. In this greater love the parents' attitude is leadership, guarding and guiding into best conditions for fullest expression. This love is inclusive and frees the mind from all ideas of ownership of the child, at the same time gives a clear vision of its requirements.

The child is a soul with immense possibilities. The infant is not merely an animal " with no language but a cry." He is an embodiment of all forces and faculties. No, no, the child is not an animal to be stuffed with food and dazed with doctor's doses, nor a body upon which to exhibit embroideries and artistic needlework, but rather a soul that, to grow its best, must develop in freedom through the fostering care of love.

" Childhood comprises the earliest and most active period of the growth of a human being. Its laws are laws of growth, which attain an additional significance by the greater flexibility, by the greater power of assimilation, in short by the greater impressiveness of its organism in this period of life." Now, at this impressive, mobile age, what have parents and teachers to do for a child's best progress, best understanding of life and his relations to it?

Months before the child is bom, he is ceaselessly active; consciously or unconsciously the soul, through motion, is making a demand for a larger life. In fetal life his acrobatic performances are not hindered by bands and blankets, by the Russian swaddling pillow or an Indian backboard. If bodily activity causes soul growth in the matrix, shall it not be permitted and encouraged as the child is ushered into the life of a larger experience ?

Some eminent psychologists hold a contrary opinion and have experimented upon the use of the swaddling clothes of primitive races. One writer had his baby strapped to a board like the Indian papoose. His theory was that a child has at some time to give up its will, and this, one of the ways to obtain the result.

A lady eminent in the Child Study movement pins her baby in a blanket when she puts him to sleep, preventing all motion of arms and legs. Another mother, a friend of hers, who thought this rather cruel treatment, resorted, however, to wrapping a Turkish towel around her baby's legs as a device to prevent his falling off the bed. She found this to work well. These mothers reasoned that at this time it was the child's business to be quiet and go to sleep, and any means that conduced to that was a blessing. It may have the effect of a straight jacket for the insane; when resistance is found perfectly useless the irritable mind yields to necessity. Possibly in the systole and diastole of a child's life, in its natural night and day experiences, it needs times of restraint as well as times of activity, and it may prove that for some very nervous and irrepressible children, the straight-jacket treatment is the most humane.

Many seem to sleep only when forced to. An infant that is wakeful may sink into slumber when the head is tucked under mother's arm and firmly restrained.

Some of the customs of different people are at least interesting;

many devices give safety to the child and secure freedom under limitations. The Chinese mother living in a boat-house carries her baby upon her back until it is old enough to crawl and walk, and then she tethers it to a cord, so if it chances to fall overboard it is easily rescued. Both the Japanese father and mother by a different contrivance carry their babies upon their backs. As children they are trained to this; when not more than eight years of age a large doll is strapped to the back, its weight increased until by the time the child is ten he can easily carry a baby. The hours are long in which the baby is kept in this one position. It feeds, sleeps and wakes, while the other child, its nurse, may play with his companions or assist his mother in labor.

Our own babies in perambulators and carts have freedom under limitations. It often depends upon the caprice of the nurse as well as the mother's devotion to spotless attire, whether the child is permitted a frolic on the grass, or to have a tour of investigation in a sand pile.

Creative energy is the propelling force of all the activities of the child. Indeed, it is synonymous with life. It is the ever present principle that is in constant manifestation. It is implanted in the child's organism at the time of conception. It is the recognition and direction of this energy that evinces the parent's wisdom in the care of the child.

In the smallest infant, creative energy is evinced in physical desires and in the almost unconscious and constant muscular movements, in the very throbbing of the fingers and toes. A child shows forth its consciousness of life in its manifold activities; it creeps, it walks, it runs; it rolls and tumbles; it finds its fingers, it plays with its toes, it discovers its mother.

What a joy to a seven-months baby is a red ball attached by a cord to his crib or buggy! Watch his glee as it swings to and fro as he steadies his hand to grasp it. A few months later what infinite resources he finds in wooden beads of the primary colors; in blocks out of which he forms his mind images, or pieces of pliant dough that yield to shapes for baby fingers.

The child is always on a voyage of discovery. His perpetual activity, his relentless destructiveness, and his passionate wilfulness are only significant signs of a desire that his voyage shall yield a rich harvest. Who dares to say him nay? Oh, man with your materialistic limitations, how can you lay the heavy hand of discipline on the growth and unfoldment of the child ? Is it any wonder, in his natural self-seeking of the unity of life, that he breaks these bonds and in his mistaken knowledge of law he seems to seek his own destruction?

Plato, Fichte, Hegel, Emerson, and Evans have shown us something of the law of life, but Froebel gives it in a clearer form and founds upon it a system of education. He demonstrates that the child's activity in play, rightly guided, may be the basis of great discoveries; his wilfulness, wisely trained, may be converted into a concentration usually ignored in teaching; his interrogations are answered by the conversion of *gifts,* clay, beads and all sorts of material, into forms of beauty and use — demonstrations of his ingenuity. Thus in an interesting and fascinating manner the child's destructiyeness is converted into creativeness; for he is a born creator.

In certain games he lives the life of the butterfly, bee and squirrel; in others he is taught to honor and respect all artisans by becoming in turn the carpenter, baker or blacksmith. In the kindergarten with what joy he sings:

> Busy blacksmith what are you doing
> At your anvil all day long?
> Horses now you see I am shoeing
> Making nails so good and strong.
> Cling clang, cling clang,
> Hear the anvil ringing,
> Cling clang, cling clang,
> While the anvil sings its song.

The child's life is filled with useful activities; he satisfies his curiosity and innate desire for new creations, giving no opportunity for expression of dangerous and disagreeable qualities.

The kindergarten gives freedom, disclosing the natural law of development in the child. It is not freedom in lawlessness, but freedom in law.

Freedom of childhood, however, means something greater and deeper and more far-reaching than Froebel expressed, and few only of his followers have divined and proven all that underlies his philosophy.

A child should be trained in love and in law, but whatever else is done for him, whatever are his surroundings he should have the right of freedom from three things or conditions: from both latent and expressed fear; from the tradition of original sin, and from ownership by parents.

Do we see a child taking the wrong road, we set him at some delightful task that leads him on the right path until his feet have become habituated to tread in that way. Does he purloin change to supply himself and his mates with sweets, you fascinate him with the manufacture of confections and he becomes delighted with the process and soon forgets that the more inferior article is obtainable with purloined pennies. Does your child run away, you send him on definite and difficult messages that require thought and command his most concentrated action. He is made to know that he is responsible, and by the responsible act has a consciousness of belonging to the family life.

What soul is great enough and strong enough in divine wisdom, to have perfect confidence in the law of unity for his child's development? Can you look into your child's eyes and say confidently, I trust you? Further, can you fill your heart so full of trust and confidence that you can in the silence send it on thought waves to the innermost consciousness of your little one? Can you do this in spite of repeated prevarications and disobedience ? Can you forgive even seventy times seven? If you can not, you do not realize that he is a manifestation of the universal law of life and, too possibly, that his prevarications and disobedience are the direct result of your distrust. " A suspicious parent makes an artful child."

We must free children from the bondage of " original sin." Already most of us have omitted this from our creed, but alas! it is still in traditional thought, and we talk of the Adam in a child, of human tendencies, of natural traits, of inherited waywardness.

One has said " the child who lies upon its mother's breast is nearest to the portals of heaven," but mistaken man has sent forth the edict that the child is prone to evil, that his heart by nature is wicked, that there is no good in him.

What an inheritance to give an innocent child, but blessed privilege to have had a glimpse of the law that proves this a false doctrine. We now know that we are and all have been children, as Carlyle phrases it; light sparks floating in the ether of Deity. Nay, more than that, omnipresent creative life manifests in every child. God has not his private palace in a far off Heaven, sending his embassies to earth to do his work well or ill according to man's deserts. He has never given authority to an opposing power whose deeds are darkness, meting out misery and desolation.

Evans says, " An infant is the divine flower that is to ripen into the mature fruit of manhood. No man ever looked into the face of a new-born babe without a feeling of respect and veneration amounting almost to worship. Hence the divinity most adored in the Roman Catholic Church is an infant. Maternity is the divinest function of human nature. The worship of Mary by millions of people is an instinctive recognition of this truth. Maternity is only secondary to the divine operation that goes by the name of creation, and a genuine motherhood stands next to the Godhead. And what shall I say of the product of this proximity? Only that there is a point in our lives where God and man, divinity and humanity, intimately and minutely blend in one, and that is in infancy and childhood."

In adult age, in order to get into closest proximity to God and union with Him, we must return to the divine innocence of childhood, for, unless we become as little children we can not enter the kingdom.

Froebel says: " The destiny as well as the vocation of man as an understanding and rational being, is to bring his nature — the divine in him — into complete consciousness, to vivid recognition, to clear insight, and with self-determination and freedom to practice all this in his own life. In himself man is to represent the God-life, that which he most truly and deeply is, his real being." " It is for no idle dreaming that man, the soul, is sent to dwell in nature, to wear clay and eat the fruits of the earth."

To recognize the inner nature as a part of the divine, and then to make it manifest in action, is that for which man lives. The metaphysical teaching of to-day is to bring man first to consciousness of his interior unused power, and then to put that power in action upon the plane of daily affairs.

This latent power is the unity of Froebel, is omnipresent love and life, the conscious recognition of which transforms all lives. This omnipresent life is good, is beneficent, and is manifested in the little child in love.

According to our faith and persistent application of this truth shall the blessed children be freed from the traditional teachings that even new-born babes are sinners? From this day on we remove this curse from childhood and let it blossom in the eternal effulgence of divine love and wisdom.

Total depravity is abolished from our creed. All sons of women, all daughters of men inherit by the right of birth and genius a perfect soul. Life's experiences, life's education, being, doing, living, all combine to make this perfect soul manifest in the flesh.

Last but not least, childhood must be freed from ownership by parents. This is the foundation principle of all rights of men and women.

" One's own life is included in Divine Life, and the child's life must also be so regarded." All claim of ownership in the child ceases. One comes to understand that he is only the guardian, the child is an independent being, an individualized manifestation of the universal spirit.

One enjoys the growth and development of a child and revels in its happiness, but if the parent's love is freed from selfishness, vanity and ambition, this lets him live in freedom, in the fullness of love. What is freedom? Does freedom mean lawlessness and license? Does it mean that the child shall be given the hammer and looking-glass, or a set of tools and a clock, his creative powers allowed to operate in destructive channels? Does it mean banishment and estrangement? Who will care for the children if parents do not own and have complete authority over them? Will you send them to a heartless, loveless state institute as suggested by Schindler in his dream of young West ?

The American Government, the American flag, the Constitution of the United States all stand for liberty. No man can own another.

NO SOUL CAN OWN ANOTHER.

The master does not own the servant; the husband does not own the wife, nor the wife the husband; neither can parent own a child.

If one has no right to give a bill of sale for a child, is he necessarily freed from all relationship with him and responsibility to him? A merchant does not own his clerk, still he is not absolved from duty to and interest in him. A husband does not own his wife, but her interest is his, her happiness his first and last thought, her well being his day and night dream.

So when one ceases to consider that he owns a child, when his love for the child is born of divine wisdom, it includes in its manifestation every relation and sentiment that can exist between them. This is an unselfish love and will lead parents to make the best provisions for the child's development. The long swaddling clothes of

209

conventionalism will cease to be their fetish; they will go to the very heart of nature for wisdom and guidance.

Long, long must we all live in the law of unity and in the freedom of divine love before we fashion not only our lives but our most secret motives by keeping close to the heart of the Infinite.

When parents cease to think that the child has come into this world for their pleasure, their happiness, their aggrandizement, when their selfish human love is transformed into an all-inclusive divine love, then will he have such soul-development, such transcendental powers as has not yet been known to man.

We now have great prodigies in Art, in Music, in Literature, in Philosophy and Metaphysics, but they are only the merest dreams, portending how the childhood of the future shall magnify the law in men of wisdom and power.

The souls that are born into earth's conditions in unity with the law, and under the power and inspiration of good only, have really a birthright of freedom, and will manifest diversity of gifts, gifts of healing, of prophecy, of statesmanship and philanthropy such as the world has not known.

The Catherines of Siena, the Emersons, the Savonarolas, the Christs will be the rule and not the exception.

This birthright of freedom we demand for every child, knowing that it is a birthright of illumination and power, a birthright of transcendentalism converting and transforming the earth into an eternal paradise.

Let lovers consciously set the seal of God on the child; he is divine, he is created in an orderly plan, he is not an exception to the universe of things. He is the product of love and law. As we emerge from the shadows of the past, from the giving of power to evil to the rule of the All Good, we free the child and give him the vivifying, growing, creating possibilities of all his energies.

The law of love begets the love of law.

—*Colville.*

All souls are atoms of one spark divine,
And are as one when bowing at Truth's shrine;
All thought, all greatness since the ages roll
Is but the upward step, the onward march of Soul.
From Earth to suns, from truth to Truth afar,
Our souls may to perfection step — from star to star.

CHAPTER XXVII.

FROEBEL'S LAW OF UNITY.

God created man in his own image, therefore man should create and bring forth like God.—*Froebel.*

In " The Education of Man" Froebel not only lays down theories upon which to found a system of education, but gives us a philosophy of life. On the first page he says: " In all things there lives and reigns an eternal law. Looking from the material to the spiritual and tracing the connection of all things, one with another and with the universal law, there must lie at the foundation of this all-ruling law an all-working, self-animating, self-knowing, therefore eternally existing unity."

" This unity is God," and he goes on to say —

" All things exist because the divine works in them."

" The divine which works in each thing is the nature of each thing."

Here we have a statement which, although it holds the dust of the earth as a sign of the law, still sees the soul as its own master, lord over nature, subject only to the Supreme of which it is a part; and while it declares the power of God as the First Cause of all effects, still shows the separate workings of that power which gives to each thing an inner nature, an essential being of its own.

When Froebel uses the word GOD, he does not mean the God of traditional teaching. Knowing this his philosophy and theories are better understood. God to him is the all-ruling law, kosmic love or universal life of nature manifesting in diversity.

In the application of the science of being, Froebel constructed a

212

system whereby self-revelation is accomplished in the child; where the child's development is considered and the leadings and environments made to conform to that development.

Both teacher and parent must see in every child divine possibilities. No child is conceived in wickedness or born in sin. His origin is from the universal source, he is the image and likeness of God. The business of parent and educator is to make this image and likeness manifest.

Froebel's ideas are adapted to the entire period of life, but he devoted his special thought to very young children; the first five years being the most pliable period of man's nature.

When we see the marvels accomplished by the kindergarten for the very young, wisdom demands that all education and home training, all development, shall be founded upon the same principles of self-revelation.

Self-activity of the mind is the first law of instruction of an ideal training; slowly and continuously and in logical succession it proceeds, from the simple to the complex, from the concrete to the abstract; so well adapted to the child and his needs that he learns as easily as he plays.

Every child must know that the wide field of knowledge is for him, and as he grows and lives in nature and in the atmosphere of scientific research he is made to feel his powers and his ability for attainment. He learns that investigation always brings reward; self-consciousness is lost in natural development, for the soul in its expansion knows its right to fullest bloom. It gives out its fragrance in artistic creations, in the poetry of a Lowell, in the architecture of Ruskin or the inventions of an Edison. These are culminations not of genius, not of the few favored ones, but of every soul led to show its inherent divinity.

A child should be no more conscious, in the sense of worldly pride or vanity, of any attainment than the bird is of its song. Any momentary exultation is only an invoice of the soul's progress, as one in ascending a mountain gets new and larger views.

Every child is the epitome of love, life and intelligence. The effect of education is to bring forth, to show forth this love, life and intelligence — that which the child already embodies. He is no more considered an empty vessel in which to pour facts and figures, but he is akin to a seed that contains the germ of the entire plant; the acorn is the oak in embryo; the child is the man in embryo and includes in his nature all the possibilities of manhood. As you plant the acorn in proper soil, give it food, moisture and sunshine, so you place the child in proper environments; you give it home and school influence according to its needs, and then you let it grow and shine; you let it grow and shine.

We are just learning the significance of the word *let.* Let means to loosen bonds; to remove limitations; the watchword becomes " I love and I trust." In loving and trusting we give the child opportunity to use his natural energies. By gradual sequence we lead this energy into constructive lines. The baby has his ball and colored beads; the child from blocks builds mills, bridges, lighthouses, cars and engines. The youth makes discoveries in the laboratories of physics and economics; he molds the plastic clay into forms of beauty; he represents his growing thought upon canvass, in fact he builds and constructs according to the evolution of his creative thought. What has been called education — reading, writing and arithmetic — becomes means to an end — they are for the child, not the child for them. They are tools of service, implements for opening the gates of wisdom, for throwing wide the portals of discoveries within the growing reach. A child gets best development of his inherent possibilities through directed activities.

In the kindergarten self-revelation is accomplished. Wherever a similar system is adopted for those more advanced in years, where the leadings, environments, indeed the whole curriculum of his life is made to accord to that development, there we find the greatest progress in actual growth. Not that the child can read the greatest number of pages, or cipher the most sums on a slate, but that through his own research, through his own application of principles, through his own discoveries of the relation of all things he develops thoughts and powers within himself, and through this development he is ready for greater undertakings. He learns to create by creating. By a natural law the doing is the road to active thinking.

The child must be freed from the paralyzing destructive *do not*, and placed under the life-long power of doing, of creating.

His creative energy should be directed into channels of usefulness. He scatters coal out of the coalhod, he splashes water on the floor, he upsets the inkstand. By a little wise leading all this restlessness can be turned into constructive channels, into creations. These delight his heart and his mind expands with new powers. He is busy from morning to night in his child doings. Listless, restless inattention becomes earnest concentration.

This is not done by words, by commands, by repeated " do nots," but is accomplished through interest in the life of the child. Verily you live with him; you think his thoughts; you feel his feelings; you desire his desires; you create with his creations; you know the steps he will take; you know when he is at the chrysalis stage, when he is a caterpillar creeping, creeping, creeping on the ground; you know when he becomes a butterfly, when all his activities are awakened. Out you go with him hand in hand to the field of discovery. With what eager interest he breaks the twig or bores into the maple tree for the sweets that are coursing up and down to feed the awakened life. How quickly he sees the first crocus, the hyacinth, the liverwort, the anemone; he listens to the bluebird's song, the catbird's mew; he knows that the robin has returned to its nest; he watches for the oriole to occupy the cradle that has all winter been deserted. Each spring all of these enticing wonders of nature have new meaning to him. The alertness and eagerness of the child opens for one's own mind new fields of interest. *A little child shall lead him.*

In Froebel's Law of Unity there is no separation in training mind, body and spirit. You can not take this body by itself and make it do one thing, neither can you take the intellect by itself and get any satisfactory results. Back of intellect and body, back of soul and intuition, is the spirit.

It is known that we can command, control and regulate our thoughts so as consciously to discern the power of the spirit, to intelligently permit the divine principle, the kosmic unity, to show forth effectively in accomplishment.

THE LAW OF UNITY

embraces this training of thought, this harnessing of all the psychical activities of the man so that they shall ever and always wheel into line and serve him. Who of us were ever trained to think effectively? Who of us can concentrate upon any problem and solve it, much less guide our thoughts into contemplation of the deeper meanings of all things, into the knowledge of the life universal ?

In time this thought training will begin with the birth of the child and will become the most important factor in his education during his entire life. He will not only be told to think, but will be shown how to think; not only commanded to have pure and lofty thoughts, but will be directed plainly and unerringly how to set all the soul's processes into effective service.

Education is the development of the divine at all ages of life. There are no graduating limitations, no finishing days, no thirty-year mile stakes to the man that knows he is created in the image and likeness of God. He is a living spiritual being; the divine life permeates his life. He recognizes this in fact and in fulness, and in his recognition he manifests more and more day by day the perfection of His nature.

Education based on the unity of life illuminates all speculations of the soul and theories of spiritual life. It discloses the golden thread of all truth and knits together apparently divergent systems. Material science becomes spiritual science; energy, law and intelligence are

216

revealed in all of nature's activities, in all arts and sciences, in chemical action, in photographic processes, in the blending of colors on the artist's canvas, in the marvels of electricity known only by its effects. So with the law of spirit, the law of being; we get knowledge of the cause by the effects, it becomes a science.

Froebel says: " The inner being, the spirit, the divine essence of things and of man, is known by the outward manifestations." As we study the processes of nature, as we see the acorn fall from the grand old oak to produce another oak, as the orchard bloom reveals with certainty the autumn fruitage, as the bee builds its six-sided cell, its honey pot for his winter's supplies, and the ant his almost human dwelling, our hearts stand still with awe at the intelligence directing and impelling all.

We come to know the ONE intelligence and its law of expression in diversity. The law is always true to its kind. A rose is always a rose, the May-apple is ever a May-apple. We roam the woods for the haunts of bee and squirrel, we rise at early dawn to hear the love notes of the feathered songster, and to discover the abode he has with more than architectural skill builded for his young. We review our lesson in unity and diversity, and as streams their channels deeper wear and time impressions stronger make, we become more and more conscious that nature is ever a revelation of love as law and law as love.

What of the child — is he an exception to the order of all life? Has divine intelligence failed in the creation of human beings, or have we in our shorter vision put the seal of depravity on the divine image, distorting that image as by the law of refraction and reflection the image of a wand is distorted in water? Is there no truth in the saying that God made man in his own image and likeness ? Are all nature's productions governed by love and law except the child you welcome to bless your home? Think of it fathers, think of it mothers, shall we not seek the highest inspiration, the deepest love and conjure the bravest words to reverse the traditions?

Look at the baby but to-day ushered from the maternal matrix. How we admire the rosy ruddiness in face and limb, how flexible every joint, how perfectly adapted is every part of his body to each function. In the law, freedom of bodily activity supplants the swaddling clothes of conventionality; love and trust take the place of fear and anxiety; a natural, joyous unfoldment is not hampered by the jest, ridicule and prevarication of unwise elders.

You plant a climbing rose by your home. You water it, you enrich the soil, you put a trellis upon which it may climb, but you never seek to convert it into a blackberry or sweet brier, you never once feel that the incident of its being in your yard gives you the power to change it and set it about other business. You know you can not alter its rose nature. You may dwarf it or make a gigantic specimen of its kind, but it is still a rose. You know that a power greater than yours possesses that rose-life; it is within and without.

Recognizing individuality in the child, the law in manifestation as we see it in the rose, parents cease saying *our* and *my* children. The incident of birth is only a fact giving them the privilege to clear its path of weeds and brambles, to let in the sunshine that the light and shine of its own soul may become responsive to it. In the law of unity one is bound to all life and all men; in the law of diversity, the law of expression, soul life — each is unlike every other human being.

We do not form character of all children in the same mold as so many bricks. We rather rejoice at diverse expression as they unfold in freedom.

In relation to the cause or source of life all are equal; the God of one's life is no respecter of persons; the special unfoldment, the personal character is diverse, manifesting according to the application of principle. In this knowledge servility ceases and dominion begins.

In consciousness of our divine nature we become independent of opinions and fashions, we have our own ideals and work them out according to the impelling, pushing force that created them. We make obeisance to the God-life, the Infinite I of the child, and know that no clay, putty or paint can fit the cubes of his nature to the circle of conventions; that no silken cord or golden thread can imprison the natural faculties.

THE LAW OF OBEDIENCE.

Government is accomplished through the power of love and confidence. A beautiful lady said to me, " I desire to join a child-study round table. One thing I do know and that is to require obedience of my child; what I tell it to do it must do." I held my breath a little and said: " Are you sure, dear little mother, that sometimes your child may not be wiser than you; may not by some leading know its own requirements? Are you confident you always understand the situation? Do you always read the child's mind ?"

To understand child nature and to wisely direct it, one must be imbued with the larger love; the mother must be conscious of her own divine nature.

This larger love enables one to know the cause of seeming waywardness; to meet the child's activities on the plane of its development; to guide instead of chiding; to lead it to inventions and constructive doings that forestall the dwarfing and destructive " do-nots."

Usually the obedience required by parents is instigated by selfish motives. The child must keep still for the mother to take a nap; must be quiet at the table so others can talk; must not do this or that, for it interferes with the pleasures of elders.

At any moment he must leave his little world, no matter how absorbing, to answer some requirement of the parent. Any play, work, book or companion is deemed of less importance than a whim or command of elders. A constant interference in his active world creates a rebellion — arouses the combative spirit.

AVOID ISSUES.

Issues should be avoided. If parents fall into the law of the child's doings, they will seldom have to exact obedience. In a sense the child expresses his life in freedom — in liberty — but requires direction. You do not give a child of fourteen months rocks to throw through windows and into the china closet. You rather give him a hammer, a pine board and some tacks, quietly showing him their use; with blocks you lead him to construct cars, houses and familiar objects. I have seen a baby boy, who when a man became a mechanic and inventor, sit for hours removing and replacing the cover and dash of a toy churn, while noises and ordinary amusements would not pacify him.

You teach the child adaptation, and use of articles he comes in contact with; water is not to throw on the floor, fire is to handle only under limitations.

Does a child contrary to your wishes and judgment run away, seeking playmates and amusements you deem unfit for him?

How do you know what leads him to this ? Possibly he is resenting limitations you have put upon him. Perhaps your home and yard, even if well appointed for amusement, are not large enough for him. You do not wonder if a farmer tires of his broad acres, the free air and his independent life, and seeks a wider scope for his entertainment and advancement. You raise no objection if a city lady exchanges a large fine home, for the freedom and solitude of the camp or the country. Then why should not the child with its quick impulses, its untrained imagination, seek its pleasure outside of the home limits? Often the best way to overcome a disposition to run away is to let it have its freedom. Through this freedom he naturally meets with difficulties that prove to him that home is after all a better place.

Trust and confidence begotten of love work wonders. It must be a love that sees the divine in the child and that permits its growth according to his peculiar nature. A child's combativeness, his resistance to your will, is an instinct for freedom, an instinct for the development of individualism. He has a mind of his own.

In nine cases out of ten his resistance is aroused by a spirit of criticism, faultfinding or sarcasm from those who care for him. A parental interest in his games and sports, in his lessons and adventures, indeed in his entire life, will change the combative spirit to a sweet and willing response, to a desire to conform to reasonable requests.

This is obedience, the only true obedience. It is obedience in law, but a law that is the outgrowth of love. A forced obedience, where the child holds a mental resolution to pay back when he gets big enough, is not obedience. It is as if you beat the rose for lying on the ground when you give it nothing to climb upon.

Love must be the foundation of every law, every rule, every regulation, and a love that is divested of the seeds and rootlets of selfishness. Love is a great chemical solvent, it is a consuming fire, dissolving as in a crucible hate, revenge, resistance.

Fathers and mothers, let the divine love manifest in your own souls. When disagreement occurs between you and your child say to him " I love you, I love you; my love is so true that it sees not your resistance, sees not your waywardness, sees not your selfishness. My love creates a contagion in you my child, a contagion of love that shall bear fruit in harmony and peace. My child, I love you." Try this in silence, in the stillness of the soul. Love heals the wounds, allays anger and opens the eye to wisdom. Love leads and directs the law of expression.

You have learned so well the creative and constructive power of thought in healing and all of life's relations, remember it in your dealings with the child. His mind is free from the teachings of tradition; he knows no fear, is all trust and confidence. His heart is responsive and is ever ready to meet the smile, the affectionate thought, the encouraging word. You have only to touch his divinity with the flaming torch to have it shine forth in joy and gladness.

SPIRITUAL LIFE OF THE CHILD.

Froebel says the highest office of education is to train the spiritual in man, that is to make him conscious of his spiritual faculties, and conscious of the absolute back of all of these; to feel the Love-life in his soul. In nature study he finds that love is the cause of life's beginnings and will conclude there is only one force in nature, love, and that all beings because they live in love, live for love.

The child sees the delight of plant life, the ecstasy of birds, the joy of all living creatures, because they manifest love. He will come to hug himself for joy on account of the glimpses he gets from day to day of the truths of nature. Under this pressure of joy he grows and expands and makes room for more joy; and is not joy religious?

Froebel says: " The idea of God is born of the vision of nature." " In all things the same spirit, the same spiritual divine laws operate; the spirit of nature and man are one, they have the same source which is God." While you do not talk about God, you would not lead the imaginative child mind to build a personal God, but the religion of nature inspires him with aspirations and morality compatible with nature.

All growth, all development of man, is conscious or unconscious manifestation of mind — a pushing forth of inherent intelligence into soul expression. Conscious growth, together with the knowledge of the expression of love, of unity in the diverse manifestations of nature, constitutes education. It is man's knowledge of himself and his relation to all things. When a child becomes conscious of divine intelligence, operating, guiding, perfecting his own life, then it is that he knows that the same intelligence shows forth in every tree and plant, in sky and water; in sound and color. He discovers his unity with all life. A soul's knowledge of its Godhood or Godliness reveals the Godhood of every other soul, and the intelligent divinity in all the universe of life. Froebel says: " The destiny and calling of all things is to develop their true idea, and in so doing, to reveal God in outward and through passing form. All has come from God, and through God alone is conditioned." In proportion to man's recognition of the divine principle (Unity) in himself, in that proportion does man see love, law, life and intelligence in all things. He comes to know that the grace and beauty of the willow nature can never be perverted or distorted into a spruce or a bamboo.

The lion is always a lion. In his shaggy mane, in his expressive, resonant voice he manifests the lion principle and must always express the lion nature. Man sees unity in diversity; life, law and intelligence in each created thing.

When all education and all life is based on this law of unity, perfection, divinity in man will show forth in child-life, in blooming youth, and in the sweetness and loveliness of maturity.

In the law of unity man recognizes his kinship with God, his boundless resources, his unlimited powers. Froebel founded his system of education on the inherent divinity of the child. He recognized in every child an undeveloped, unmanifested God, that each soul has within itself all possibilities, and by and through processes of development — education — these possibilities may be attained.

The education that recognizes the divine in the child, that calls forth this divinity in observations, in applications, in creations, is mighty in purpose and power; the seal of it discovers the kingdom of heaven in every soul, and this discovery illuminates every path of investigation, every line of research. It gives the child freedom to grow, *to be* and *to do;* to develop resources in himself hitherto unknown, to attain to powers undreamed of, to manifest in greatness, in accomplishment and service beyond any record of history. A new heaven and a new earth open to him because he is led to understand the law of his nature.

All things present new meanings. His concepts are based upon ideals, images, you may say, while the numberless manifestations of nature reveal to him new laws and new forces. He revels in inventions, constructions and creations, and these are not confined to material things and material science, but as he grows to manhood show forth in all the interests of the world; in political and social science, in financial economics, in adjustment of great municipal and national interests, in homes of altruism, in artistic and poetic creations, in oratory and prophecy.

Education that is vibrant with divine unity, magnifies the law and gives a development that manifests in achievement in every department of life. It is life, love and intelligence shining through the soul's illumination of its own creative powers, its own greatness. This shining forth, this illumination permeates every avenue of life. It is the divine life of man, the child in fruition.

Children delight in the simplicity of plants, the intensity of stars, the purity of living waters, the solidity of rocks, the beauty of flowers, the grandeur of mountains. As one has said, " This river, this harvest, these vine branches, this sky, this sun, and even our flesh are particles of God."

God, love, unity in plant, in leaf, in man.

We still our voices and hear the great heartthrobs of love in all nature. We breathe in the grand harmonies of sound and color; and as we receive we give. Our hearts swell with the consciousness of the divine within us, and we shout it forth to all people. The reverberation of our *joy* touches humanity. We feel the heart of the world beating in our breast.

As the majestic sun ascends in flaming splendor; as the bird thrills us with melody; as the color and perfume of flowers awaken raptures in the soul, so we send forth to all people the gospel of love; for a little child through the law of love has turned the key, opened wide the door and let us in.

CHAPTER XXVIII.

BOY LOVER.

For his age a boy may love as ardently as a man, but the man is bigger.

The boy in High School lives the romances of history; he is thrilled with heart-experiences portrayed by Shakespeare's master hand; is entranced by the Iliad of Homer, the Divine Comedy of Dante; or from day to day he is feeding upon the thrilling novels found at book stalls. Although he seems absorbed and lost in these creations of imagination, he suddenly awakens to a romance of reality,

HE HAS FALLEN IN LOVE.

One girl is the only girl. All the forces of life, all plans, all schemes with boys, all loves for parents or friends, all are submerged in this one great passion. His every act is colored with it, his voice betrays it, his eyes bespeak it, his walk, his every movement disclose it.

The love tones of voice can not be concealed; the love glance of the eye is an open language; the love attitude of body speaks the heart love. The teasing, rollicking impetuous boy becomes absorbed and moody, by turns is gay or reticent. The exuberance of boyhood is transformed into the seriousness of youth.

The boy in love is a symbol of concentration. All thoughts center in the one. He plays football and golf for the one; in algebraic formula and chemical affinities he sees the one; in Greek myths and Latin story he reads of the one; his day dreams are filled with expectations and plans for the one; his night dreams repeat these plans.

225

His soul is filled with this one love, his heart is absorbed by this one grand passion.

What is it? Does he stop to analyze it? Does he know from whence it comes? Does he imagine that no other person has had a similar experience and that this girl is the only girl that *could* so transform him?

He can not be reasoned with. The girl has no faults. She is the one priceless pearl. There are no battles too hard to fight, no worlds too difficult for him to conquer. Days, weeks, perhaps months, this emotion possesses him; or possibly it is the one love of all his life.

This boy-passion should not be treated with raillery and sarcasm; both he and his friends must know that this love affair —

THE SOUL'S AWAKENING,

is the witch's wand to introduce him to himself, and the magic glass through which he discovers his human relations. He climbs a mountain peak and gets glimpses of the world; he outgrows his knickerbockers; the things of yesterday are toys, the books are primers and school associates younglings. The man of him grows apace; he has wisdom equal to father and mother, scorns opinions of teachers, dares his chums to combat in sports and study, and aspires to business.

He is exhilarated, but not drunken; he is awake, wide awake. How much is revealed to him! how industrious he becomes! how short are the days for accomplishment! study, work, recreation, are crowded into the few hours.

Love shows him that he is to be a family man, a business man, a world's man; he is no more somebody's youngster but a grown-up of affairs. The world looks large and he has a large place to fill.

In his heart is a mate who through the law of love compels him to sing his best song and plume his feathers. His lessons become easy, his duties light, and other athletes look out for scores. Surely he is at

226

the very top!

Love's search-light enters his heart, for he must know how and where he fits. He begins living for another. Are head, heart and hand in training for life's accomplishments? Does he always think the thoughts that love impels, speak the words it indicates and do its bidding?

The word character blazes forth with new meanings. He not only wears a tie or boutonniere to please the eye of this one girl, but the man of him must bring out the woman of her, molded and polished, fitted for union. He sees and knows that she has needs beyond gratification of the eye, the pleasing of the senses; that she has a garden in which are flowers that must have the right treatment in order to bloom, upon which his shoes may not tread.

The experience of an early love, be it evanescent or permanent, has effected a larger awakening than school culture or home discipline. All drills, all exercises, all mind and body training take on new meanings. There are no more frills and furbelows, but soul vestures, the garments that make a man.

He does not strive for championship at baseball simply to win; he does not dig out the hard problem for the high marks; he does not write essay or oration for the prize, but in his awakening he knows that all application and all efforts develop latent faculties and call them into line. They are manhood's tools for service. No more shall it be said that a boy has fallen in love; rather that he has *awakened in love*.

Passing from the bud of youth to bloom of manhood, from the first period of intoxication, he seeks the equipments for the man — the regalia of honor and service. He does not sit around in a daze and dream, puling in his baby clothes, but, facing life's realities, more alert, more alive, making for himself the shining raiment of aspiration and an enduring garment of activity, he becomes clothed in his right mind.

The soul awakened by love knows no bounds; intuition and

inspiration become active; understanding the unity of life, all interests go out from self to worldwide interests. The man of him reveals inherent powers and possibilities. He is alive to new pursuits.

GENDER SENSE.

Accompanying or possibly preceding love's awakening, is the development of the gender sense; the boy is thrilled with the power to create. He is no more surprised at his love romance than he is with the changes that take place in mind and body. In mind his thought is quickened and perceptions awakened. He sees with new eyes and hears with new ears, his heart is attuned to new symphonies. In body the growth of hair upon face is manhood's insignia; the change of voice is a sign of power, and passion's thrill is latent creative energy demanding activity — the gender sense seeking expression.

The gender sense requires training, thoughtful and extended training, to make it serve man's needs and highest aspirations.

A boy gets a smattering of all sciences, with enough Latin and Greek to understand their terminology; a fine training in language and literature, but the schools give never a hint of love's world; love as related to family and social life, as expressed in passion and generation; love in the highest sense, as belonging to his intuitive and spiritual life. The wisdom of the age has not discerned that the boy should have special training in his love nature.

From early babyhood the sight sense is trained to note objects, to walk in paths, to distinguish colors in the works of nature and art; the sense of hearing learns to distinguish letters, and language; it perceives the voices of nature and the tones of endearment; through a long process of education it comes to recognize the infinite tones and harmonies of opera and oratorio. As we educate eye and ear to know and appreciate great works of art, so it is a boy's privilege to train the gender sense; as an animal it may create a body, another animal, but as a *man* possessed of powers to think and to know, it may be trained to serve the purposes of life, to be strength of his strength, to be an impelling force in the world of art and construction.

Gender sense, inherent in man with life itself, is not awakened until he has reason and knowledge. As sight is the seeing sense, gender is a two-fold sense, *loving* and *creating.* It has a double function, one of the heart and one of life; one the cry for companionship, one the impulse for reproduction, the two working together or separately.

The boy in love works out the gender sense through emotions and feelings on the love side; he experiments with unused tools; through years of experience, sight and hearing have been at his service, but the gender impulse has had no experience; as cupid it must fly with a clipt wing. The boy may have conjugated the verb love in English, Latin and Greek; he may have read " Evangeline," " The Lady of the Lake," " Enoch Arden," and a host of others, but all to him is like a dream until he loves. He learns love through loving.

The gender sense, on its creative side, is not so new; from babyhood it has builded, invented and constructed; chu-chu cars, tops, kites, horses, engines, have, one after another, called forth the creative faculty; as boy-man it demands a new creation; one of its kind. Shall this demand be a school-boy shriek, or the controlled, directed command of manhood? Shall it be the whoop of an untrained savage or the resonant, harmonious tone of the musical artist?

As a boy has learned arithmetic and algebra through mathematical principles and formulas, so he can learn the principles and formulas of creative energy; he commands a service from this knowledge not to be compared with the bookkeeper's art or counting-room accomplishments.

A boy can know very early that:

First, creative energy has its origin with life itself. It is not of the body but of the spirit, and is man's greatest gift — the power to create, sublimest thought of all!

Second, through the knowledge that creative energy is of the spirit, it may be appropriated to any and all uses of life. It need not necessarily be expended in reproduction of the species.

Creative energy has its origin in spirit, not in matter. It is coexistent with life itself. In all forms of animal and vegetable life is found duality, masculine and feminine qualities, seeking through the gender sense place and opportunity for perpetuation.

In plant the law is fulfilled by attraction of pollen to pistil, in animal by union of sperm to germ. This union in each is impelled by the kosmogenic force of the universe, the spirit of all things.

Long since, a boy has learned that there can be no effect without a cause, no creation without a creator. He has often been delighted with the machinery of watch, wheel within wheel, working with exactness and regularity. He knows the watch in his hand is evidence of a maker, a creator.

The telegraph and electric light are the effects of a cause, are the wonder workings of electricity, a force in nature that no man has yet been wise enough to define, subtle and potent, *known only by its effects*; the kosmic mind or the spirit of the universe we must know and understand through results. Creative energy, the miracle of sex union, the perpetuation of life are *effects,* are manifestations of infinite intelligence, in all and through all, one law, one mind.

As one knows that a clock is not made without the thought-power of the maker, as a telegram can not be sent without the unseen, subtle force that flashes the message, so no one thing from man to mole can exist without spirit or power to produce it. All life's processes evince the intelligence of this power.

Without man's volition the lungs, as a spongelike bellows, indraw air which oxygenates the blood through porous tissue and by expiration expel impure air. The heart valves send blood to every part of the body with unerring certainty and regularity.

Animals and plants are adapted to the environments in which they must live; birds fly in the air; fish swim in the water; the cactus thrives on the desert, the lotus in slime and mud; the eidelweiss in mountain snows. They are the diverse expressions of the one life, each fulfilling the law of its kind.

The five ordinary senses evince the creator's intelligence by organs adapted to represent the special function; the eye is a perfect seeing instrument; the ear a complete hearing machine; the gender sense, the sex impulse, has organs equally fitted to their functions.

Male and female created He them; two sets of organs are required to express this sense; one planned for and adjusted to the other, and to these is given the high office of begetting life, the miracle of generation.

Creative energy may be appropriated to all of life's uses. If creative energy is of the physical alone, we could have reproduction on the physical plane only, but man's ability to invent, to construct, to master conditions in any department of life, may be through the application of this energy.

The gender impulse is not to be treated as an enemy, as something to be killed out, to be annihilated; no, no! welcome it as the herald of life and vigor, learn to appropriate it to special pursuits, to some chosen study, some certain work or definite occupation; if in school, an original essay or romance, a picture; if a mechanic, some new device or invention; if an office-boy or clerk, some new and special interest in the business.

The farmer boy finds varied and absorbing interests; he makes new devices for labor-saving improvements in caring for stock; he engages in enterprises for extending business. The quickening creative force applied and appropriated, puts new vigor into old lines of work, at the same time is eminently inventive in new lines and resources.

Creative force can be utilized by a process of mental training, which training is valuable for every youth. Its origin is coexistent with life, is God-given. In essence all created functions are good;

everything has its use, what higher one than to produce life; what faculty of man proves his union with divine life more than his ability to create?

Recognize passion as an insignia of love and life. There is nothing base in man's nature. Functions may be perverted, but there can be nothing unholy in natural adaptation and use.

A small boy who stamps with his feet, drums with his hands, and whistles and wriggles, by wise leading is taught to sing songs of joy and patriotism and train every muscle to rhythmic motion. When he drummed and whistled and wriggled, both tune and rhythm were out of place, but some kind friend found the note of harmony and his soul shines through the body, reflecting poise and power.

As the little boy's feet and arms, untrained, failed to perform their part, so the gender sense may misrepresent the true life. Learn its natural, its creative power, then dropping it from the mind; forget it as you forget head, hand or stomach in their perfect working. The busy boy never is wondering what the stomach is doing with the piece of gingerbread his grandmother gave him; forgets his hand when building a sail boat or molding plastic clay; forgets his feet when roaming in the woods for nuts or forsaken birds' nests.

As the musician fills his soul with the harmonies of infinite tones, making technique secondary, so the boy lover trains the creative powers into active service; he does this through physical and spiritual development.

All athletics and out-door sports are at his service; boating, swimming, ball games, the interesting nature-study rambles. The gymnasium and a simple home apparatus supply special needs for bodily activity   (see Supplement *ff*).

A system of physical exercise founded upon the law of activity and repose requires no apparatus, but is remarkably effective in giving bodily strength. This may be called Mental Gymnastics.

This system combines alternate resistance and relaxation — for instance, push the arms slowly to the highest reach, always imagining an object of resistance, then slowly relax. Push out and down in the same way; move the body forward and back and rotate it. Exercise feet, hands, fingers. Lie flat upon the back, relaxing every muscle; then reach both feet and legs far up, pushing — pushing. Again relax, then raise the body, resting on hands and feet. Also perform this last face downwards. By a slow movement throw the head forward on the chest, then back as far as possible; make side movements the same.

One is surprised how much *stiff-neckedness* is overcome by these head movements. They give special relief where the mind refuses to work after a long strain or when one becomes sleepy.

Perform all these exercises slowly, impelling the full force of the mind into them, then relax, abstracting the mind as fully as possible from every part of the body. Every muscle can be handled in this way, and the practice gives one an immediate and ever ready means of rest and relaxation.

This method is a constant practice of some of our busiest men and women. Its knowledge gives added power to every youth. You put into practice the law of activity and repose, so wonderfully illustrated in all of nature's processes; it is a voluntary demonstration of that law.

When you return from school, your head confused with the many problems presented by many teachers and books, your body refusing to obey the mind, do not be so foolish as to run to mother's pantry for refreshment, or to some unfrequented corner to become absorbed in a dime novel; a few moments only of the above athletic practice will change the tension of thought, will put into activity all of life's forces. Change is always rest. This special change is ever at hand. After this you are ready for the piano, for the studies outlined for another day, or for a social evening with family and friends.

These exercises are especially valuable if there is any abnormal expression of the gender sense, if creative energy seems too active or too dormant. Through them one secures adjustment of forces according to the law of rest and activity. The circulation becomes free and normal, the ruddy glow of health supplants pallor, robust strength succeeds weakness.

TRANSMUTATION OF FORCE.

Every boy is familiar with chemical changes; oxygen ancl hydrogen become water, wood and coal are transformed into heat and gases; liquids become solids and solids liquids. So passion, representing the sexual instinct, the gender sense, may be transformed in the life of man and become, through conscious willing, the impelling power of all of his activities.

In the transmutation it thrills and vivifies all bodily functions; it arouses mental processes and awakens spiritual perceptions.

Nature ever teaches us the law of rest and action, the sleeping and waking, the seed time and harvest; two forces, the uniting and dividing, centripetal and centrifugal, the inner and outer, a giving and receiving; the silence of inaction and the trumpet tones of music and oratory. In the understanding of this law one's own thought is stilled to be supplanted by kosmic forces. One gives up his own " I told you so," his own hard combating methods, for the incoming sweep and surge of the God-power, impelling, pushing, demanding fruition. Daily habits of stillness, of entering the Silence, enable one to be conscious of latent powers, and more definitely of controlling and appropriating the forces of life. Creative energy becomes transformed into physical strength and mental activity. In this certain law the alembics of life are under control. The fulness and power of the law of rest and activity will lead into paths of greater light and wisdom (see "Willing and Letting," page 91).

To realize the strength and power of creative energy, to become one with it, is to have a god-likeness — to become master.

Your train is not run by a wild engine to be side-tracked or ditched, but you are the engineer and conductor combined; you have placed a headlight on the engine, your hand on the lever, and the pent-up forces of your life are directed on the double track of rectitude and righteousness. It takes you into the populous world of barter and traffic, or out, out to wild and unexplored regions. Wherever you go, whatever you do, this headlight and this lever are your twin associates, not only guiding and guarding your every act, but leading you into new fields of discovery, new possibilities.

You have often had manhood's ideal set before you; in these pages is given the possibility of attainment. To get perfect command and control of creative energy may require time. However, in the light of truth, there is always hope. Put the seal of blessing on all your powers, know that the divine plan enters into all of God's creation and that the gender sense is no exception to this plan.

Of course different experiences come to different individuals; but always and always remember that any voice of passion is the voice of love demanding a creation, and a fulfilment of that demand in vital and important activities may become a habit; it is a transmutation of the physical into the spiritual, of what has been called lust into love. Patience and persistence will enable you to be conquerer.

Early learn to meditate on the great things of the world; think of the grandeur and greatness of mountains, the limitless expanse of sky, the broad prairies, the great throbbing heart of humanity. Take any one of these and dwell upon it until the mind is taken off of self and finds itself in harmony with all life and all nature. A frequent repetition of this practice renders the mind receptive to thoughts possessing real power in themselves. New impulses will be revealed, promptings and inspirations not before experienced.

Hold to high ideals. Look about you in history and literature for noted examples of attainment, remarkable men whose life-work has contributed to the world's progress — Plato, Socrates, Emerson!

Does not the acorn contain the oak in embryo? So in every boy's nature is the seed of nobleness, grandeur and efficiency. The soil in which it is planted, the environment of culture and all institutions of life do their part in development of the man-oak, but what is the boy's part? Differing from the oak he has the power of knowing his own inherent qualities, and also commanding them into service. Shall we say that the man-oak is a god-man, with the nature and functions of man and the likeness and possibilities of a god? Shall not the acorn possibilities be fulfilled ? May not the human intellect unite with the divine nature in youth in such a manner that he can utilize his own powers and know his own greatness?

An oak must always be an oak, but man in the diversity of gifts may utilize these in a diversity of avenues. The original genius lies in the enticing land of music, but the musician may be an orator as well. He has a double speech for those who listen. He reaches the heart through the tones of harmony and through the silvery voice of oratory.

A mechanic or artisan flashes an invention upon the world — a cable or an airship — but the possibilities of his nature may show forth as a painter or sculptor. The genius in him is not an acorn genius but a god-genius, and in the law of unity and diversity shows forth in manifold creations. Franklin, our "poor Richard," is a type of a god-man. Is he better known as an inventor and a printer than as an ambassador and statesman? Could he give us a picture of his private life, would he not tell us that his success and renown came from the fact that he had confidence in the god-seed of his life; that in early youth he was awakened to his possibilities and powers? Franklin united science with religion and proved his faith in God by having faith in himself.

Do you know anything of the boyhood of William Morris or Ruskin? Have their lives no fascination for you? They lived a real fairy story and touched the world with an enchanter's wand. How did they do it? How could they arouse such a world of interest in art, economics and state-craft save that it first existed in their hearts? The knowledge, the awakening, made it possible for them to be England's twin god-oaks.

The seed of life is god-seed. Engrave this upon your heart, and you shall hold the key that unlocks the castle of attainment; in this castle you make your choice of the fruits of life.

Do I speak in parables ? Go back over all the pages of this work and, somewhere, you will find the word that interprets this page.

It is your privilege to take possession of the riches that lie hidden in your own soul; this is the fairy land that all may enter and from its treasures enrich the world.

> I am the master of my fate,
> I am the captain of my soul.

CHAPTER XXIX.

GIRL LOVER.

In every marble slab there dwells a madonna.

A girl in the adolescent period is the flower of humanity. Sweet sixteen! how royally she comes in the bloom of youth and the blush of womanhood. The free elastic step, the joyous merry-making, the independence expressed in speech, in walk, in pose of body, in garments that defy imitation, are a combined prophecy of the new woman.

You do not hear " Father says," or " Brother says," or " Teacher says," but " I think." She even questions Emerson and Ruskin, and is prepared to settle all problems of life. In school she is taught to rise to her feet and not only give orally and independently what she has found in books, but she is encouraged to have an opinion upon every subject. She analyzes, infers and compares, but, at last, perhaps comes to conclusions with surprising quickness and alertness. Intellect is quickened by intuition. She has original ideas and she gains confidence in their expression. She is free and independent in thought

The age has made her what she is.

The century just passed has been notable for a defense of free speech and free thought. Its impress is stamped upon the youth of the land. Girls, as well as boys, study the science of government, the relation of capital to labor, sociology, economics. They would be bewildered with the many problems presented for discussion, were it not that in each they find the thread of unity, the one law of life that holds all secrets in the heart of man, and that is the law of love.

The maiden is not the shy maiden of one hundred years ago. She is not sitting in the chimney corner to be sought by some youth. She is rather the frank comrade of her boy associates, side by side with him in intellectual pursuits, with him planning pleasures and recreations, and often and often his equal in rowing, swimming, cycling, tennis, golf and other athletics. Flirtations, giggling and diplomacy to gain a point, all these are supplanted by a healthy, frank and free association, where small talk is at a discount and influence of freedom and equality are visible in the opening of the flower of womanhood.

In life's adjustment, sex differences are disappearing. Athletics and pursuits that cultivate alertness, agility and bravery in a boy are equally desirable for a girl. Music, needlework and other fine arts that bring out sweetness and tenderness in a girl will do the same for a boy. Strength and wisdom are not typical of manhood only. For all pursuits women require wisdom and physical strength.

For the vocation of motherhood, more than all else in the world, she demands vigor and robustness of body and a trained intellect that shall not only be prepared for the ordinary functions of life, but that shall stand guard for emergencies and the great unlooked-for events. Very early the girl should be conscious that the joys and blessings of maternity carry with them a duty and foresight in training and preparation.

As a child she evinces this instinct in her love and care for dolls, and the true mother is on the alert to convert this mimic life into a preparation for real life. Older children, too, care for younger in the same way: bathing, feeding, dressing, and making garments.

One day a young girl was passing a severe criticism on the way the children of a certain family were dressed, there being no fitness or appropriateness in their apparel; " she should think their mother would be ashamed to send them to school in that way." Her own mother remarked that perhaps this mother had never been taught to sew and care for clothes, perhaps she did not even have dolls to dress and likely never made her own clothing. From then on this little girl evinced a special desire to know how to make both doll and infant clothes. It seemed an awakening of the maternal in her.

Most girls have times of this awakening and often it occurs very young. Parents and friends should not treat it with ridicule or lightness, but recognize it as the natural outpicturing of the inner thoughts. In no direction will child-confidence be rewarded as in this, especially at the adolescent period; hopes and joys of parenthood should be frequent subjects of conversation. When a girl realizes that she is preparing for motherhood, the activities of life take on a new coloring. As she has evidences of her divine womanly powers, her life is quickened by earnestness and seriousness— yes, by a joyousness of content.

Very early, perhaps, she becomes a lover. The maiden does not fall in love, does not awaken in love, she loves. How shall I picture her, a soul listening to the song of birds, a heart enraptured with strains of music, a dream of fairyland, the enchanter's wand touching the closed lids which open with a glad surprise. The world becomes a moving panorama of all that gladdens the senses; hillsides that are a tangle of loveliness; moors and prairies whose vastness is the measure of her mind's expansion; skies whose blue typifies the purity of her soul; waters whose ever changing restlessness, depth and placidity mirror the stirrings, the joy and peace of her heart; the long, solitary walks in shaded woods, where there is nevermore loneliness; the morning song bursting rapturously from her own lips. Oh, the joy of living, for the maiden loves! No wonder Emerson said that " All the world loves a lover," for her love, her joy, is a contagion as it thrills and throbs in her heart; it sets up a vibration of joy in every other heart.

As we are charmed with the mating song of birds, so her morning carol sends joy to our hearts; as though it were set to a tune we sing —

I love, you love, she loves;
We love, you love, they love.

The love gets into our feet, we enter into the whirl of a windmill game, or all join hands in a grand right and left.

Shall she still this joy, shall she trample out this love? Shall we call it names and pronounce upon it a death sentence? No, no! it is a kosmic law, seeking expression. The feminine of her soul is attracted to the masculine heart, fulfilling the law of duality. She is filled with the prophecy of a purpose in life, and the light, rollicking character of her joys change for those of deeper significance. She may know Latin and Greek, she may know art, architecture or statecraft, she may be versed in philosophy and ethics, but any and all of these are simply adjuncts to the main import of life. They are frills to the garment, for wifehood and motherhood are inherently the culmination and manifestation of creative energy — the love force of her soul. This love power is deeper and more enduring than race development or proclivities.

Motherhood is one of the eternal verities, self-existing and indestructible. Education may guide it, social conditions may so warp that it seems misshapen and misfitting, but coexistent with life itself it demands expression. The activities of business, of politics, of literature and art can not erase it.

As Elizabeth Cady Stanton says: " Men and women will love each other, love their children, and be loved by them in turn, no matter what happens,— even if the world turns upside down. You might as well talk of the animal deserting its young; of the bird in the tree forsaking its unfledged little ones, because of a great thunderstorm or some convulsion of nature, as to say that social upheavals or changes weaken or destroy human affection. None of these convulsions now sweeping over society will change what nature has made unchangeable,— love. In the material world we have positive and negative electricity, the centripetal and centrifugal forces, balancing each other. If these forces were thrown out of equilibrium for five minutes, we should have material chaos. So, in the social world, we have the two diverse elements, complementary of each other, the masculine and the feminine, and the perfect adjustment of these two great forces is as necessary to the preservation of the order of the social world as the balancing of the centripetal and the centrifugal force is to the maintenance of order in the material world."

Girls must remember that love is the most potent power in the universe; it is the cohesive and attractive force of all things. The atom by its central molecular affinity of love joins other atoms to produce stone and rock. The creative principle through the duality of sex in plant and animal life by the force of love reproduces its kind.

" Love is the energy of nature and all creations tend irresistibly toward the maximum of love."

What is true of plant and animal life is true of man. Sex attraction is not a race belief, is not a matter of education, is not a product of society or art; it is natural and enduring as life itself.

The young girl who has been trained to recognize fundamental truths of sex, through the strong stirrings of her soul, reaches out to know the masculine heart, and from her inmost and highest nature through love and her intuitions, is inspired at all times to do and to be her best; to read thoughts of her associates, to give strength and life to those who need it, but always and always to respond gladly and willingly in her feminine nature to the highest and best in the masculine nature.

In this training, shyness, reticence and undue modesty are removed, yet in frankness, ingenuousness and free life there is nothing of the hoyden. It is difficult to describe in cold words, but she is neither brazen and bold nor reticent and bashful, resorting to deceit and *finesse* to gain a point.

True to her inner nature, true to principles of love and wisdom, she is simply herself, an individual personality — living her own life and being true to that life, she is true to all with whom she associates. She knows that, according to law, there is an adjustment that must bring true relationship which works out in harmony and justice to all.

A girl natural and free may have strong impulses in her sex life. She will have the need of activity and must use all means for self-control. The creative impulse must be set at arduous tasks, requiring concentration, attention and execution. Surface frivolities are not sufficient; work and sports are demanded that absorb her inventive faculties. (See " Creative Life.")

Teachers and parents must be on the alert to supply wholesome outlets for activities; books and dry facts will not do this. There must be something of absorbing interest. It is better that this something engage the attention of the entire school or family — girls and boys together. Comradeship is a great factor at this period of life. We can not expect either a boy or a girl to go off alone and learn an appointed task; the social nature is strong in them and what can be done in groups is more easily accomplished.

More and more educators are coming to understand that inherent faculties must find expression, that construction and invention are natural attributes. Opportunities to express these attributes must be given in the routine of school work.

The pupils build looms, weave mats and baskets make tents, and by gradual sequence in the use of clay, wood and metal construct dwellings. Go into any well arranged manual-training shop and watch the eagerness and interest in the work. The faces glow with enthusiasm and the hours are far too short for the accomplishment of plan and execution of designs. The traditional three R's are supplanted by creative art, which includes drawing, painting, clay modeling and tool work. Under these heads the teacher formulates his program, and constructive activity forms the center around which radiate language, number work, history, literature and many of the sciences.

The impelling force is creative. To be making something is as natural as breath itself. The mind is no more considered an empty pot into which to pour facts and figures, but a soul of immense natural capabilities that is seeking opportunities for expression. The teacher is only the leader; he does not even clear the path of brambles, he simply points the way.

It is difficult to specialize the activities that utilize creative energies. The girl should be set about originating entertainments and excursions that are the outgrowth of her studies. Suppose it is a trip on the Nile, a sojourn at Bombay, an evening with the Greek poets, living tableaux of the Vale of Cashmere. What subjects for study and research these present! Habits, customs and dress, together with native products, as well as the art and literature upon the chosen theme, all serve as an outlet for tremendous energies. A room full of boys and girls can be enlisted in some such a theme and latent talent discovered in the pupil.

In home life the tiresome stitching of long seams, the routine work of washing dishes or sweeping, all may be done cheerfully, but when it has passed the educative stage, it ceases to contribute to development; then, it may be done as cooperation in utility service, and should be supplemented by that which serves to bring out the best in the girl.

The occasions should be frequent when her associates are invited to an evening in which games are introduced that require skill and activity. Tableaux, charades and living pictures all serve this purpose. Often and often parents call in neighbors' children to entertain them. They read to them, furnish music, stereopticon views, pictures, but an evening in which there is a plan for original work by the children themselves is not only more enjoyable, but serves a better purpose in the evolution of character. All these give training of inherent powers, an evolution of the self within.

Girl life should not be a continual ride in a merry-go-round, but rather a voyage of discovery, a realization and an application of her own powers, and at the same time an adjustment in social life and to conditions. The deeper and more earnest the participation in every-day affairs and in the entertainments of life, the more surely this object is accomplished.

Mary invites her friends to a Japanese tea. How interested and enthusiastic she is in all the preparations. Her friends are asked to bring screens, kokimonas and curios, and to wear kimonas and tabis. Chairs and tables are removed from the room. The gay party, after being seated on the floor, recite with interest tales of Japan. They recall what they have read and heard of these people, their temples, their art, their family and social life, their love of nature, their simplicity and their courage.

Mary has previously prepared some rice and cake to serve with tea in tiny cups. She explains that it is not practical to supply raw fish and *saki,* but is pleased that they seem well satisfied.

An evening like this familiarizes the awakening mind of youth to the real Japan, and at least gives zest and interest to the reading about this country.

DEVELOPMENT OF SOUL POWER.

In a natural evolution of the soul, it is free to know its powers and capabilities and the adjustment to material environment is possible.

A girl's conversation will not be full of *bows* and *beaux*, of the latest cut of skirts of sleeves, whether she will be ostracised if her dress is one inch shorter than her mates, or her tam-o' shanter is an " off " color, or whether the boys are doing so and so, or some other way. She is so full of the real import of life that she has no time or thought for these. Helen of Troy becomes her own soul, full of victories. Joan d'Arc is a symbol of the overthrow of malice, jealousy and revenge, and Lucretia Mott, of peace and good will to all. Then the stories she tells, the songs she sings are songs and stories of conquest and victories, not for the adulation and flattery of youth, but conquest and victories of that which gives strength to character;

a victory of love shining forth in every act, in every desire, in every thought.

Is this victory more a feminine grace than a masculine trait? No, no. So it might be reiterated that for a pliant soul, what will lend sweetness and loveliness to a girl, will add gentleness and grace to a boy; what will give robustness, alertness and independence to a boy, will give the same to a girl. Differences of character, of ability, is not seen more between boys and girls than between those of the same sex; so, shall we not think of both girls and boys as souls, equal in privileges, equal in inherent faculties, equal in power of expression. Individual differences are not alone attributable to sex. When we come to this conclusion we will not hear boys say, " I can not understand girls; I do not see into a girl's nature." We will not hear a girl say, " I wish I could know the heart of a boy. He is a riddle I can not read." Remember that no one soul always knows another; but if we can realize that each has emotions, aspirations, desires and needs equal to every other, then the mystery is not so great.

Remember, too, the eternal unity — the one absolute principle of all life; this is the foundation of male and female, or rather the kingdom where there is neither male nor female. Then, soul will answer to soul and speech to speech in a universal language. The one life, and that life the product of love — a love that is intelligence itself, and the story of stories, and song of songs — is that a realization of that love is, of itself, a conscious awakening of its inherent power, *is of itself* an opening of faculties, a prescience that adjusts difficulties and straightens out tangles. A soul that knows love, sees loveliness; that feels love, lives righteousness.

> A block of marble caught the glance
> Of Buonarotti's eyes,
> Which heightened in their solemn deep
> Like meteor-lighted skies.
>
> A brow was lifted high and pure,
> The waking eyes outshone,

And as the master sharply wrought,
    A smile broke through the stone.

The stately bust and graceful limbs,
    Their marble fetters shed,
And where the shapeless block had been,
    An angel stood instead.

Sculptor of souls! I lift to Thee
    Encumbered heart and hands;
Spare not the chisel, set me free,
    However dear the bands.

CHAPTER XXX.

THE AWAKENING.

O joy, joy insuperable, in his heart he knows the Arisen One.

In his loneliness of despair, life must find the Life, for joy is gone, and life is all that is left; it is compelled to seek its source, its root, its eternal life.

Man is impelled to seek knowledge of his divine self by many and varied experiences, through affliction and suffering, through disease and disaster, through the great human unrest demanding peace and satisfaction.

Religion has long revealed to man his redemption through faith; science now proclaims it through knowledge. It is a revelation of the Self, a consciousness of the Absolute; the *esse* or limitless, boundless source becomes *existence,* from *existo,* coming out of.

The within is in evidence; divinity impelling humanity; the soul expresses the activity of spirit. The awakening is a knowledge of this activity, a realization of inherent powers, a knowing of the Absolute as omnipresent, omniscient force.

The awakening of true being is an illumination. In religious parlance it is a *conversion,* a knowledge of the light that lighteth every man that cometh into the world   (see Supplement *g g).*

By faith one *sees,* feels, knows the truth of his being. The inward Christ speaks to the Adam consciousness and reveals its ever growing and increasing power, its limitlessness and boundlessness. One is no more finite man, but, becoming *at one* with infinity, realizes that somewhere deep down in his nature is infinity — the divine Self.

Life is a continual process of *becoming,* of growing consciousness.

Having once experienced the vision of life, having had a consciousness of the higher self — the Spirit — one has started for dominion and can never retrace his steps until he has reached the throne of being and becomes Lord of all.

The soul's awakening may be momentary, a glimpse only, but this glimpse, this moment, is evidence of its possibilities, and bids to press on and on to greater heights, to larger experiences.

Sincere desire and forms of meditation and concentration hasten this awakening. Make a picture of a perfect man; call to him as though he were far off; bring him to your consciousness. What do you see one straight of form, lithe of limb and perfect in poise, the face and eyes reflecting beauty of the soul's kingship. That vision of loveliness is the Self — the embodiment of peace and power.

You now woo it with endearments, with thoughts of confidence, with love's adulations and blessings. You open your arms, you embrace it — you become one with it — and the natural man through the influx of the spiritual man, through a union of the finite and infinite, becomes the perfected one.

Man comes to know that spiritual consciousness may not be permanent until intellectual faculties are brought into harmony, and bodily functions proceed in an orderly manner; attainment is possible through adherence to ideals. These ideals are desires, born of emotion and feeling. They are the fruit of sense perception and serve us well as we delve into the innermost recesses of life and discover its possibilities. They are the gateway to knowledge opening the doors of revelation. They bid us to the feast and conduct us to the promised land. As one gets glimpses of the perfected self, he comes into greater realization by repeated recognition. In a realization that is constant one can never be sick or miserable, can never know any lack.

The Spirit of knowledge is a revelation of one's Self, and only through experience does one know that Self and its power, know the difference between intellectual attainment and spiritual consciousness.

Personal consciousness of kosmic mind is

INITIATION.

All religions, all orders of mystics, all sects, are seeking this consciousness. To know the source of life is the hunger-cry of every soul; to feel the presence of the ALL life is the consciousness of victory —of power. Upon this one simple fact or process of the soul, religions and philosophies are founded, volumes and volumes written, brotherhoods and mystic orders exist. *All that has been hidden shall be revealed.* It is given to man to find that which he seeks. As nature is prolific in forms and manifestations, as the mind and character of every man differs from every other man, so the ways and means of knowing God are various.

The intelligence projecting and impelling all life gives us birds, insects, fish, plants and trees in such variety and abundance that each is a study of a life time. The ornithologist, the zoologist or the botanist must devote all his time, years and years, to become an expert.

To the Forestry building at the World's Fair in Chicago many countries sent from three to five hundred kinds of trees, while Brazil and Australia each had over eight hundred. It would take weeks to learn the names of all these, let alone the character and use.

Man in his formation, in variety of characteristics, evinces a more marvelous manifestation of intelligence than all else in nature. Nations, countries, neighborhoods and tribes give us a deep study of habits and customs. Art, literature and science each evolve according to national characteristics. When the one goal of life is to become conscious of God, when the mountain peak is oneness of kosmic and personal mind, or rather man's consciousness of his own divine nature, it seems natural that there would be many ways of experiencing that consciousness. Where, how, or when man has this experience, it is precious to him, so precious, such a deep heart experience, that it is no wonder that he should seek the hermit life, the cloister, or give it the protection of orders and secret societies. The real secret, the initiation, is, however, with each soul. Joining orders, depending on rituals and symbols, is something like building a fence around your dooryard: you shut yourself in more than you shut others out. You put a premium upon freedom; your life becomes a play world from which you debar your fellows. Christ's teaching is a protest against all secret orders. *Ye shall know the truth, and the truth shall make you free.*

When Christ came to earth the world's most sacred truths were hidden in monasteries and brotherhoods. It is conjectured that, during the unrecorded years of his life, he lived and studied with some of these orders. He gathered the truths of the cults and condensed them in simple forms for all people. Without ceremony, without symbol, from his heart treasure, he spoke to the heart of humanity. He gave to the world the wisdom of the ages — truths that can only be measured by the depths of the ocean or heights of mountains. Without incense, without robes, without ritualistic forms, he says, " Come all ye that are weary and heavy laden." Come all, no degrees, no human symbolic conceptions, but simply COME, and drink freely.

Secret orders, forms and symbols representing esoteric experiences, arise as a consequence of man's dependence upon material things and his education through sense perception. They recur in different ages and different generations in answer to the cry of suffering, of sick souls demanding crutches; man's dependence upon forms is good as long as he is a child in spiritual knowledge and requires these helps.

Many are led to join societies and orders under the hope that they may find an easy road to the mountain top. No doubt every religion and every leader of both new and old cults possesses a measure of truth; the method of presentation, the forms in which it is clothed are adapted to the needs of some classes of mind, and have a meaning in the world's progress. All learn, however, that religion — the awakening — the true initiation — is a personal experience.

One has said: " There is no purifier in this world to be compared with spiritual knowledge. He who is perfected in devotion findeth spiritual knowledge springing up spontaneously in himself."

Who is perfected in his devotion? That one who adheres to his ideal of a perfect self and seeks to have that self incarnated in his life. He may accept this ideal as a fact, but it is only through a spiritual assimilation that he enters into true knowledge and experiences the awakening.

Intellectually he may hear a statement of a truth daily, but if it does not enter into the heart it has no vivifying power. The awakening truth emanates from the center of being; one becomes identified with it, is governed by it; he thinks it, speaks it, lives it.

The spiritual life is the awakened life; it is a consciousness of knowledge not found in books, of processes not learned through intellect, of possibilities without boundaries and limitless. The awakened soul sees the same powers and possibilities in every other soul, sees that the awakened Christ is for all; with hope, with calm confidence he awaits fulfilment of expectations.

The ways are many and winding to the shining heights of spiritual consciousness. There is no straight and direct road to the mountain top; one must proceed over rugged cliffs, through the darkness of canyons, by the narrow, icy ledge, and beneath the threatening avalanche, ever anon as he ascends being rewarded with distant visions of grandeur and magnificence.

Two seldom follow the same path in making this mountain ascent. One may gain it through the tortuous and devious paths of intellect; he studies, reads, compares and sifts; he knows all religions and all philosophies, and at last, through some illumined word, perceives the truth of truths. Another, through some experience — a sorrow perhaps, a business failure, an unrecognized achievement, a useless

252

battling against odds, in any situation that makes human effort seem powerless — all at once gets a glimpse of the light.

Another through the " Mysteries of Matrimony," through the love-life in its dual expression — conjugal union, discovers resources and powers indwelling in the masculine and feminine natures. Man's close kinship with the Creator is thus accentuated, for out of the heart of being is revealed infinite possibilities.

Another, through vision, through dreams, through clairvoyance, or some new experience of the soul's power, knows spiritual life and thus becomes conscious of that life. Another, in cloistered cell, abjuring family ties, social life, ambition's power and fame's fruition, verily loses his life that he may gain it; in the silence and the stillness to him is revealed the Christ.

Another, through the harmonies of sound, the tone symphonies of voice and orchestra, is led from material concepts to the realm of infinite possibilities of the spirit. Another knows and feels the oneness of Spirit through nature's great throbbing soul. His perceptions are awakened and moved by the song of bird, the murmur of brooks, the expanse of prairies or the majesty of mountains. He sees the life that is his life in stream, flower, beast and man. In the silence of the wood his soul enters into communion with the perfected man that is pictured in perfected nature. No bird's carol is more alive with joy and praise than his awakened soul, no child more gleeful in his play than this heart that can never again be alone, for it is attuned to the infinite harmonies of life and rejoices in its own powers.

Thus with or without creed, with all books or with none, the student or the laborer, the recluse or the man of affairs, all, all may know and realize the spiritual life, may have the soul's awakening that brings peace, poise and power.

That day — the day of deliverance shall come; in what place you knew not; it shall come, but you know not the time.

THE LOVER'S WORLD,

A

WHEEL OF LIFE.

SUPPLEMENT.

First comes thought, then vision, then knowledge.

THE LOVER'S WORLD.

SUPPLEMENT.

A supplement is both explanatory and corroborative. The practical workings of many theories advanced in " The Lover's World" is found in the following pages; while extracts from books and correspondence give the ideas of many people. The reader, in the supplement, is put in touch with the world of thought and thus will find aids to progress in many lines, while upon controverted points, the opinions of fearless and advanced thinkers are quoted. Man's greatest need is to think, to see and to know. Some one word from the many here collated may lead him who desires truth to think; from sifting and gathering ideas and facts he will obtain glimpses of truth, and through practice and observation of law he will acquire knowledge; he becomes what he wills to be.

This may not be an instantaneous experience, but according to the testimony of most people, the perfect life, in which one has health and control, is a building-up process. A little here and a little there; line upon line. A giving up the inherited errors of tradition, the blotting out of old thoughts, and day by day letting in the shining light of new truths. Keep the mind ever recipient to the influx of kosmic love and thus in the heart will the kingdom of heaven be established. The Wheel of Life will not sink into ruts or be tossed about in stony places; it will never become wabbly, for perfect adjustment of center to circumference renders it possible for it to run on the road of pleasure. and satisfaction and to limb: the mountain of power in safety. For the progress of humanity and that the secrets of life may be further disclosed, correspondence is solicited.

Alice B. Stockham, M.D.

1388 Washington Boulevard

PAGE 17, *a.*— *Philosophers' Ideals.*

George S. Morris, interpreting Kant, says :

Kant was not so much the builder up of a system, as one who cleared a space upon which a system could be reared. He was a conqueror rather than a founder. He may be regarded as a Julius Cresar, as Hegel was the Augustus, of modern philosophy. His work was thus critical rather than constructive. It was to, break up the hard and crude notions that men had of a solid, material world, wholly independent of spititual presence, and to substitute for this the thought of an ideal world, which is for and of the spirit alone.

God can be conceived, defined, and demonstrated only as he is first known. And he is and can be known only as Spirit. And he can be and is thus known by man, only because man is spirit. Man, considered *per se,* or according to his true intention and characteristic nature, is spirit; his knowledge is the process of spirit, or is spiritual knowledge, and the perfect object of his knowledge, as such, must and can only be of kindred nature. The instructive purport of all that

257

Kant accomplishes for the science of knowledge consists in the demonstration that that which is called physical knowledge, and which appears at first to consist only in a mechanical relation between knowing subject and known object, implies, as its condition, *spiritual knowing,* or the unifying, illuminating, all- pervading activity of self-consciousness. All of man's knowledge is thus spiritually conditioned. He knows the world only because and so far as he finds himself in the objects which the world presents, i. e., only because and so far as the world is steeped in and exists through the present power and life of spirit, and so exhibits, in object-fashion, the rational and orderly, or synthetic, forms which can alone correspond with the forms of a spirit's subjective knowing activity. Further, his knowledge of the physical universe is a relative, incomplete, imperfect, non-absolute kind of knowledge, in this sense, namely, that man does not find in the universe as such the whole object which his nature fits and requires him to know. He finds there, in other words, the life and power and forms of spirit, but not spirit *per se,* not absolute spirit, complete and without qualification. In his knowledge or consciousness of the world man finds, indeed, his "other"; but this other, while his, i. e., while formed of the web and woof of a spiritual nature which is his also, is yet less, in point of fulness of spiritual being, than himself. On the other hand, in his knowledge, or consciousness of absolute spirit, man finds again his "other," but truer and more complete than before. He finds not only himself, he finds that which is more than himself, by as much as the perfect is more than the imperfect. For man is imperfect spirit; he is spirit in process of self-realization; and in his consciousness of absolute spirit he is conscious of the transcendent, living ideal and type of his true, completed, spiritual self. (It is on the hypothesis of this consciousness that the rationality of such a requirement as the following alone can rest: " Be ye perfect, as your Father in heaven is perfect.") He is conscious of a divine self, which is the precondition and goal, not only of his own, but of all real being. If there exists such consciousness, there exists the consciousness of God.

Moreover, the process by which religious philosophy recognizes and demonstrates God is founded in the science of knowledge as a spiritual process, and not merely, as sensational psychology regards it, a mechanical one. We have seen heretofore that the act of *knowing,* as a spiritual process, is an act whereby those terms of apparent opposition, subject and object, are brought into harmonious union and identity of nature. And the further analysis of the case shows that this reduction of opposites to unity is not an arbitrary act on our part. No, the finite act of *knowing,* on man's part, is simply equivalent to a demonstration that from the beginning and from everlasting the opposition was only relative, and that the appearance of absolute opposition would not have existed for us, but for the original restriction of our point of view within purely mechanical, sensible, and finite limits.

So God, as the absolute object of knowledge, comes to be conceived and known, not as pure subject, nor as pure object, but as the everlasting precondition of the distinction between subject and object, as the present condition of their possible synthesis in our knowledge, and as the one in whom this synthesis is eternally and completely actualized. In short, God, as spirit, is that which only a spirit is capable of being; he is in his nature subject, plus object, *plus the absolute organic unity* and identity of both in an everlasting synthesis of life, which is absolute energy of *mind and of love.* Thus alone is he capable of being the "author" of the "world," which, ideally and strictly defined, consists, first of all, in nothing but the apparent and partial diremption of subject and object, and, then, in a process, the law of which is but the law of the restoration of the separated terms to that unity in which alone the true nature of each is completed.

The statement of Fichte is, briefly: The *I* is the source of two forms of activity. The one stops, say at the limit, finite, the other presses beyond into the infinite. Being so unequal, the two forces can be compared, and thus recognized by the *I*. Though their inequality is thus the means of their recognition, yet, since the *I* is one, its activities should be one. The *I*, therefore, can not rest content with this inequality, but demands that it should be removed. Since the infinite force represents the reality of the *I*, the *I* demands that the other should be made equal to it.

The *I* feels its limit because it presses beyond it; and it presses beyond the limit because it divines something to which it has not yet fully attained. For these results are needed different forms of activity that can be compared between themselves.

The *limit* is the world of objects within which the soul seems to be inclosed. These form a limit because they do not follow the wish and will of the *I*. They are not precisely what it would have them. They are thought of as representing a force outside the *I*. This force and its results are compared with the ideal of the *I*, and found wanting.

The *I* has only two forms of activity. One is the objective activity just described; the other is the absolute activity, by which it affirms itself. The objective activity, as the name implies, is limited. It goes as far as the object and there stops. The other is described as pressing beyond this limit, out into the infinite. The contrast between the two is what makes it possible to recognize each. The *I* would know nothing of its infinite activity if it were not for its finite, objective activity; and the reverse.

The *I* brings these forces into comparison. If they are thus brought into relation, they should be absolutely equal. This equality is demanded by the fact that the *I* is one. It can tolerate, therefore, no difference within itself. All its activity must be one. The act of positing the object is its activity. Therefore, the *I*, comparing this activity with its infinite activity, demands that the two shall be equal and alike.

Hegel knows absolute spirit as self-revealed and makes this transcendent objectification a part of the essence of the Divine Being;

creation is a free act, and the universe is the outcome of the Divine glory, synthesized by a *loving will*.

Beauties in the outer world, as perceived by us, are dependent upon the less or more of the Idea exhibited in them. All men, therefore, should be more beautiful than animals, all animals than plants, and plants than inorganic existence. But as even human life, in its individual or social aspect, fails to reveal the Idea perfectly, being full of contradictions and inharmonies, therefore man, who aspires after the perfect, and will be content with nothing less than the highest, eliminates all imperfection from the Idea, as he finds it reflected in his own mind.

There are passages in Hegel which seem to show his recognition of the truth that the emotion of the Beautiful is the coalescence of the subjective soul with the objective soul of the universe; as when he says of the subject, " It becomes itself concrete in the object because it takes knowledge of the unity of the Idea and its reality."

" In the First Principle, which as a concrete one must have imminent relations, *Love* is the *prius*, as the very definition of *Life*. Life could never have existed on our planet unless the principle of the universe were loving."

Froebel was a student of the German philosophers, accepting many of their ideas, but by far more than any who preceded, put his philosophy in a practical form. His theories of education, which are fast permeating all systems of pedagogics, are founded upon the innate divine nature of man. On the first page of "Education of Man" he says: " In all things there lives and reigns an eternal law. This all-controlling law is necessarily based on an all-pervading, energetic, living, self-conscious, and hence eternal Unity . . . ."

This Unity is God. All things have come from the Divine Unity, from God, and have their origin in the Divine Unity, in God alone. God is the sole source of all things. All things live and have their being in and through the Divine Unity, in and through God. All things are only through the divine effluence that lives in them. The divine effluence that lives in each thing is the essence of each thing.

" It is the destiny and life-work of all things to unfold their essence, hence their divine being, and, therefore, the Divine Unity itself — to reveal God in their external and transient being. It is the special destiny and life-work of man, as an intelligent and rational being, to become fully, vividly and clearly conscious of this essence of the divine effluence in him, and, therefore, of God."

" The precept for life in general and for every one is: *Exhibit only thy spiritual essence, thy life, in the external, and by means of the external in thy actions, and observe the requirements of thy inner being and its nature.*"

" If man consciously and clearly recognizes that his spiritual self proceeds from God, that it is born in God and from God, that it is originally one with God, and that consequently he is in a state of continuous dependence on God, as well as in a state of continuous and uninterrupted community with God; if he finds his salvation, his peace, his joy, his destiny, his life (which is the genuine and only true life as such), and the source of his being in this eternally necessary dependence of his self on God, in the clearness of this knowledge, in living and constant obedience to this knowledge in all he does, in a life, indeed, fully unified with this knowledge and conviction — he truly, and in the full sense of the words, recognizes in God his Father. If he acknowledges himself to be a child of God, and lives in accordance with this, he has the Christian religion, the religion of Jesus."

" In the entire process of the development of the crystal, as it is found in natural objects, there is a highly remarkable agreement with the development of the human mind and of the human heart. Man, too, in his external manifestation — like the crystal — bearing within himself the living unity, shows at first more one-sidedness, individuality, and incompleteness, and only at a later period rises to all-sidedness, harmony and completeness."

" For does not the same one Divine Spirit live and work in man and in nature? Are not man and nature the creatures of the same one God? Must we not, on this account, necessarily find unity and harmony and obedience to the same law in the spirit of nature and in the spirit of man, in external forms and forces, and in internal formation and thoughts?"

" Mathematical forms and figures should not, therefore, be considered as put together in accordance with external, arbitrary causes, but as the necessary outcome of a self-active, inner force, acting in all directions from a central point."

" Man is by no means naturally bad, nor has he originally bad or evil qualities and tendencies; unless, indeed, we consider as naturally evil, bad, and faulty the finite, the material, the transitory, the physical as such, and the logical consequences of the existence of these phenomena, namely, that man must have the possibility of failure in order to be good and virtuous, that he must be able to make himself a slave in order to be truly free. Yet these things are the necessary concomitants of the manifestation of the eternal in the temporal, of unity in diversity, and follow necessarily from man's destiny to become a conscious, reasonable, and free being."

" Whoever, then, considers that which is finite, material, physical, as in itself bad, thereby expresses contempt for creation, nature, as such — nay, he actually blasphemes God."

" Hence the only infallible remedy for counteracting any shortcoming and even wickedness is to find the *originally good source*, the originally good side of the human being that has been repressed, disturbed, or misled into the shortcoming, and then to foster, build up, and properly guide this good side."

Froebel's interpretation of Christ gives the essence and life power of Jesus' teachings and shows that he thought that it is possible for every human being to realize the within Christ. He says: " Jesus himself, in his life and in his teachings, constantly opposed the imitation of external perfection. Only spiritual, striving, living perfection is to be held fast as an ideal; its external manifestation, on the other hand — its form — should not be limited. The highest and most perfect life which we, as Christians, behold in Jesus — the highest known to mankind — is a life which found the primordial and ultimate reason of its existence clearly and distinctly in its *own being*; a life which, in accordance with the eternal law, came from the eternally creating All-life, self-acting and self-poised. This highest eternally perfect life would have each human being again become a similar image of the eternal ideal, so that each again might become a similar ideal for himself and others; it would have each human being develop from *within*, self-active and free, in accordance with the *eternal law*. This is, indeed, the problem and the aim of all education in instruction and training; there can and should be no other."

Plato terms the absolute, the *good*; Aristotle, pure energy; he states that energy of mind is life; St. John calls it Love. All these designations rightly interpreted, express the same truth of absolute fact. They show that philosophy proceeds or is derived from the universal source and is adapted to the many-sided human manifestations.

PAGE 27, b.—Romantic Love.

" Romantic Love is a modern sentiment, less than a thousand years old.

" Conjugal Love is, indeed, often celebrated by Greek, Hebrew, and other ancient writers, but regarding Romantic — or pre-matrimonial — Love (which alone forms the theme of our novelists), they are silent. The Bible takes no account of it, and although Greek literature and mythology seem at first sight to abound in allusions to it, critical analysis shows that the reference never is to Love as we understand it. Greek Love, as will be shown hereafter, was a peculiar mixture of friendship and passion, differing widely from the modern sentiment of Love.

" It is because among the Romans the position of woman was

somewhat more elevated and modern than among the Greeks, that we find in Roman literature a vague foreshadowing of some of the elements of modern Love.

" In the Dark Ages there is a relapse. The germs of Love could not flourish in a period when women were kept in brutal subjection by the men, and their minds refused all nourishment and refinement. The Troubadours of Italy and France proved useful champions of woman, as did the German Minnesingers, by teaching the mediaeval military man to look upon her with sentiments of respect and adoration. Yet their conduct rarely harmonized with their preaching; and the cause of Romantic Love gained little by their poetic effusions, which were almost invariably addressed to married women.

" Not till Dante's 'Vita Nuova' appeared was the gospel of modem Love — the romantic adoration of a maiden by a youth — revealed for the first time in definite language. Genius, however, is always in advance of its age, in emotions as well as in thoughts; and the feelings experienced by Dante were obviously not shared by his contemporaries, who found them too subtle and sublimated for their comprehension. And, in fact, they were too ethereal to quite correspond with reality. The strings of Dante's lyre were strung too high, and touched by his magic hand, gave forth harmonic overtones too celestial for mundane ears to hear.

" It remained for Shakespeare to combine the idealism with the realism of Love in proper proportions. The colors with which he painted the passion and sentiment of modern Love are as fresh and as true to life as on the day when they were first put on his canvas. Like Dante, however, he was emotionally ahead of his time, as an examination of contemporary literature in England and elsewhere shows. But within the last two centuries Love has gradually, if slowly, assumed among all educated people characteristics which formerly it possessed only in the minds of a few isolated men of genius." — "Romantic Love and Personal Beauty," *Finck.*

The devotion of an Indian woman, who casts her body upon the funeral pyre of her husband, has often been related in story and song as an illustration of conjugal attachment. One knowing Hindu thought sees in this act no evidence of her affection. By some unconscious occult means the *suttee* has caused the death of her husband, and she throws herself upon the burning mass to expiate the wrong she has done. She may never have had one affectionate thought toward the man whose body is being incinerated.

Unless one has been in that land he can not realize the great gulf there is between men and women, particularly among the Brahmins. While attending a convention at Adyar, the woman question frequently came up. Brilliant men who had come from all parts of India to attend this meeting had never thought of the native women being present, and, although many of them were quick in perception, keen in analysis, fluent in expression, born orators, and on many subjects had broad opinions and liberal thought, yet when it came to the question of the position of woman, they were unreasonable and obdurate. There was no argument or phase of the subject that made the slightest impression.

How well I remember one evening as we all sat upon the floor in Hindu fashion, asking and answering questions. There were seven of us American women present; some had spent many years in India, others, like myself, were only visitors, and while by some contradiction of reason, they bore for us great respect and reverence, yet for the native women they only expressed disgust and hatred. There was one young man, however, who was an encyclopedia of facts in regard to philosophy and history in India, who, strange to say, was a great champion of women; he had himself chosen his own wife, had had her educated; had plead for equal education of girls and boys; he recalled from his reading the facts of women in past times, who were eminent in philosophy and literature. The position he took in defense of woman called forth the bitterest animosity on the part of the other men present. They, as one man, were saying that woman's education should be for domestic life only; that she should know how to keep her house and to cook her husband's meals, this was the sum of essential knowledge. The question was asked, " Where do you place woman, any way?" With flashing eyes and clinched fist one most eloquent in expounding philosophy answered: " Above the chattels and below the dogs." Picture it, imagine it! In such a condition what place for sentiment, what occasion for romance?

PAGE 36, c.— Atlantean Races.

" What little we know about the social organization of the fourth race during the Atlantean period, shows that in the upper and influential classes at all events women had a very much more independent and commanding position, than with us. Strength is the determining factor in the relationship of the sexes, as in so many other concerns of physical life, and in Atlantis among the upper classes the occult powers, wielded by both sexes alike, dismissed mere muscular superiority into the region of negligible quantities. Women, there seems reason to believe, possessed these powers, and may often have been able to employ them even more effectually than the men. The results were visible in what seems to have been — if not a social preponderance of the women — at least a social and political equality. Women not only exercised sovereign power in states very often, but were appointed rulers of provinces in some cases, a system which modern civilization has not yet been quick-sighted enough to revive, though it has lately had the object-lesson of supremely successful female sovereignty to guide it in that direction.

" Now the great principles of alternation or oscillation are continually operative in nature's working on the large as on the small scale, and probability points to its operation in successive root races with reference to the social and political relationship of the sexes. In the fourth or Atlantean root race, women were, if not predominant absolutely, approximately so. In the fifth root race they have been subordinate. It is a reasonable inference that in the sixth root race their turn will come again. That result, as regards its obvious causation, will not improbably be due to the reviving importance in human affairs during the sixth race of occult forces that have been in obscuration during the fifth. Again the women may be found, for choice, the stronger sex of the two, and then the customs of society and politics will adapt themselves to that state of things.

" In connection with this conjecture it is worth while to observe that the characteristics of each great root race are in some limited degree foreshadowed in the corresponding sub-race of the preceding root race. We are now in the fifth sub-race of our fifth root race, but the sixth sub-race is actually in process of development in the United States of America. The probabilities are that when the sub-race is fully developed — which will not be for many generations to come — the women will somehow have acquired a stronger and more influential position than has been usually their portion in the civilizations of the recent past and present. Indeed, in the freedom of American women even now from some of the conventional restraints that are till operative with women in Europe we may fancy we discern the first glimmerings of the coming dawn."— *A. P. Sinnett.*

" But this fact, of man's non-perception of it, does not make the tragedy less. Far back out of the brows of Greek goddess, and Sibyl, and Norse and German seeress and prophetess, over all this petty civilization look the grand untamed eyes of a primal woman the equal and the mate of man; and in sad plight should we be if we might not already, lighting up the horizon from East and West and South and North, discern the answering looks of those new comers who, as the period of woman's enslavement is passing away, send glances of recognition across the ages to their elder sisters." —
" Love's Coming of Age," *Carpenter.*

PAGE 37, *d.* — *Women Do the Courting.*

The women of some aboriginal tribes do the courting and make all advances for procreation, also through them descend right of royalty and property. This is the case with some native Alaskans and the Nairs in India. The latter reside mostly in Trichur, on the western coast south of Bombay.

The Nairs choose their husbands, and if for any cause they wish a separation, their word only is necessary. They do not require a process of law for a divorce. However, separation is not common among them.

In as far as externals represent life the custom of according to women superior powers is good. Nowhere in India does one find better houses, more profitable industries and finer schools. The men do not seem to sense their inferiority. They are lawyers, teachers and inventors, while labor is about equally divided between the sexes. The property descends through the females. If there are no girls, a sister or sister's girl inherits it.

PAGE 38, *e.* — *Educated Women.*

" Opportunity for the higher mental development was not given to woman until thirty years ago. The State University of Michigan was the first institution of true college grade to open its doors to her. That was in 1870. Cornell followed in 1872, being the first private college to become coeducational. Other colleges in this class have followed slowly. There was an interim of eleven years before the next move was made by the Massachusetts Institute of Technology. The ultra conservatism was due to the fear that coeducation would lower the standard of scholarship on account of the supposed inferior quality of women's minds. Experience in coeducational colleges has proven, however, that the average standing of women is somewhat higher than that of men. Several years ago the University of Wisconsin made an investigation, and found that women ranked in scholarship considerably beyond the men. President Angell, of the University of Michigan, has repeatedly laid stress upon their excellent scholarship. When, in 1893-94 a committee of the faculty of the University of Virginia made inquiries in regard to this point from a number of coeducational colleges, the testimony received was remarkably in favor of the women students. In England the success of women in collegiate studies has been established beyond a doubt by the published class lists of the competitive honor examinations at Oxford and Cambridge.

" The avidity with which women have taken advantage of the opportunities offered is a proof of their appetite for advanced learning. In the coeducational colleges the increase of women students is relatively greater than the increase of men. In 1890 there were studying in coeducational colleges 16,959 men and 7,929 women, 31 9-10 per cent of the students being women. In 1898 women in these colleges formed 36 1-10 per cent. Between 1890 and 1898 men in educational colleges increased 70 per cent, but women increased 105 4-10 per cent. If this rate is maintained, women in the future will outnumber the men in colleges and universities. In the collegiate department of the University of Chicago they are already in the majority. There can be little doubt, judging from the present outlook, that the future women of the leisure class will attend college as generally as the men of that class do now. Already girls form 56 5-10 per cent of the pupils in all secondary schools, and 13 per cent of the girls, against 10 per cent of the boys enrolled, are graduated from the public high schools.

" The fact that women excel as teachers proves that they do more than master their studies: they also retain them, and are peculiarly gifted in the power to apply their knowledge and impart it to others. Judging by the present ratio of increase, the very immediate future will see all the elementary and secondary teaching of the country in their hands. Already women have entered the field of college professorship and held their own. The broader and more general development of the future is bound to break down every barrier of prejudice that now makes impossible competition with men for university professorships.

" The question of the health of women must surely be regarded as settled, in view of the test of the past three decades, when thousands of men and women have worked side by side in coeducational institutions, with no larger percentage of withdrawals on the part of women than of the men. Indeed, the health of the college-bred girl over that of her non-college-bred sister is recognized everywhere as superior."—*Cosmopolitan*, May, 1902, *Lavinia Hart.*

" Women were admitted to Oberlin from the beginning, in 1833, and so far as I know, it was the first college to give women equal advantages with men. The degree of Bachelor of Arts was conferred upon a woman in 1841.

" Prior to that, women had graduated from the ' Ladies Course.' From the beginning they were to take the ' Classical Course.' "

PAGE 45, f. — *Fecundation.*

" The love-songs of bird the amorous croakings of frogs, the antics of brightly-plumaged male birds in view of their expected mates — these and a thousand similar phenomena are all the expression of intense emotion which has only one aim in nature — to bring the sexes together in the act of copulation. And as we are animals by undoubted parentage, all human wooings have the same ultimate end, without which the sex-life of even spiritual man is incomplete. This act of intimate physical union is, indeed, the sexual phenomenon *par excellence.*" — " Science of Sex,"·*Godfrey.*

" The whole conception of sex as a thing covert and to be ashamed of, marketable and unclean, will have to be regenerated. That inestimable freedom and pride which is the basis of all true manhood and womanhood will have to enter into this most intimate relation to preserve it frank and pure — pure from the damnable commercialism which buys and sells all human things, and from religious hypocrisy which covers and conceals; and a healthy delight in and cultivation of the body and all its natural functions, and a determination to keep them pure and beautiful, open and sane and free, will have to become a recognized part of national life."

" While the glory of sex pervades and suffuses all nature; while the flowers are rayed and starred out toward the sun in the very ecstasy of generation; while the nostrils of the animals dilate, and their forms become instinct, under the passion, with a proud and fiery beauty; while even the human lover is transformed, and in the great splendors of the mountains and the sky perceives something to which he had not the key before — yet it is curious that just here, in man, we find the magic wand of nature suddenly broken, and doubt and conflict and division entering in, where a kind of un-conscious harmony had erst prevailed." — " Love's Coming of Age," *Carpenter.*

PAGE 50, *f* 2.— *A Child's Lesson.*

" It was not without much anxiety that I took the first step on a road I intended to explore alone. Chance favored me. I was in Java, and amongst my servants was a dressmaker, married to the groom. This woman had a dear little baby with a velvety brown skin and bright black eyes, the admiration of my little daughter, whom I took with me to see mother and child when the baby was a few days old. While she admired and petted it wonderingly, I said to her: ' This pretty little baby came out of Djahid like the beautiful butterfly came out of the chrysalis, it lay close to Djahid's heart, she made it, and kept it there till it grew. She loved it so much that she made it grow.' Lilly looked at me with her large, intelligent eyes in astonishment. ' Djahid is very happy to have this pretty baby. Djahid's blood made it strong while it lay close to her heart; now Djahid will give it milk, and make it strong, till it will grow as big as my Lilly. It made Djahid ill and made her suffer when it was born, but she soon got well, and she is so glad.' Lilly listened, very much interested, and when she got home she told her father the story, forgetting nothing. But beyond that, she did not refer again to the matter, and soon forgot all about it. The birth of Djahid's second baby gave me the opportunity of repeating the little lesson. This time she asked some questions. I explained many things to the eager little listener, very simply, and told her that the mother kept the child within her, and took great care of it until it was old enough to endure the changes of temperature, etc., and showed her how a mother's joy and love made her forget her pain. The little creature, suddenly remembering that she must have given her mother pain, kissed me tenderly. That was a flower of love and gratitude, which it was my happiness to see develop on the fruitful soil of truth. I analyzed a flower, I pointed out to her the beauty of coloring, the gracefulness of shape, the tender shades, the difference between the parts composing the flowers. Gradually, I told her what these parts were called. I showed her the pollen, which clung like a beautiful golden powder to her little rosy fingers. I showed her through the microscope that this beautiful powder was composed of an infinite number of small grains. I made her examine the pistil more closely, and I showed her, at the end of the tube, the ovary, which I called a ' little house full of very tiny children'. I showed her the pollen glued to the pistil, and I told her that when the pollen of one flower, carried away by the wind, or by the insects, fell on the pistil of another flower, the small grains died, and a tiny drop of moisture passed through the tube and entered into the little house where the very tiny children dwelt; that these tiny children were like small eggs, that in each small egg there was an almost invisible opening, through which a little of the small drop passed; that when this drop of pollen mixed with some other wonderful power in the ovary, that both joined together to give life, and the eggs developed and became grains or fruit. I have shown her flowers which had only a pistil and others which had only stamens. I said to her, smiling, that the pistils were like little mothers, and the stamens like little fathers of the fruit. Thus I sowed in this innocent heart and searching mind the seeds of that delicate science, which degenerates into obscenity if the mother, through false shame, leaves the instruction of her child to its schoolfellows. Let my little girl ask me, if she likes, the much dreaded question; I will only have to remind her of the botany lesson, simply adding: ' The same thing happens to human beings, with this difference, that what is done unconsciously by the plants, is done consciously by us; that in a properly arranged society one only unites one's self to the person one loves.'" —" Love's Coming of Age," *Appendix.*

PAGE 58, *g.*—*Sex Perversions.*

Sex inversion and perversion assume many forms and in turn cause many diseases. Excess of passion followed by abuse, illicit gratification and seminal loss in men are most common. With many good men this is the nightmare of their existence, overwhelming and blotting out all joy and comfort; day and night this is the devil pursuing them, alas! too literal in his persistence and persecutions to be termed a myth. He storms the citadel of good purposes, stings all aspirations and gnaws at the heart's core. He is serpent, insect and beast in one, and with Job one wrestles day and night.

There are many sex perversions, but the inordinate, unsatisfied passion with its constant demand is the most frequent. The cause is largely in the common error that the union of marriage is local only, and hence only local relief is sought. Every thought and all pleasures are centered in the organs themselves and expected to be accomplished in the shortest space of time.

Fear of child-bearing is also a factor for preventing the natural instinct of life. Married women have been led to think conception can not take place except through a relation where husband and wife participate equally. For various reasons she may desire to defer the bearing of children and her fear of conception causes her to repress the instinct that produces life.

Usually in repression there are conditions of contrasts in different parts of the body; some parts evincing great tension, others are weak and relaxed, while moods and emotions are contradictory. No one knows how to take her as she passes so often from gaiety to sullenness, from laughter to tears.

In women repression is often at the foundation of hysteria and mania. It is in the power of every woman to overcome this condition. Life may be manifested normally, through right understanding and proper training.

" A curious part of all the old religions, Pagan or Christian, is asceticism: that occasional instinct of voluntary and determined despite to the body and its senses. Even in the wildest races, rejoicing before all things in the consciousness of Life, we find festivals of fierce endurance and torments willingly undergone with a kind of savage glee; and during the Christian centuries — monks, mystics, and world-spiting puritans— this instinct was sometimes exalted into the very first place of honor. I suppose it will have to be recognized — whatever absurd aberrations the tendency may have been liable to — that it is a basic thing in human nature, and as ineradicable in its way as the other equally necessary instinct towards Pleasure. To put it in another way, perhaps the ordinary Hedonism makes a mistake in failing to recognize the joy of ascendancy, and (if it is not a "bull" to say so) the pleasure which lies in the denial of pleasure. In order to enjoy life one must be a master of life — for to be a slave to its inconsistencies can only mean torment; and in order to enjoy the senses one must be master of them. To dominate the actual world you must, like Archimedes, base your fulcrum somewhere beyond."— " Love's Coming of Age," *Carpenter*.

" Moreover, the ideal of science is self-control, not self-restraint; and that control is directed towards the rational use of faculties, not towards their suppression. There is something here far finer, far loftier, than the mere crushing of fashion, the binding of body and soul in the miserable chains of asceticism."—" Science of Sex," *J. A. Godfrey*.

PAGE 59. h.—Transmutation.

There may be a satisfactory exchange of sex magnetism without the complete union of the organs, and a practice of this exchange is an aid to self-control. One correspondent writes: " Love embraces can be very complete without the contact of sexual organ, but the union of the sex organs does add to the soul union."

" Sexual instinct may not manifest itself as passion, but only as a strong love affection, a reaching out for an ideal companion, one who will love and caress." This is not the same as repression, but is rather a complete and satisfactory soul union.

" A man seeking to transmute must try to lift mind and soul to high things. I have nothing to do with Cowan and Kellogg: their continence is *repression* and fighting all the time. This fighting and self-repression is the severest possible nervous strain a man can endure. Fighting is self-destruction. The subconscious mind must be worked and trained to ideals through mental and spiritual methods, transmutation gradually becomes automatic. Continence is the physical and bodily expression of purity. It is also the measure and index of one's power. If he can contain without injury he can project germs for the physical, mental or spiritual with more power. As measuring the coiled-spring power of the spiritual organism, it is invaluable."—*C. A.*

276

" It is man's conception of an act that purifies or prostitutes it."— *Gordon.*

PAGE 61, *i.*— *Forms of Blessing.*

" In one of the Upanishads of the Vedic sacred books (the Brihadaranyaka Upanishad) there is a fine passage in which instruction is given to the man who desires a noble son as to the prayers which he shall offer to the gods on the occasion of congress with his wife. In primitive, simple and serene language it directs him how, at such times, he should pray to the various forms of deity who preside over the operations of Nature: to Vishnu to prepare the womb of the future mother, to Prajapati to watch over the influx of the semen, and to the other gods to nourish the fœtus, etc. Nothing could be (I am judging from the only translation I have met with, a Latin one) more composed, serene, simple, and religious in feeling, and well might it be if such instructions were preserved and followed, even to-day; yet such is the pass we have come to that actually Max Muller, in his translations of the Sacred Books of the East, appears to have been unable to persuade himself to render these and a few other quite similar passages into English, but gives them in the original Sanskrit!"—Pages 16 and 17 " Love's Coming of Age."

The marriage ceremony of the Syrian Greek church is very long and full of occult meanings. " Their whole ecclesiastical celebration of the marriage sacrament, the many phrases impressively beautiful and serious, demonstrate that in the olden time there was an acknowledged sacred meaning in the *Mystery of Matrimony.*

" Before a marriage, the priest examines the candidates. For them to attempt and presume to be parents without themselves knowing that which it will be their duty to teach their children, is declared to be shameful and sinful. In the ceremony occurs these words: ' Thou who by thy presence didst bless the marriage of Cana of Galilee; to show that lawful union is thy will, or the procreation of offspring therefrom; bless this marriage, that sobriety and such fruit of the womb as may be profitable, may be bestowed on these thy servants.'"— *Anna Ballard.*

PAGE 62, *j.*—*Sexual Science.*

" There should be a regular science of sexual intercourse. At it is now, man is like a brute and sacrifices everything to haste and force. Moderation and delicacy are more important than almost any other relation." —*H.*

" Each person in sexual life, as in eating and drinking, must live to his highest. He must be a law to himself; the right of others and the rights of children must be respected. Those who are tremendously sexed can not be treated like those who are moderately sexed."

" With regard to control of the sexual propensities, the most effectual method is in the cultivation of a higher idealistic habit of thought. Yet I do not place myself in the position of one advocating a life of strict celibacy habit for all. Our conduct must be conformable to our stage of evolutionary development, and what would be practicable for a few, would not be adaptable for the many. I believe that the highest ideal, the one which we should hold in mind as the ultimate goal, is celibacy except for procreation; not that there is any specific evil in the relation, but because the creative energies involved are divine and sacred. I hold intuitively to a so far undemonstrated theory that perfect control of the creative function leads to a higher psychic and spiritual development. Nevertheless, under a just social system, there would be no more evil in participating in this relation, for the pleasure involved, than there is in eating savory foods for the gratification of the sense of taste; for the food we eat calls into activity in the processes of digestion and assimilation energies just as divine and sacred.

" By a just social system I mean one in which there is no such thing as an illegitimate child and maternity is protected by the state. But such a state can exist only in theory now, as at least a majority must evolve to that stage of mental and moral advancement to make it possible. The ideal I picture for woman is as mother and teacher; I would make the latter so broad and comprehensive as to satisfy the ambition of any racial woman. I do not like the tendencies of the times to force women into money-making life, yet I am proud of the woman who sees conditions as they are, and tries to make the best of circumstances."—*W. L. G.*

Among methods of sexual control diet has helped many. Most writers have advocated going without supper as aids to mastery. Since the *no breakfast plan* has become prominent, many have found helps in that. One writes : " Finally, I was led to study diet. I soon saw that diet had much to do with sexual feeling. Then I found that fasting would control passion very effectively. When anything is the matter, or when I feel no especial appetite, I skip one or two meals. It is a never-failing remedy. All the inner works have a chance to get into a good condition. Have you ever made any personal experiments to test Dewey's ideas ? It has been four or :five years since I have eaten breakfast regularly. The physical and spiritual are so blended that it is difficult to tell where one begins and the other leaves off . Fasting seems to allow the physical needed rest and reacts upon the spiritual, giving greater clearness and insight. No one believes more thoroughly in the spiritual than I, but the sound mind in the sound body and the pure spirit in the pure body seem to be the highest ideals. Spirit expresses itself through body, but a clean wholesome body reacts on the spirit also . . . . Then I was circumcised: at the same time I had my boy circumcised . . . . then I found that the mind could direct the thought energy when it pleased. Then came the idea of the breath as a means of helping the mind to act, and the practice of breathing to a particular part of the body. I can now cause the most obstinate erection to subside at once by simply driving the blood away from the sexual organs by thought I have what I call my *germ* book. When I feel passion strong upon me and every nerve is thrilling, then I thank God and quietly turn this great force upon my problems or studies; then the tension subsides and my spiritual germs are thrown out, some of which astonish me. I put them in my book for future use. Why, in one-half hour I often see more than I could work out the rest of my life, so vast are some of my upward leaps of mental energy. So vivid is the imagination, so clear is the mind that I revel in the wide outlook and infinite capacities that I feel. Many could learn to do the same. In short, one might become a power, a genius, instead of merely satisfying animal nature, and retarding the unfoldment of soul power. A friend says it is enough for a man to sit near a woman. The necessary interchange will take place unconsciously. I believe a man can generate in himself the love power so that ultimately an interchange may not be necessary. Otherwise there would be little hope for those who are unmarried."—*H. O.*

" I think the *new-thought teaching* would have caused me to leave my good husband if I had not met you. It seemed to me cohabitation was the lowest act a human could perform. This seemed as bad for my husband as myself. I thought he was killing himself. . . . Anyway, I always felt degraded for days. . . . I do feel so different now. As you told me, I *blessed the power in him*. I had him read *Karezza* aloud and to himself. While he has not been able to control each time, yet it is all so different!

" A lady came to me for her head and nerves. She told me that her husband sometimes had her nearly crazy; that when she consented she got no relief; that she could not sleep afterward and all next day trembled like a leaf. I gave her *Karezza* and she said it was laughable the way he treated it. He would read awhile, then throw it across the room, then after a little read again.

" One night he told her he was going to try the *new theory.* She said it was the first time she had not hated him in the act. I told her I guessed she would need no treatment for her nerves. . . . So you see, we may drop a seed here and there, that will bring forth after the third generation.

" I am convinced that the race will be saved by just this knowledge you present so beautifully.—Yours with love," *Celia.*

PAGE 71, *k.—Drop the Chin Upon the Breast.*

Rev. C. H. Mann, in a little brochure entitled, " What God hath Cleansed," gives some theories that should prompt investigation by physiologists. In the following extracts one has a glimpse of his ideals:

" The elevation of this feature of man's life consists in sanctifying what has heretofore been regarded as common or unclean. The lover, and the just married, who have in the past held a supreme position, will hereafter be regarded as merely the images of devotion and romance, while only the life-long married and the regenerated-married will be regarded as its realizations.

" Still again, the elevation of this love will revolutionize our conceptions of many of the features of the marriage relation. On no subject have there been greater misapprehensions than concerning the central and supreme characteristic of the marriage relation, that which constitutes it absolutely unique among human relationships — the sexual organs, and the relationships which spring from them. So distorted have been our thoughts and lives in reference to them, that they are not regarded as proper subjects of conversation in society, and the gravest ignorance and the most unworthy conceptions concerning them prevail among us. The grade of their life, their beauty, their dignity, and their glory have been lost in the sphere of shame which has been placed about their consideration.

" These functions are not of the same grade, but are discreetly one above another — each in the order named being, by a distinct step, of a higher grade than the one mentioned before. How different and how more wonderful the work of the stomach than that of the fingers; and how different and how more wonderful than both is the work of the brain! There are degrees of life, of which the muscular is the lowest, the assimilative the middle, and the brain the highest. Notice how the muscles deal with substances merely as to their outer form, handling them from the outside, and making them in their outmost shape serve the purposes of the body, while the assimilative system treats substances as to their chemical constitution, extracting from them the elements which may be made to nourish the body, and rejecting what can not be thus used, accomplishing that transcendentally wonderful thing, the creation of bone and flesh and blood and brain from food. The brain, above both of these, is the source of their life, and is the end for which the others exist and perform their uses.

" In this trinal order of function where shall we place the sexual organs? Where but in the highest, the grade of the head? This is shown negatively from the fact that these organs have nothing to do functionally with either the muscular or assimilative systems, though their position associates them with the trunk rather than with the head; but that the sexual organs belong to the order and grade of the head is positively demonstrated by the nature of their secretions, which are of the brain order of structure. *The germs of life in the secretions of the sexual organs are, as it were, little brains of human beings*. This structural peculiarity places them at once upon the highest plane of order, even upon the plane of the head of the body.

" But as we contemplate the body as an interdependent community, we find that the sexual organs are a remarkable exception. They do not sustain such a relation to the other parts of the body. These organs are entirely separate from this community as such. The community can exist without them. These organs do not render any service to their neighbors in the body. On the contrary, they contemplate a new creation; they seek to make a new man, outside the community with which they are connected. They represent not mutuality of service which is charity, but the bestowal of life without hope of a return. They therefore transcend the representation of charity, and are an image of divine love which seeks in creation the formation of recipients of life outside itself. From this aspect of their nature the organs of sex as contrasted with the other organs of the body represent the love of the Lord as contrasted with the love of the neighbor."

It may prove that the function of the brain creates thought while the sexual organs create life. It is as if man had two centers of creative activity; one of thought and one of life —one independent of the other.

May it not be that the resting the chin upon the breast causes a pressure at the upper vertebrae, on the spinal cord, and thus disconnects the physical relation of the two brains? At all events, the *dropping of the chin* is important in securing transmutation.

Dr. Mann proceeds:

" The brain takes cognizance of the world through the eye and ear, which perceive the objects about them as to the qualities with which the brain is concerned, namely, as expressions of life. The brain puts itself forth into the world for the purposes of the creation of life through the organs of sex. These organs, therefore, are related to the head for the expressions of its purposes on earth, as the hands and feet are to the muscular system, and as the mouth is to the trunk. The sexual organs are the brain's instrumentality for putting itself forth into the universe. It is true that the brain makes use of the hands in the execution of its purposes, and of the vocal organs in the utterance of its thoughts; but such use is as servants. The organs of sex are the brain's only organs for the direct ultimation of its very self; the other expressions are the ultimations of the muscular and assimilative systems in obedience to the brain."

Speaking of spiritual children:

" This embodies the doctrine that from the conjugal union, whether in heaven or on earth, such offspring is produced. This spiritual proliferation which is the ground for this act in heaven, where natural procreation is impossible, is ample ground for its practice on earth, when such procreation is impracticable. That nothing less than this spiritual offspring should be always contemplated in this act we most cordially hold; but that it should be entered into only for the procreation of earthly children, is a doctrine which would lead the married partners who observed it to forego one of the richest opportunities placed in their hands by the heavenly Father for the implantation and the unfolding of love and truth in the soul.

" Others, moved by the ideas of the earthly utilitarian, ask why such acts should be indulged in when no earthly service to the neighbor is contemplated. But might it not as well be said that the hands should never be put to so useless a service as hand-shaking; nor the lips to so empty an act as kissing? Marriage union contemplates a purpose in the regenerate life in addition to the procreation of children. To the regenerating man it is an expression of heavenly as well as natural love, and thence is a source of spiritual as well as natural benefit.

"From these things we conclude, both from the ground of their nature, their quality, and their order in the body, and also from the ground of their spiritual correspondence, that the sexual organs are the highest, the purest, and the most holy of all the external parts of the body. While the abuse of what is highest is most degrading and leads to the deepest hell, its right use leads to a correspondingly higher heaven. It is of supreme moment, therefore, for the very purity of our thought and life, that we should regard these things with the profoundest reverence, and should think of them as we think of holy things, and especially that we should be conscious of innocence in the thought of them. And when man and wife come together in the divine nearness which the Lord has made possible, they should feel that they are entering together the holy of holies of life, coming into the most nearly divine relationship it is possible for human beings to enter."

One recent author claims that the curative power of the body, called by physiologists "vis natural," is redeemed sexual life; the same author claims, that all diseases and all suffering in childbirth is caused by the wrong conception of sexual energy. No doubt most sexual derangements of both men and women arise from this fall of man, a fall from a true conception of natural powers.

Some authorities claim that the semen, after it is secreted, may be returned to the blood and converted into nerve, brain and muscle. This is a transmutation on the physical plane only — and makes of man a material machine.

One man, very much interested in Social Purity, has prepared with great care a lecture to be delivered to boys of the adolescent period. In this lecture he lays great stress upon the semen by a physiological process being changed into brain and nerve cells. He claims that boys can not be appealed to on the mental plain, forgetting their knowledge of and interest in myths, in stories of heroism and bravery, in all that awakens strength and mastery and leads to victory.

PAGE 73, *l.* — *Plan and Pleasure.*

" Oh, yes, to your question. The union is always controlled. In Sir J—'s case this is now done without conscious exertion of the will. Such an exaltation of his whole nature ensues as gives what he calls ' automatic ' control. Our whole spirit and soul participate. What is commonest is sensitiveness of conscience. We see how selfish our lives have been, and we are going to work with and through you for the present. Of that I will write more at length when I have read ' The Wedding Night.' To return — as for my own control, it is difficult only when we have not had due anticipation and preparation.

The day previous I refuse myself to all and spend the day with Sir J—. We read some intellectual or spiritually suggestive, mentally stimulating book part of the time. We speak much of our love, of our children. Of the things that are excellent. So the day passes. Then comes the sweet experience. I, too, require to make no conscious effort of the will to avoid the climax which formerly was so quickly and so violently brought on. Now there is only a wonderful exaltation of spirit, soul and body, during which we believe that great character changes are going on because the wish to live for others does not pass, nor the new vision into the qualities of things and ideas, but abides. Along with this is indescribable physical rapture for both of us. It is not the old, violent excitement, followed by lassitude. There is no reaction. We sink into the quiet sleep of healthy children afterward. Imagine the difference. Without strain or undue excitement, the delicious interblending of spirit, soul and body lasts nearly one hour. Then we are quiescent, and open to each other all that we are seeing. Our pulses subside, and quietly, gently, without exhaustion or reaction we both are profoundly satisfied — satisfied, not satiated. How fresh and vigorous we are in the morning! What a contrast from the bad former days." — Gratefully, *Lady J.*

" When the sex passion becomes divorced from the expression of true love, and is used as end in itself — the production of pleasure — then the higher capacity of love fades away. Impurity strikes at the very root of all love, and blights all the love life of the individual." — *Dr. Luther Gulick.*

PAGE 74, *m.— Law of Agreement.*

A gentleman residing in Chicago has practiced the controlled union sixteen years. He is a materialist, believing that matter is self-existent; besides he and his wife have often been on the point of separation, so it is not love's fulfilment. Upon this one point, the *Karezza* practice, they are agreed. They make plans and fulfil them. It is according to the law of agreement. Through this practice the wife was cured of long-standing uterine disease.

PAGE 86, *n.*— *Home Department in the Government.*

" This is my thought. We do not so much need *organization* as the *systemization* of government. In this systemizing the interests, educational, scientific, industrial and ethical, of every child and every home must be protected and developed. A bureau of correspondence and a special department in the government, with a woman holding such a portfolio in the cabinet, will be in the line of such a system."— *Elizabeth M. Boynton Harbert.*

PAGE 88, *o.* — *Sexual Perverts.*

" In the case of hermaphroditic organisms, where the sex organs are imperfectly developed, it will be found that psychic force, the mother's mentality, was exerted in a very marked degree. It began early enough in the gestative period and was strong enough to arrest the development of one set of generative organs, forcing a different set into prominence because the mother's mind was specially directed to the kind of organ which she desired in her child. Therefore each deformity is more or less marked.

" In a mild form of sex perversion it is noticeable that the male looks and acts like a female, or a woman is mannish in appearance, in action, or likes and dislikes. In the first case, the mental influence of the mother was directed more to a desire for a child who would be a girl, and in the latter case, a boy; but Nature had determined otherwise, and the mother interfered with the process. As her mind was not directed to the organs of sex, they were not affected, the brain cells alone being influenced by such interference.

" The 'tomboy' is generally an interesting creature while still a child; but she rarely develops into a thoroughly feminine type. She is prone to be of the hard and angular sort. But she is not so unbearable as the effeminate man.

" A prospective mother, who dwells on the question as to her child being a boy or a girl, is liable to create a brain structure in it which, if a girl is wanted and a boy is the outcome, will likely be of an effeminate character. He may be opposed to normal relations with females and prefer male associations because of his general femininity. He will be, if I may be allowed to use a slang phrase, a *sissy boy*, and may develop into a nonentity or a pervert." — *Bayer, U. S.*

PAGE 91, *p.*— *Mind Cure in Japan.*

It is a curious fact that long before the advent of Christian Science or Mind Cure in America, there arose a sect in Japan that taught and practiced the art of healing. This shows that there is a universal law and that its application is equally universal. This sect is called the Kurozumi Sect of Shinto.

" Kurozumi Sakyo was born in 1780 in the province of Bizen. From his early years he was remarkable for piety and filial affection. While still a child he firmly resolved that, for the sake of the joy it would give his parents, he would strive to gain the praise and esteem of men. When about twenty years old, there arose in his mind this thought: ' He who steadfastly refrains from acts which in his heart he knows to be evil will become a *kami*— deified spirit.' From that time he exercised the greatest circumspection concerning his conduct, carefully avoiding all known wrong. In the autumn of 1812 he lost both of his parents, there being an interval of only seven days between their deaths. This affliction caused so much grief that he himself became ill. His disease developed into consumption, and in the spring of 1814 it seemed to all that he had not much longer to live. It was while awaiting the death which he supposed to be inevitable that he made this vow: ' When I die and become a *kami*, I will devote myself to the work of healing the diseases of mankind.' As a preparation for his departure, he worshiped first the sun, then the celestial and terrestrial *kami*, also his ancestors, and especially his parents, to whom he returned thanks for the many favors which during their lives they had heaped upon him. Having done this, he calmly awaited the approach of death. Now, however, a new thought entered his mind: ' By grieving over the loss of my parents I have inflicted injury upon my own soul, and have become filled with the negative, gloomy spirit *(in-ki).* This is the cause of my poor health. If, now, my soul can only imbibe the positive, cheerful spirit *(yo-ki)* the disease will of itself disappear. True filial piety should lead me to incessant care for the nourishing of my own soul.' From that time he commenced the practice of considering everything he saw or heard as a blessing bestowed by Heaven, and as such to be received with gratitude. When in this way he applied himself earnestly to the nourishment of his soul, he began to recover his health. Here was the great crisis in the history of Kurozumi.

" One day, soon after the events already narrated Kurozumi crawled out from his bed, and, though as yet he had hardly the necessary strength, he bathed himself and then commenced to worship the sun. At once, just as frost vanishes before the morning sun, so did his illness depart, leaving him in perfect health. At the time of the next winter solstice, while again engaged in worshiping the rising sun, the positive spirit so penetrated his breast that he was filled with thoughts of joy and gratitude. Unconscious of what he did, he continued to drink in the sunlight, until his heart suddenly became pure, and he for the first time ' laid hold on that life which vivifies the universe.' He was at that time thirty-five years old.

" Not long after, a maid-servant suffering from an attack of colic was driven almost crazy by the pain. Kurozumi, moved with pity, breathed out upon her the positive spirit with which he himself was filled, and the girl was immediately healed. From that time he commenced the practice of breathing upon those who requested his aid, while he also taught them to care for the welfare of the soul as well as for that of the body. Those suffering from chronic diseases experienced instant relief, and were thus led to investigate the teaching of their benefactor.

" The sect, though of such modern origin, has gained a large number of adherents. Its success is largely attributable to the healing of disease, which its believers profess to accomplish by means of various rites. There can be no doubt that, as in more or less similar methods of treatment found in western lands, there have been remarkable cures.

" In the practice of this religion one must first understand what is meant by the life and death of the soul. Whenever a person thinks of his blessings and joys, his soul becomes filled with the positive, cheerful spirit. Hence it lives, and as a consequence his diseases are healed, and whatsoever he undertakes prospers. That is what is meant by the saying, ' Good luck comes in at Laughing-gate.' On the other hand, when a person is always complaining, ' This is very disagreeable,' ' That is a sad state of affairs,' then the negative, gloomy spirit prevails. Thus disease is produced and goes on increasing until the man dies, while before his death everything he attempts is attended with difficulty and failure.

" The difference between a *kami* and a man is simply one of the heart. When a man frees himself from desire, he has power over heaven and earth, he can work miracles, he becomes one with the celestial and terrestrial *kami*. On the other hand, a man who is filled with carnal desires that lead him to like some things and to dislike others, will get angry, will grieve over events, and will lose his hold upon truth. Hence he has no power to work wonders; he is a mere man.

" Kurozumi taught that men should always recognize the blessings of Heaven, and should not yield to desire; but, being filled with the positive spirit, should perform aright their appointed tasks.

" Healing of disease is the gate by which men enter the Way. There are two kinds of disease; that of the soul, and that of the body. The former consists in a wicked heart. It is cured by instruction, sermons, etc. The common methods of healing infirmities are prayers, incantations, or the aid of physicians. Kurozumi taught that if a man recognized the divine mercy, and with his whole heart meditated on the blessings he received, he would be healed of his diseases. This would furnish new cause for thanksgiving, so that, with a heart full of gratitude, courage, and life, he would faithfully serve his feudal lord and his parents, would perform his appointed tasks, and would have his wicked heart replaced by one of righteousness. In this manner the healing of bodily infirmities would be the gate by which a man enters the Way. If, however, healing of the body is not accompanied with reformation of the heart, it would be just as though one depended on mere forms and prayers for a cure.

"Again he said, ' If the soul lives the body lives also. Death commences with the soul, and with it the body perishes. When a man is grateful for his blessings, when his heart is alive and he is filled with the positive spirit, then even the most dangerous diseases are healed. If death does not enter the soul, then man is immortal with the universe.

" Method of imbibing the positive spirit. Expel all the breath from the lungs. Do this three times. Then, banishing all other thoughts, let the whole heart be filled with gratitude for the blessings bestowed by Heaven. Turn the face toward the morning sun and slowly inhale the positive spirit. Hold in the breath for a short time, then turn to one side and let it slowly pass out from the lungs. When eight or nine tenths have escaped, inhale as before. The breath inhaled should be as much as possible; that exhaled should be a little less. — *Andover Review, June, 1889, Otis Cary.*

The fetal circulation is independent of the mother — that is, the placenta does not grow to the uterus, the fibres and blood-vessels interchanging and interlacing. The placenta lies against the uterus, a very thin membrane between the two — the nutrient blood passing to and from by a process of absorption. Any effect the child receives from the mother must be through a mental process, not unlike one mind affecting the other in ordinary life. The child is wonderfully protected in fetal life and seems no more liable to take on diseases in the prenatal condition than to have them engraven into his being when running on the street. A mother need have no more fear of marking the fetus through fright, through mental or physical disturbances, than she has of affecting the child in the cradle by similar causes. She has only to love and bless the infant in its independent life.

PAGE 109, *r.— Robust Woman.*

" Oh, for a school of wise motherhood — one which shall teach girls before marriage the importance of cultivating self-control, peace, and harmony of thought during the pre-natal months, and one which shall impress every woman in the land with the necessity of finding resources within herself for enjoyment, instead of aimlessly seeking to be amused.

" The first thing on rising in the morning, fill the lungs with full, deep inhalations of fresh air, and say to yourself: ' I am breathing in happiness and usefulness.' When you exhale slowly, say: ' There go my discontent and restlessness into thin air.'

" Take three of these breaths at least. Then as you prepare for the duties of the day, say: 'I am happy, busy, useful. I am a reflection of God's mind — I love, rejoice, and am happy.'

" Say it to yourself a dozen times in the day. Look at your husband

and children, and say: I love them — they are blessings; they are gifts from God, and I am happy and grateful.' ●

" Go to sleep saying these things. After a few days, or a week, you will find your mind awakening from its torpor, and its restless discontent leaving you. The moods will return, but you must keep at the assertions, and you will conquer them. Try and think what you can do each day to help some one less fortunate than yourself.

"Keep your eye out for other people's troubles, and your own will vanish."—*Ella Wheeler Wilcox.*

Page 111, *s.— Motherhood Protected.*

" The freedom of woman must ultimately rest on the communism of society — which alone can give her support during the period of motherhood, without forcing her into dependence on the arbitrary will of one man. While the present effort of women toward earning their own economic independence is a healthy sign and a necessary feature of the times, it is evident that it alone will not entirely solve the problem, since it is just during the difficult years of motherhood, when support is most needed, that the woman is least capable of earning it for herself.

"And since motherhood is, after all, woman's great and incomparable work, people will come to see that a sane maternity is one of the very first things to be considered — and that really, though not the only consideration, it is a work which if properly fulfilled does involve the broadest and largest culture. Perhaps this might seem to some only too obvious; yet, when for a moment we glance around at the current ideals, when we see what Whitman calls ' the incredible holds and webs of silliness, millinery and every kind of dyspeptic depletion' in which women themselves live, when we see the absolute want of training for motherhood and the increasing physical incapacity for it, and even the feminine censure of those who pass through the ordeal too easily, we begin to realize how little the present notion of what woman should be is associated with the healthy fulfilment of her most perfect work. A woman capable at all points to bear children, to guard them, to teach them, to turn them out strong and healthy citizens of the great world, stands at the farthest remove from the finnikin doll or the meek drudge whom man, by a kind of false sexual selection, has through many centuries evolved as his ideal." " Love's Coming of Age," *Carpenter.*

" The reproduction of the race is a social function, and we are compelled to conclude that it is the duty of the community, as a community, to provide for the child-bearer when in the exercise of her social function she is unable to provide for herself. The woman engaged in producing a new member, who may be a source of incalculable profit or danger to the whole community, can not fail to be a source of the liveliest solicitude to every one in the community, and it was a sane and beautiful instinct that found expression of old in the permission accorded to the pregnant woman to enter gardens and orchards, and freely help herself."—Pamphlet on "Evolution in Sex" (p. 15), *Havelock Ellis.*

PAGE 115, *t.*— *Economy in Cooking.*

In preparing rice, the cook will not only boil enough for the day she wishes to use it, but will have some to set away for rice cakes, for croquettes, for omelets. In cooking lentils, she will save the water to use as stock for soup, and also have enough for a dish of baked lentils, lentil hash, lentil gravy. Making cornmeal mush, she will remember that nearly every person is fond of fried mush and that also what is left is good to use in puddings or griddle cakes. In cooking lima beans she knows that the left-overs are good for succotash or make an excellent salad. All the legumes are richer, more nourishing, more palatable and more wholesome for slow cooking; the temperature should be kept just at or below the boiling point. This can be accomplished by setting the vessel, in which they are cooking, back on an ordinary range. Any person with a little tact can originate an appliance for slow cooking that I am pleased to call a *kozy kooker.* This consists of a lamp with a double or round burner set under a standard made of zinc or sheet-iron. On top of this put a piece of asbestos; upon this set the bean pot and cover it first with an ordinary tin pail and outside of this a wooden pail. This may be an ordinary bam or tobacco bucket, or it may simply be a wooden jacket that comes around five-gallon gasoline cans. These cookers may not be had on the market, but any person with a little ingenuity can rig one out of very inexpensive materials, and it will be found invaluable; the food prepared in them is more palatable and wholesome and it will prove a great economy in fuel.

A modification of this makes a good camping outfit; also in case you have not hot water in the house, by having a jar set over the lamp and within the jacket, one can always have hot water on hand. This is one of the appliances used in the Pratt Institute, as an outgrowth of the invention of Edward Atkinson, whose Aladdin oven is so far-famed. Atkinson constantly reiterates that you must " box up the heat." Every gas, coal or wood range wastes fuel. Future economics will give many *kozy kookers.*

At Vrilia Heights, Geneva Lake, Wisconsin, we always have a kozy kooker founded on the above principle. A wooden cheese box is covered with asbestos and this put over a sheet-iron frame, upon which the cooking utensil stands. An automatic lamp, on the principle of a student lamp, supplies the heat. This holds a quart of kerosene oil, which lasts twenty-four hours. This kozy kooker does all our slow cooking, soups, lentils, beans, rice and Indian puddings, and Boston brown bread. Besides, when not required for cooking, it keeps a constant supply of hot water.

PAGE 116, *t* 2.— *Home the Arena for Woman.*

She may vote, speak, legislate, may be a doctor, a preacher, an educator; she may be a poet, an actor, a sculptor or orator, yet her instincts and affection demand and procure for her a domicile called home. Business or pleasure may make her a world-rover — a globe-trotter — but her heart always longs for and looks forward to the rest of home, to the joys and peace of its retirement. Though she may never have married she provides this for herself, making it an ideal representation of her taste and requirements.

Elizabeth Blackwell, the first woman in the United States to take a medical degree, after long years of a busy professional life retired to a beautiful, romantic home, Rock View, at Hastings, England. One ascends many stone steps, and high up on the cliffs overlooking the sea, finds this remarkable woman, eagle-like, resting in her cozy nest, unmoved by the storm of ocean or tumult of human life. Here she has lived many years, satisfying the natural longing for a home.

Prof. James M. Hoppin, in writing of Rosa Bonheur in " Eminent Women," says: " Rosa Bonheur, with all her untamed instincts, still showed a love for the home-life that was intense. She lived for some years in the sixth story in a house in Paris (the Rue Rumford). This house consisted of four very small rooms opening out on a little terrace. This she made into a little garden among the chimneys and tried to satisfy her longing for animals of her own by installing here a pretty long-wooled sheep, which also served for a model for the young artist.

" After the sale of some of her pictures she bought a real home, comforted her craving for family life by adding to her ' stock' — horses, goats, cattle, donkeys and dogs, besides rare fowls and birds. Though she delights in her art she never loses the keener delights of home-making and living.

" The little cottage standing back from the street is embowered in foliage. It was modestly furnished, except her atelier. This was hung with green velvet and filled with exquisite objects of art, pictures, bronzes and pieces of armor. It was opened for receptions on Fridays.

" She worked early and late; entertaining visitors with her brush in her hand, and still wielding the scepter while listening to those who read to her or rested her with music."

PAGE 117, *u.*— *Cooperation.*

" In the human body every part, organ and member exists for the whole. The less a particular organ or member asserts its individuality, the more perfect is the general health, and hence the more perfect is the state of each individual member and organ. That is to say, in a state of health the person does not know he has a stomach, or liver, or brain, or any other organ or member. The moment any one of these becomes known or is felt, there is pain, derangement, or disease of some kind. Strange to say, the less any organ or member asserts its individuality, so that its possessor is conscious of it, the more perfect an organ or member it is. The more it sacrifices its individuality, the more real individuality it possesses. The less a person's stomach is felt, the more perfectly it does the work of a stomach — the more perfect and individual a stomach it is. The less the brain or head is felt, so that it never aches, the more perfect a head it is. Who will say that a jumping tooth is more perfect in its individuality than as though it were never known or thought of? Is a gouty foot more perfect as a foot — more really itself — than a foot which goes its daily rounds, walking perhaps many miles, and never comes into the thought at all? Certainly not. Thus every organ of the body, in a state of health, sinks as it were into non-entity, becomes in a sense as though it did not exist, and in so doing it becomes a more perfect organ and member — more really itself, to do its own work and not another's. Thus it loses its life but saves it. In surrendering its individuality to the general economy, it possesses a truer and more marked individuality.

" Let the hand say, ' I will not serve the body longer, I will assert my individuality and live for myself; I will remain at rest in a sling, and receive of the general vitality, but render no adequate return.'

After a year of such rest is it more perfectly a hand? Certainly not. It has not preserved but lost its individuality. It has become a weak thing — a mere apology for a hand. Only in forgetfulness of its own needs by working for the general good, can it preserve its individuality as a hand. And so, no matter what use a man's talents determine he shall serve — whether professional, mercantile or mechanical — only by performing his use to the general good, and sinking himself in the weal or woe of the body politic, can he preserve his own proper individuality. Organic unity, like that of the human form, is the only possible condition of freedom."—*New Church Messenger.*

Great comradeship is developed by union of forces in the activities of the home. When several take hold of a big job the labor is lightened. Washing, ironing, housecleaning, pickling and preserving all cease to be drudgery when members of the family join together, and, with song and story, make recreation out of what has been called labor. Great baskets of peas, pans of fruit disappear under the magic of many nimble fingers. So, also, the everyday doings, like dishwashing, lose their recurrent monotony in cooperation. I knew several families where the husband and young men assist in the after-dinner work. The day at office or shop may have been filled with tangles and problems, but the joy they put in this home-helpfulness is far mere successful as a recreation than dozing or smoking alone in the parlor while mother does it all. This assistance is rendered as a privilege rather than as a duty. It is a division of interests and labor. Even a visitor ceases to be a stranger when he can join in the service that helps to build a home of love.

PAGE 117, *u 2.— A Woman Manages Her Household.*

A long time ago I knew a beautiful woman who was very unhappy in her home life. She had a gifted husband, beautiful children and a luxurious home. As an only daughter she had been reared to think and act independently. In her education she had had advantages far beyond girls of that day; among them was the friendship of a sweet-spirited student of Emerson, who led her into a life comporting with that of the great philosopher. What was her unhappiness? Why, her gifted husband assumed dictatorship of the home. She could not place a piece of furniture, order a meal, invite guests, purchase garments for the children, except by his order. The style of her dress, the mode of hair-dressing was from day to day by his command. The thralldom was so great that it became unbearable and threatened the destruction of the home. Counseling an elderly friend, she was advised to quietly, but firmly, declare a rebellion — that is, to make a stand to rule her own household. The house-cleaning season was the opportunity for the trial. As each room was renovated she ordered the adjusting and settling. She avoided an issue — making few changes and saying nothing.

In time the storm came, but she smiled pleasantly and told him quietly and firmly that hereafter she must have charge of the home, directing servants, caring for children, etc. She recalled to his mind that she never dreamed of interrupting or even offering a suggestion in his business, and that the home-making was her business, which she should attend to at the best of her ability. The remedy in her skilful hands worked like a charm. They found plenty of mutual interests and also that the domestic machinery creaked and groaned far less under one superintendent.

PAGE 127, *v.— Games in Education.*

Who has not seen a room full of comparative strangers, silent and bashful, set at their ease by the introduction of a live social game? Wall-flowers cease to be in fashion, large but awkward hands and misfitting clothes are forgotten.

What is the charm of a picnic? Why does the early introduction of

" Drop the Handkerchief " and " Copenhagen " break down all caste lines ? Everybody soon knows everybody. Every soul shines to meet the shine of other souls.

Games are not merely pastime. They are educative. According to the character and the leadership they may be made as valuable to the child's development as any bookcraft or constructive work. " The spontaneous play of the child discloses the future inner life of the man."

Games of action, pantomimes, dramas and stories bring the world to the child. The common games, such as "Drop the Handkerchief," "Three Deep," Hash, Hash," that every one knows, give an outlet for restlessness, develop alertness, a sense of justice, each for all and all for each, and most of all aid in the child losing what is called self-consciousness. Really he learns to know his true self.

Any strong dramatic incident in history gives a foundation for a game. These games give interest to the constructive work of brush and tools.

Only recently I saw a class, aged ten to twelve years, at a reception, play they were Indians. They had constructed a tepee and their teacher was the chief. Dressed in improvised Indian costumes they marched in file, laid in ambush and went off hunting. Then they had a council of war. The whites were encroaching. They sat on the floor around the wigwam. They were told by their chief to be brave, to be patient, they had a right to their lands; there were good braves among the pale faces; wait, wait and not kill. At this time a young Miss, as William Penn, came in and in eloquence expressed good will and peace. The treaty was finally established by the Indians giving as much land as could be surrounded by a buckskin cut in fine cords. This was simulated by taking a string from a ball of cord and measuring the entire room. All of which the Indians yielded to William Penn.

By virtue of the laws that must be observed in games one comes to know that he is a unit of the whole; that while he is one of the party he is no greater than any one else.

Guessing games, like "The Lawyer," charades, "Dumb Crambo," etc., quicken the perceptions. The latter is of special interest to both old and young. It is drama, pantomime and conundrum combined. It gives every one a chance and affords amusement and instruction

PAGE 137, *w.—Healing, How Accomplished.*

" Spirit is the substance or underlying reality of matter, and thought is the creative power of the mind. All we can know of ourselves or our bodily conditions is in our mind, is the product of thought. A pain must be in thought before it is felt, and if not in thought has it an existence? If we could exterminate it from thought, would it not be annihilated? Is it not cured when banished from thought? A positive thought of health or wholeness transcends one of pain and suffering. The sane mind becomes master of the situation and compels Satan, in the shape of erroneous thinking and false beliefs, to leave. Here is the grand remedy — the long-sought panacea. It is a fundamental principle phrenopathic method of cure. Grasp the idea in its fulness and you have an infallible and universal specific." — *F. W. Evans.*

"Remember your higher self, your spiritual self is whole and always well. In making the positive declaration — I have light, health and strength, you make it of the spirit, and by your recognition you give power and mastery to the spirit, and it manifests on and through the body in health and strength. You free the body from its limitations of wrong thinking and make it an expression of your higher self."

" Man must be taught to forget the body and become spirit. The body is, in itself, lifeless, motionless, and sensationless. It has neither thought, intelligence, nor feeling. All these are in the soul. To perceive this is a long step toward recovery. The physical organism is the most unreal part of human nature. This must become to us an ineffaceable conviction, and be so inwrought into our very being as to change our mode of thinking, feeling, speaking, and acting. In addressing the invalid, the body should be ignored, and we should speak as a soul, and from the soul, to the soul of the patient or sufferer. We then speak from the Divine realm of causation, and have a power over disease that can not be gained by occupying any other standing ground. The man who is bound with the iron fetters of sense, and is in the underground dungeon of materialism, can afford but small aid to another in the same condition with himself. To possess the divinely ordained power of mind over matter, and of soul over body, he must be himself unshackled and born into the true liberty of spirit. This is a Divine healing force — the power of God and the wisdom of God unto salvation. It constitutes in us a point of attachment between the soul and the creative Thought, and repairs the broken link which has disjointed us from God. The utterances of such a person will be the echo of God's ideas, and have the authority of Divine oracles. His mind vibrates in harmony with the Infinite Mind, and his thought becomes one with the power that created and upholds the world, and is perpetually exhibited in Nature's laws.

" The immortal soul-principle gives the body all its life and power. It is the vital, formative, organizing and governing principle in the organic material. Hence, the fact so often brought to our notice in the Gospel narratives, that the conversion of the soul and the cure of disease went together in the practice of Christ, so that the new spiritual state might have a solid basis of physical health on which to permanently rest. The changed soul makes for itself a new bodily condition, or outward expression, in harmony with its altered spiritual status."—F. W. Evans.

" Our bodily condition is the result of our way of thinking. If we would change it for the better — as from weakness to strength, from disease to health, from pain to ease — let us *imagine* or *fancy,* or *think* and *believe,* that the desired change is being effected, and it will do more than all other remedial agencies to bring about the wished-for result."

Health is as contagious as disease.

" We all know remarkable people who have the wonderful faculty of turning common water of life into the most delicious wine. Some people turn everything they touch into vinegar, others into honey. There is something in the mechanism of some minds which seems to transmute the most somber hues into the most gorgeous tints.

" Their very presence is a tonic, which invigorates the system, and helps one to bear his burdens. Their very coming into the home seems like the coming of the sun after a long, dark arctic night. They seem to bring the whole system into harmony. Their smile acts upon one like magic, and dispels all the fog of gloom and despair. They seem to raise manhood and womanhood to a higher power. They unlock the tongue, and one speaks with a gift of prophecy. They are health-promoters. They are death to dyspepsia, and increase the appetite."

" The man who daily goes about his business in a conscious realization of the all-power and all-presence of God — the Divine Mind —and that he is under the care and control of that Mind, has a sense of confidence and trust in his own destiny that he can not and does not otherwise possess."—*Septimus J. Hanna.*

God is all-powerful and ever-present. Therefore there is no other power or presence, and the spirituality of the universe including man, is the only fact of creation.

" Christian Science silences human will, quiets material thought with Truth and Love, and illustrates the unlabored motion of divine energy in healing the sick."—" Science and Health," *Eddy.*

" As we grow into a broader knowledge of the great and inexhaustible source, so shall we become established in the state of divine wholeness."—*Lucie G. Beckham.*

" We should never fear God. God is love, why should we be afraid of love?

" My substance is the Infinite mind. From that source I draw all my supply, because I am a perfect spiritual being; there is no reality in disease, pain or suffering. The soul can put off and put on.

" Whatever it puts on, eventually appears in the body. Whatever it puts off eventually disappears from the body.

" Graft a blue plum branch on a red plum tree, the fruit will be blue. The fruit is according to the graft not the original tree.

" We *choose* what fruit we shall bear."— *Ursula N. Gestefeld.*

" The great central fact in human life, is the coming into a *vital conscious realization of our oneness until Infinite Life, and the opening of ourselves fully to its divine inflow'.*"—" In Tune with the Infinite," *R. IV. Trine.*

" Let it not be forgotten that thinking of high and noble things is a *building process.* Not only are mansions in Heaven, but right here in our present life.

" We must realize that we are children of God made in His image and likeness, and that we have His dominion. His power is ours, we need not be weak. His life is ours, we need not be sick. His riches are ours, we need not be poor."—" Bible Sunshine," *Theodore F. Seward.*

" With the new conception of God I am none the less religious, none the less devotional, for now God the Supreme Love, God the Supreme Intelligence, is to me the transcendental but ever revealing mystery, and this God I adore . . . This is the God who heals our sickness."— *Kate Atkinson Boehne.*

" There is health, strength and joy unlimited waiting to manifest through you, waiting until you are transformed by the renewing power of mind. No disease, no pain, no sorrow can stand before the sweet clean thinking of a mind in tune with infinite wisdom and love."—*C. L. Brewer.*

"All methods which induce a supernormal state disclose the

perfect *rapport,* and the power of intense attention and of unerring and rapid response of the profounder Self. . . . Beneath this manifestation there is a deeper and more general activity of the whole being, that continually tends to become personal, to modify, amplify and exalt the personal status and powers."— *Joseph Stewart.*

" It is the invisible, quickening power that awakens our consciousness of the Truth of Being, and spiritual discernment thus becomes a joyous reality."— *A. P. Barton.*

"It is centrality, unity, consistency. It is harmony, love, power, the silence of the primitive forces regained, the genuine and complete dedication of self to the purposes of God."—"Living by the Spirit," *Dresser.*

" Healing ministration is not merely religious attestation; it is also scientific, because service is a fundamental law " — *Henry Wood.*

" The mind is molder and keeper of the body."

„ This rational conception of *Allness,* individuality, permanence, eternity, and freedom from all laws, is the divine in man; when this wonderful reason comes to life and dominates the whole self-conscious mind, then is man's kingdom and power and glory restored to him; he no langer eats grass like an ox, or feeds upon the husks of sense-life, but resumes the throne of might and reason."— *George Burnell.*

„Surely, as I have thought so shaII it come to pass." — Isa. xlv, 24.

" He sent his word, and healed them, and delivered them from their destruction."— Ps. cvii, 20.

" For they are life unto those that find them, and health to all their flesh."— Prov. iv, 22.

" Beat your plowshares into swords, and your pruning hooks into spears: let the weak say, I am strong."— Joel iii, 10.

" Who forgiveth all thine iniquities; who healeth all thy diseases; who redeemeth thy life from destruction : who crowneth thee with loving kindness and tender mercies: who satisfieth thy mouth with good things: so that thy youth is renewed like the eagle's."— Ps. ciii, 3, 4, 5.

" For the law of the spirit of life in Christ Jesus hath made me free from the law of sin and death. But if the spirit of him that raised up Jesus from the dead dwell in you, he that raised up Christ from the dead shall also quicken your mortal bodies by his spirit that dwelleth in you. Because the creature itself also shall be delivered from the bondage of corruption into the glorious liberty of the children of God."— Romans viii, 2, 11, 21.

" And the prayer of faith shall save the sick, and the Lord shall raise him up."—James v, 15.

PAGE 140, x.— *Aids to Attaining Silence.*

There are many forms and processes of concentration, some of which prove valuable to one learning mental control; these include the use of crystals, beads, posturing and breathing. The use of any of these only lead to the process of activity and repose. The method is as follows:

Place a globe of water on the stand in easy range of vision or a crystal only in the hand; with close attention gaze into the globe or crystal, at the same time still the thought and relax the body. Let the crystal represent nothing to your mind and become nothing; filter out every notion you have formed of life — the mind must become a blank. Let the breathing be slow, deep inspirations, with almost unconscious expirations; mentally let go of all normal thought, then the essential self may operate freely. The globe represents the nothing and the all, but confusion arises if you see both in the crystal at one and the same time; you see nothing at first and will to let go;

you become the blank that the globe symbolizes, and then you will that the higher life, the higher love, the Christ life, shall possess and appropriate all your faculties and function; then it becomes the *all*.

Many are helped by contemplating vastness — the ocean in its moods, high mountains, the expanse of prairie, the sky, the ever-present, unending sky, all aid in opening the consciousness to spiritual realities. One may in time abandon all of these, and come to know that at any time and in any place thought activity can be silenced. The mind may be abstracted from the body; soul, as it were, goes out that spirit may enter. It is the ebb of thought, feeling and self- consciousness, followed by the flow of activity from the source of life.

One needs to learn to empty the mind, to cease all thought, in order to learn control of the mind. Abstract the mind from the body, through this very abstraction one gets control of intellectual processes and physical demands. There are people who have this power of abstraction to such an extent that they can sit under a surgical operation without any feeling of pain. Not long since a gentleman of this city had a growth removed from the side of his face and with looking-glass in hand followed the surgeons knife with the interest of any other on-looker and with as little sensation. What had he done? He had withdrawn his mind from his body.

By understanding this law of letting go, even very sensitive people may have teeth extracted without pain; besides, burns and bruises become as nothing.

" A leading dentist was engaged with some gentlemen in discussing the virtue of remedies used to avoid the pain caused, when a lady who wanted one of her molars pulled entered the office. The dentist, in order to prove what he had been saying, told her he had some of the new remedy and would use it so that she would not feel any pain. She was well pleased, and, after being seated in the chair, he rubbed a little water on her gums, and pulling her tooth tossed it up to the ceiling, exclaiming: ' There! That didn't hurt any, did it ?' The lady was positive that she felt no pain, and went away praising the new remedy."— *Oshkosh Northwestern.*

" A lad, seven years of age, was brought to me to have a tooth extracted; both I and the father told the child he must expect the operation to be severe — that teeth could not be extracted without pain. The consequence was the child, terror-stricken, began to scream the instant the instrument touched the tooth, and long after the tooth was out cried and groaned as if in great suffering. Some months after, the same child was brought to have another tooth pulled. In the meantime I had been having some special lessons upon mental control. I thought I would try and experiment upon the child. I took him in my lap and began tickling him and found him very ticklish. After playing with him some time, I said, 'Johnny, now you can keep from being ticklish, if you choose. You think right hard that I can't tickle you, and you will find I can't.' He soon found my words true. ' Now,' I said, ' I am going to pull your tooth. You remember how it hurt you before? Well, now you can keep this from hurting you just as you keep me from tickling you.' He said: ' Why, how?' 'Simply think hard that I can't hurt you, just as you thought hard I could not tickle you. Will you try it?' The little fellow agreed and the tooth was extracted without any evidence of pain."— *E. V. W.*

PAGE 145, *y.*— *Dancing.*

Notwithstanding that the natural exuberance and joyousness of youth is expressed in dancing, among the religious and people of high moral purpose there exists what seems a prejudice against it. Every nation has its dance — the Norwegian and Hottentot, the Chinese and Amazon, all express life in dancing. " Dancing, like a corporeal poesy, embellishes, exercises, and equalizes all the muscles at once." Dancing has within itself elements as fitting to race characteristics as laughter. It is poetry in motion and has its place in the arts of life.

In families, neighborhood clubs and social functions, it has for the individual great power of throwing off tension of the day's doings, or restraint of self-consciousness. A bashful man forgets his feet as they move to the rhythm of music.

As a social factor it has cohesive qualities. Dancing requires necessary forms of etiquette, but gives freedom in these forms. The shy man or maiden becomes the social companion. The quickening, enlivening power of music speaks through bodily activity, awakening insight and perception. The reticent man bows his admiration to a shy maiden, who responds in movements of grace. The objectors to dancing say that it arouses passion, that it leads from virtue to vice. Has this been proven? And if passion should be aroused, does not the dance give an opportunity for interchange of masculine and feminine elements that satisfy passion? Those who have much experience claim this.

A young man of fine physique was an intimate friend of our family. He taught dancing as a profession, and danced the round dances with all his pupils. He testified that the more he danced the less he realized the demand and existence of passion. He contended that dancing was essential to social purity.

PAGE 149, z.— *Less Sleep Possible.*

Personally, I never required much sleep; four and five hours have usually been sufficient, but still I have wasted many years vainly striving to acquire the ordinary sleep habit. When once I had it settled that it was not a necessity, I was able to utilize the waking hours to advantage.

One entire family in Chicago, from conscientious convictions, spend but four hours out of twenty-four in sleep.

A visit to Mr. G-----'s home at midnight found the husband, wife and child sitting about a table. Mr. and Mrs. G----- were reading and the child was playing with pictures and a slate. Their hour for retiring is 2 o'clock a.m. They rise at 6 o'clock, and Mr. G----- is always at his store at 7. There he is on his feet the entire day, save an hour spent at luncheon.

" When my day's work is over," said Mr. G-----, " I return home and we usually spend an hour at the dinner table. That we look upon as the principal daily event of our home life. After dinner we either go to the theater, visit or entertain friends. We are rarely ever out later than 12 o'clock. From then until 2, our hour for retiring, we spend in reading. From 7 a.m. to 6 p.m. each day I devote to business; our evenings we usually spend in recreation and two hours are given to reading. Necessity and the natural aversion I have to sleep forced me to the practice. Since beginning it I have never had a spell of sickness, and the same may be said of my wife and child."

Mrs. G----- said that she felt drowsy when she began to accustom herself to the prolonged wakefulness and was often compelled to take a nap during the day, but now she never craves more rest than the allotted four hours. The child, she said, they have broken into the custom merely by training and not through force. They gradually cut short the number of hours of his rest until now he is able to remain awake each day as long as his parents.

" Dr. James Legge, professor of Chinese in the University of Oxford, retired each night at 10 o'clock and rose at 3 a.m. One hour less would have done him just as well. He lived to be eighty-two years old. Brunnel, the world's greatest engineer, worked twenty hours a day. His associates say that he hardly ever went to bed. He worked until late in the night, slept for two or three hours in his arm-chair and at early dawn was ready for the work of the day. He is said to have never seemed tired or out of spirits. During the great siege of Gibraltar Sir George A. Elliott, afterward Lord Heathfield, never slept but four hours a day for four years. He was eighty-four years old when he died.

A flock of sheep that leisurely pass by,
One after one; the sound of rain and bees
Murmuring; the fall of rivers, winds and seas;
Smooth fields, white sheets of water and pure sky
By turns have all been thought of, yet I lie
Sleepless.

Many have found relief by having the room partially lighted, then, with a fixed stare, gaze at some one object, forcing the eyes to remain open. By a contrary action of mind the eyes soon close in sleep.

Deep, slow breathing often relieves the tension on the brain, equalizes circulation and sleep follows.

Practicing the *Silence* (see page 137) brings one that deeper consciousness which gives a more satisfactory rest than sleep, and precludes the necessity of passing into the unconscious state. When sleep ceases to be one of the seeming necessities of life, then one devotes wakeful nights to writing, reading or some favorite pursuit.

PAGE 160, *bb.*— *Ten Rules for Artistic Gowns.*

The following rules were adopted by the committee of final appeal on World's Fair exhibit of Society for the Promotion of Physical Culture and Correct Dress:

I. The lines of the gown follow those of a natural body as represented in classic sculpture. The armhole describes the top of the shoulder joint, the sleeve follows the shoulder line, or at least does not contradict it; the gown gives room for the waist region from below the bust to grow gently larger as it approaches the hips, the front line directly below the bust having a gentle outward curve; the whole presenting the contour of the Venus de Milo.

2. Every part of the gown is suspended from the shoulders. A yoke or an easy waist is a convenient method of suspension.

3. The dress is loose enough to permit free and graceful movement, allowing a possible suggestion of the play of muscle. It appears to be easy by an absence of seams stiffened by whalebones.

4. The form of construction is suited to the fabric, simple forms for heavy goods and gathers for thin materials.

5. The costume is genuine throughout, being just what it pretends to be. If made of two materials, its prototype would be the gowns of the early middle ages, one worn over another.

6. The folds of the gown radiate from the only proper points of support, namely, the shoulders; secondarily, the hips. Where folds radiate, or sprig out, they are confined, or seem to be confined, by a belt, a band, a lacing, a clasp, or a buckle.

7. The gown indicates unity of purpose, each part subserving, or at least not contradicting, that purpose. That is, if it is a house gown, it is in every part suited to its supposed use. If a walking dress or an outing suit, it is adapted to convenience in walking, of freedom for exercise. The same rule is to be applied to the accessories of a costume. The buttons on the gown serve to button it, each having its proper buttonhole. The ribbons on the gown tie, or seem to tie, something. The wrap affords and seems to afford added warmth. The hat secures shade for the face.

8. The decoration of the gown is subordinate to the gown itself; not arresting attention before the wearer, like the lines of a diagram; not contradicting the contours of a classic figure, especially not seeming to make the lines from the armpit down approach each other like those of a letter V. The ornament serves the purpose of strengthening the edges of the gown, uniting its parts, or holding it together Where the edges of the dress join the skin at neck and wrists, they seem to blend with it, either by a gentle gradation in color, or by an uneven edge — that is, not being harsh in tint nor abrupt in form.

9. The dress, as a whole, presents no intensity of color, by violent contrasts, or by other bizarre effect above and beyond the personality of the woman arrayed in it.

10. The gown is suited to the personality of the wearer in color, texture and form; that is, it enhances her best physical features, concealing or agreeably modifying any infelicity of structure or complexion. It expresses the sentiment of her disposition, giving an expression of her gentleness and modesty, her sprightliness and vigor, her steadiness and executive ability, or her serene, majestic dignity.

The successful application of this last rule is, necessarily, the final outcome of much independent thought. It is the crowning effort and highest achievement of genius, in this greatest of fine arts, the making a glorious picture of a living woman.

PAGE 189, *cc.—Diapers Not Required.*

All animals have an instinct for neatness; the human child is no exception to this rule if suitable measures are taken to allow the natural instinct expression. The new-born baby will easily and naturally form habits of regularity in performing excretory functions if encouraged to do so. By a little careful observation, when he first wakens or has been feeding, the nurse will detect the signs of a desire to relieve himself. Let her hold him out, giving him opportunity to avoid wetting or soiling himself. An ordinary spittoon, with a hollowed and sloping flange, is the most convenient for this purpose. Put it in the lap between the knees and the child is then held comfortably without any exertion on the part of the nurse. If this method is persevered in regularly and systematically the child forms a habit of perfect neatness, so that by the time he is a month or six weeks old, when the diapers ordinarily have to be pinned closely about his hips, they may be dispensed with altogether. This is no idle dream. Forty-five years ago I knew a mother who never had diapers to wash after her babies were three months old. In those days many old ladies counseled the young mother to hold her child out at regular intervals and thus secure habits of neatness. Many mothers have written me of their great success in bringing about regular habits in their children. Think what this does for the child and for the mother. The legs are permitted natural activity and natural development. The diaper causes heat and pressure while through neglect the body is irritated by accumulated waste. It produces irritation and often is the cause of early habits of self-handling. Many deformities of hips and legs are the direct result of this padded protection. The bones, until a child is many months old, are pliable and easily distorted.

The diaper is an unnatural and unnecessary part of a baby's wardrobe. The mother who thus trains her child carefully frees herself from an enormous amount of labor both in caring for the child and in the laundry work.

If these regular habits of neatness are not established before the child is three months old, it then becomes difficult to form them before he is three years old and often result in the common habit of bedwetting. The same law holds good with the child that obtains with the animal; if you do not give him the conditions for neatness at once, his pliant nature is soon perverted into habits of uncleanness.

The Hindu mother teaches her child to relieve itself upon awakening in the morning, which is directly followed by a bath. This becomes a lifelong habit. Indeed, it is observed by many of the natives with the punctiliousness of a religious rite. Unless one knows this fact he can not understand how a baby of the Orient can at all times run about without clothing. He is taught and treated as Western people treat their favorite spaniels or cats.

As the mother cat trains her kittens, it is well that the child should be directed in its habits through maternal love and patience. Remember that diapers are not a necessity.

PAGE 193, *dd.—Teething.*

From the time a child is three months until he is three years of age, it has been quite customary to attribute all his ailments to teething. Parents forget that teeth are a product of nature and that she has instituted a wise plan to provide them.

Teething is not a disease; establish this fact well in mind and free your mind from all solicitude. A healthy child should have no consciousness of the growth of teeth any more than of the growth of hair or nails. Teething is a process of growth and the child may require more freedom to grow than usual. Should his hands and feet through excessive heat show signs of unusual activity in the forces of life, strip him off, give him a water or air bath, take him and keep him outdoors. In the summer time let him lie or sit on the ground, planting his feet in the earth. Dig in the sand, yes, even make holes in the ground and bury the feet for a time in them. The earth is a great comforter and by natural sympathetic vibrations removes fevered conditions and establishes a harmony of all functions. He needs no doctor, no drugs, only to live his natural life free from any one's anxiety. If he is still kept on liquid nourishment, he should have solid food added to his bill of fare; Wheatlet or Purina made into mush or gruel, barley or oatmeal porridge, some form of grain that contains he phosphates. If he has an inclination to bite upon hard substances, give a crust of bread, graham cracker or oatmeal biscuit. The harder they are the better he will be suited. The child's instinct for nutriment ought to guide the supply, and if he thus far has had a natural life, unhampered by the fancies and notions of many people, the mother makes no mistake in yielding to his choice. Usually his tastes are simple, demanding one or at least few articles of food.

I have seen children day after day for weeks perfectly satisfied to suck the nourishment from very dry crusts of bread. A cracker made of graham flour and sweet cream, adding a little sugar, is quite a favorite of little ones, while any of the hard crackers on the market made of graham, entire wheat-flour or oatmeal, are good substitutes.

No doubt too much clothing and too constant covering fosters sensitiveness. The face seldom feels cold; the hands, accustomed to exposure, are usually warm.

An Indian was once asked how he could endure the cold when his body was not covered. He replied: " Does white man's face get cold ?" "Why, no; it is used to it." His curt answer was: " Me all face."

It may prove that clothing affords a hindrance to circulation, to the stimulants that absorbents require from air and electricity, and thus defeats the purpose intended. The Kneipp cure introduced the barefoot fad, and thousands have proven that their feet have recovered lost circulation that has been produced by wearing impervious leather and rubbers; by very exposure the power of resistance is gained. A run barefoot in the dewy grass, on frosted ground or snow-crust, might well be adopted as a cure-all for cold feet, frost-bites and bunions. A dose of snow is a good foot warmer. The frequent exposure of the entire body to the sun's rays, to warm or cold air, is equally effective as a restorative to normal conditions. Sensitiveness to cold can be overcome by one's divesting himself of all clothing and taking deep breathing and bodily exercise in a cool room. One is surprised how soon the sense of chill is replaced by a glow of warmth and a thrill of strength; it is the joy of childhood, a sweet embrace of Nature, and she gives back principal and interest in health and vigor. To many it is the sure preventive of colds, catarrh, grippe, and all the influenza family — the clown says it becomes a whole brood of out-flu-enza.

For a more potent and deeper reason, we need to become accustomed to the uncovered body. Some nuns, in the habit of making visits to artesian baths, always brought their bath robes. The attendant asked for the reason; they replied: " Why, we must; we have never seen our naked bodies." Many people have a like experience, fostering and perpetuating a false modesty, an idea that

Nature made a great mistake in giving to man rosy flesh, supple limbs and organs wonderfully adapted to use. No man is free from shame or prudery until he delights in his body as God made it; no woman can be modest at heart, through and through, until she feels the sacredness and purity of her own flesh. If love takes us back to the Arcadian life, it may prove that a test of true modesty will be for men and women to be unmoved at the uncovered bodies of each other. The Wheel of Life in its revolutions must make every part of the life an expression of the divine plan. One wears clothes for warmth, but finds being accustomed to exposure is the best protection from inclemency; one is attired to be modest, and yet, who knows but that the fostering of the idea that there is aught to be hidden produces what we wish to avert. In an American Mission, in India, a recent convert was fitted out with Christian (?) clothes. At night, upon going to his own house, he removed the new garments, folded them carefully away, and returned to his people in his usual scant attire. Questioned by the missionaries as to his reason, he replied: " I would be ashamed to be seen wearing clothes! "

" Caliban makes the fire for me as I write. He has nothing on but a cotton wrap and a thin jersey, but does not seem to feel the cold much; and the guide is even more thinly clad, and is asleep, while I am shivering, bundled in cloth coats. There is something curious about the way in which the English in this country feel the cold — when it is cold — more than the natives; though one might expectthe contrary. I have often noticed it. I fancy we make a great mistake in these hot lands in not exposing our skins more to the sun and air, and so strengthening and hardening them. In the great heat, and when constantly covered with garments, the skin perspires terribly, and becomes sodden and enervated, and more sensitive than it ought to be — hence great danger of chills. I have taken several sun-baths in the woods here at different times, and found advantage from doing so."

" Since writing the above, I have discovered the existence of a little society in India — of English folk — who encourage nudity, and the abandonment as far as possible of clothes, on three distinct grounds — physical, moral, æsthetic — of Health, Decency and Beauty. I wish the society every success. Its chief object, as given in its rules, is to urge upon people ' to be and go stark naked whenever suitable,' and it is a *sine qua non* that members should appear at all its meetings without any covering. Passing over the moral and aesthetic considerations — which are both, of course, of the utmost importance in this connection — there is still the consideration of physical health and enjoyment, which must appeal to everybody. In a place like India, where the mass of people go with very little covering, the spectacle of their ease and enjoyment must double the discomforts of the unfortunate European who thinks it necessary to be dressed up to the eyes upon every occasion when he appears in public. It is indeed surprising that men can endure, as they do, to wear cloth coats and waistcoats and starched collars and cuffs, and all the paraphernalia of propriety, in a severity of heat which really makes only the very lightest covering tolerable; nor can one be surprised at the exhaustion of the system which ensues, from the cause already mentioned. In fact, the direct stimulation and strengthening of the skin by sun and air, though most important in our home climate, may be even more indispensable in a place like India where the relaxing influences are so terribly strong."—" From Adam's Peak to Elephanta," *Edward Carpenter*.

We would arrest a man that walks on our streets divested of clothing and put him in the lock-up, but who knows that he may not be more pure at heart than his accusers; must he be compelled to adopt conventional standards? I can not say. The psychologist of the future will have this question to settle, and in settling must help the great world to know that there is no defilement in one's natural complexion.

In the meantime, each person must make frequent obeisance to the natural charms of the color and form of his or her own body. A daily acknowledgment will strengthen him in a life of health and purity.

A late writer has said, " There is no greater blasphemy in the universe than shame of self, no greater destructive force." We redeem the body, the entire body, by thoughts of love and appreciation and unite in harmony the spiritual and physical, producing a constant renewal of all the elements and forces. It is a regeneration or daily birth in which there is no picture of decay and death, but rather an unfoldment of ever increasing perfection.

It is a false idea to think that garments are purer and sweeter than human forms.

PAGE 232, *ff.*— *Home Gymnastics.*

It is well to supply some simple apparatus, such as horizontal bars, the hand swing, the ladder, the punching bag and the trapeze. The latter is easily adapted to any home by putting to any door frame cleats with graded slots that will hold firmly a bar or pole. This can be placed or removed in an instant and is a never-ending source of recreation. Three or four boys and girls will spend hours in feats of skill and agility with this one simple apparatus. Bean bags may also be made a source of recreation. They combine exercise and pleasure, and the games can be made very interesting.

Many forms of breathing are practiced to assist in transmutation of sexual energy.

" In sexual control I get helps by breathing — ' special conscious breathing' — and I have done a little of it for *fifty odd years*, from boyhood. When I was a boy in my teens, I thought, and others thought, that I would die with the consumption, young, as both my parents did. Somehow — I know not how — I got onto the trick of breathing. It is my medicine for ennui or any complaint, and has been for more than a half-century. Ordinarily, natural breathing is *eighteen breaths* per minute. My ordinary breathing is, when at rest, *eight breaths* per minute. My *conscious breathing* — that is, when I give attention to it — is from three to four breaths per minute, and this is most restful breathing, and I could keep it up all day and all night and not feel tired! I feel the sensation perceptibly, and I *taste* the life-giving forces in my mouth."— *O. L. Barter.*

PAGE 248, *gg.*— *Conversion.*

Conversion, as taught and professed by protestant Christians until within a very few years, seemed to me more of a romance than a possible experience. My people were Hicksite Quakers, who believed in the *inner light*, but not in the atonement through the death of Christ.

At college I was associated with Congregationalists (Finney stamp) who emphatically believed in the fall of man, and the inherent vileness and wickedness of the human heart. I listened to divines who portrayed in grand eloquence the eternal destruction of the ungodly and the faith in Christ necessary for salvation. For years I sought the change of heart, the *conversion* claimed as essential to redemption. Yet to me the story and the change so pictured remained a myth; the best expression of life coming from growth and ideals, rather than from any sudden knowledge of God through Christ. An early student of Swedenborg and the science of Spiritual phenomena led only to the rationalist's view of life, conversion meaning simply a change of character.

At the present time I *know* there may be a *conversion* — an escape of the soul from a prison of darkness to the freedom of light. None may have given a satisfactory, logical statement of this change, but once experienced, logic and intellectual processes are a tangled network in comparison to the illumination. Combined with personal experience I learned the process of a *change of heart* through the teachings of Christian Science and through the perusal of Evans' Divine Law of Cure, the most remarkable and comprehensive work

320

on *healing* in modem literature. It is very simple when one knows that conversion is not a knowledge of the personal Christ—Jesus the man — but rather the Christ within, the revelation of the Essential Self to the Self. Evans says: " The principle of Christianity and of every true religion is within the soul — the realization of the incarnation of God in every human being."

Knowledge of God or interior spiritual light is known by many names. Plotinus denominates this higher faculty *ecstasy*; St. Bernard calls it *contemplation*; George Fox, the *inward voice*; Swedenborg, perception. In the Old Testament it is spoken of as The *Word of the Lord*, or *Thus saith the Lord*, while in the New Testament it is called the *True Light that lighteth every man that cometh into the world*.

INDEX

327

Epilogue by the Editor

In January 2019, I met Daniel Joslyn, a PhD candidate at New York University, in Bonn. He works on late nineteenth-century sexual mysticism and social reform in the United States. He had become attentive of my reprint of Stockham's *Karezza, Ethics of Marriage* and the statement in my Epilogue:

> „*It is time, that the scientific community recognizes her important idea of a spiritual or mental emancipation from sexual bestiality. In my opinion, Stockham is a fascinating figure for medical and cultural historiography in the overlapping fields of natural philosophy and religious thinking, mesmerism and psychoanalysis, medical anthropology and sexology, feminism and social hygiene, and last but not least humanism and pacifism. It is time to rediscover her life and work.*"[3]

Daniel Joslyn informed me about new approaches and publications of contemporary American scholars. Above all, he hinted at Stockham's magnum opus *The Lover's World, A Wheel of Life*, which I had ignored so far. This book is not available in any German respectively European library and one can find it only in a very few libraries in North America. Thanks to his information I could produce this reprint.

---

3   Reprint of the second edition: Chicago 1903; edited by Heinz Schott with an Epilogue by the editor, Norderstedt: BoD – Books on Demand, 2017 (SCHOTT's NEUE BIBLIOTHEK / 3), p. 71. – See advertisement on page 334.

Alice Bunker Stockham (1833-1912) was an obstetrician and gynecologist from Chicago, an enthusiastic fighter for a marital and sexual reform. Stockham was the fifth woman in the U.S.A., who got the degree of a Medical Doctor. Apart from her medical field she was engaged in charity and interested in spiritual topics. She also practiced homeopathy, fought against alcoholism, served probably sometimes as a trance medium, and was an active feminist, a suffragette. She became a successful self-publisher. In 1886, she published *Tokology, A Book for Every Woman* concerning the health of women followed by several editions and translations into foreign languages. Leo Tolstoy, a supporter of her ideas and a personal friend of her, was so impressed that he initiated a translation of the book into Russian. In 1900, she published by her own press the study *Tolstoi—A Man of Peace* together with the Tolstoy study of Havelock Ellis, the well-known English sexologist.

Stockham adhered to the so called "New Thought Movement". In 1886, she joined the first course on Christian Science organised by Emma Hopkins in Chicago. Many renowned women supported this movement, which was separated into two parties. One of them refused strictly any sex appeal, whereas the other one backed by Stockham pled to perform sexual life worthily. In 1896, she published a little book titled *Karezza, Ethics of Marriage.* She took *"Karezza"* from the Italian term *"carezza"* (written with a "c") meaning petting or gentle stroking. Stockham was convinced, that there was a tremendous difference between the usual copulation ending up with orgasm and ejaculation and the gentle Karezza conjunction or merging avoiding orgasm. Her magnum opus *The Lover's World, A Wheel of Life* published in 1903 (see below: Editorial Note) is based on her former work comprehending all of her theoretical and practical knowledge as a medical doctor, social reformer and spiritual thinker.

I am quite impressed by Stockham's opus combining medical, ethical, anthropological, social, philosophical, cross-cultural, mystical, and religious perspectives. In my opinion, it is a key work for understanding the social, political, and intellectual situation in the United States and partially also in Europe about 1900. I am not able to analyse Stockham's writing in detail here. Her historical sources, theoretical assumptions, and practical consequences are rather complex, whereas the guiding idea is quite elementary: Love is a marvellous spiritual ("heavenly") power framing and transcending the crude animal sphere of human beings. Stockham's concept displays a fascinating intersection of medical advice, health care, social reform, sexual education, spiritual exercise, and religious empowerment. Her idealistic views – among others she referred to German idealism and Hegel – did not impede her professional devotion as a doctor to the very earthly needs of her fellow human beings providing them with words of advice and encouragement. Moreover, her books represent health guides and instructions of self-help belonging to a certain genre of advisory literature authored by medical doctors to help their patients as well as the suffering mankind in general. Insofar, she stressed the traditional idea of dietetics originating from the ancient Greek medicine, which has been modified in many ways throughout medical history.

Stockham was a learned woman with an overwhelming pedagogical Eros – without academic arrogance and elitist behaviour. This reprint can only deliver a certain basis for further studies to detect the importance of this extraordinary woman within the context of her time. Even more significant in my view: Her ideas are apt to stimulate the discussion on the crucial problem of sexuality and love nowadays. She transcended the view of biologism, although she often invoked a plain naturalism. In her optimistic view of life she was not interested to reflect tragedy and absurdity of the human condition in a philosophical way. Her heaven on earth idea she advocated as a marital reformer did not correspond to the materialistic socialist doctrine of her time. For she targeted a spiritually founded life style overcoming animal sexuality as a reflex of instinct by self-education. In my opinion, this task is as topical today as is it was in her time. In spite of sexual revolution(s), women's emancipation, and the "anti-baby-pill" during the 20th century, the sexual misery is going on regarding the abortion and divorce rates, the debates on sexual abuse, or the odd controversy about "gender main streaming". The history of ideas resembles a treasury containing fascinating gems for someone, who is ready to perceive them. And Stockham's work is one of them.

Bonn, in May 2019   Heinz Schott

EDITORIAL NOTE

The Lover's World: A Wheel of Life was released by two publishers in 1903:

Stockham Publishing Co. (Chicago), the prototype of this reprint, and

R. F. Fenno & Company (New York).

The text of both editions is identical, but its presentation differs regarding frontispiece, layout, pagination, index, and ads at the end of the book. The Appendix of the present reprint reproduces the frontispieces and title pages of both editions and displays the ads of the New York Edition at the end. The entries of the Index refer exactly to the Chicago Edition.

SECONDARY LITERATURE FOR FURTHER READING[4]

Alice Bunker Stockham [Wikipedia article]; https://en.wikipedia.org/wiki/Alice_Bunker_Stockham

---

4   I give my thanks to Daniel Joslyn for his substantial support.

Burton, Shirley J.: Obscene, Lewd, and Lascivious: Ida Craddock and the Criminally Obscene Women of Chicago, 1873-1913. In: *Michigan Historical Review* 19, no. 1 (1993): 1–16.

Edwards, Robert: Tolstoy and Alice B. Stockham: The Influence of Tokology on 'The Kreutzer Sonata'. In: *Tolstoy Studies Journal;* Rochester, NY 6 (January 1, 1993): 87–104; https://docs.wixstatic.com/ugd/dab097_d03459b9e1b04880a51f33b9bfedfef5.pdf [May 1, 2019].

Griffith, R. Marie: *Born Again Bodies. Flesh and Spirit in American Christianity.* Berkeley: University of California Press, c2004 (California studies in food and culture; 12).

Janson, Sharon L. : Alice Bunker Stockham, Dress Reform, and "Karezza". In: *The Monstrous Regiment of Women. A Women's History Daybook* [Blog; posted on December 3, 2015]; https://www.monstrousregimentofwomen.com/2015/12/alice-bunker-stockham-dress-reform-and.html [April 4, 2019]

Materra, Gary Ward: *Women in Early New Thought: Lives and Theology in Transition, From the Civil War to World War I.* (Ph.D. diss.). University of California, Santa Barbara, 1997.

Satter, Beryl: *Each Mind a Kingdom. American Women, Sexual Purity, and the New Thought Movement, 1875-1920.* Berkeley; Los Angeles; London: University of California Press, 1999.

Schmidt, Leigh Eric. T*he Unprintable Life of Ida C. Craddock, American Mystic, Scholar, Sexologist, Martyr and Madwoma*n. New York: Basic Books, 2010.

Silberman, Marsha: The Perfect Storm: Late Nineteenth-Century Chicago Sex Radicals: Moses Harman, Ida Craddock, Alice Stockham and the Comstock Obscenity Laws. In: *Journal of the Illinois State Historical Society* (1998-) 102, no. 3/4 (2009): 324–67.

Schott, Heinz: Mesmerism, Sexuality, and Medicine: "Karezza" and the Sexual Reform Movement. In: *Cultural and Religious Studies*, July-Aug. 2015, Vol. 3, No. 4, 211-216; doi: 10.17265/2328-2177/2015.04.00; http://www.davidpublisher.org/Public/uploads/Contribute/5608e2732df5a.pdf

Versluis, Arthur: Sexual Mysticism in Nineteenth Century America: John Humphrey Noyes, Thomas Lake Harris, and Alice Bunker Stockham. In: Wouter J. Hanegraaff and Jeffrey J. Kripal (eds.): *Hidden Intercourse. Eros and Sexuality in the History of Western Esotericism.* Leiden; Boston. Brill, 2008 (Aries Book Series; v. 7), pp. 333-354.

Wilson, Jennifer: *Radical Chastity: The Politics of Abstinence in Late Nineteenth Century Russian Literature* (Ph.D. diss.) Princeton: Princeton University, 2014; https://dataspace.princeton.edu/jspui/bitstream/88435/dsp01qr46r304f/1/Wilson_princeton_0181D_11182.pdf (May 1, 2019).

Women of History: Alice B. Stockham. In: *Mary Baker Eddy Library* (Featured Articles); https://www.marybakereddylibrary.org/research/women-of-history-alice-b-stockham/ [April 4, 2019]. – With a letter from Alice Bunker Stockham to Mary Baker Eddy, September 12, 1883.

APPENDIX

CARMEN SYLVA.

Frontispiece: Edition New York 1903

THE LOVER'S WORLD

A WHEEL OF LIFE

By ALICE B. STOCKHAM, M.D.

Author of "Tokology," "Karezza," etc.

Behold! I create a new heaven and a new earth

R. F. Fenno & Company
18 EAST 17th STREET :: NEW YORK

Titlepage:Edition New York 1903

Frontispiece: Edition Chicago 1903

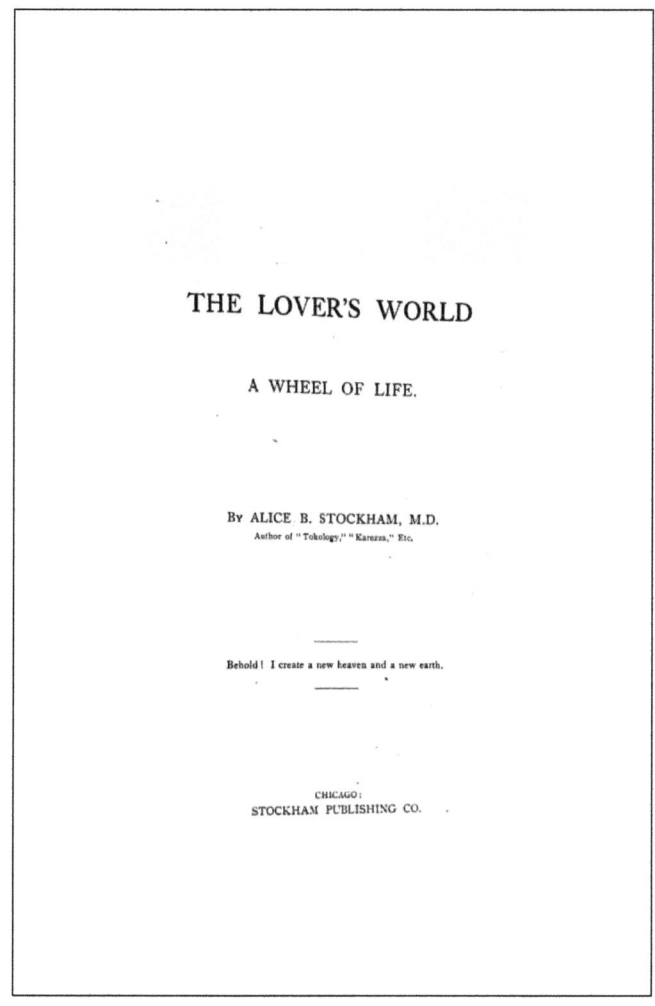

THE LOVER'S WORLD

A WHEEL OF LIFE.

By ALICE B. STOCKHAM, M.D.
Author of "Tokology," "Karezza," Etc.

Behold! I create a new heaven and a new earth.

CHICAGO:
STOCKHAM PUBLISHING CO.

Titlepage: Edition Chicago 1903

ADS IN
THE LOVER'S WORLD
EDITION NEW YORK 1903
(R. F. FENNO & COMPANY)

AT THE END OF THE BOOK

347

352

THE MYSTIC WILL

By CHARLES G. LELAND.

THIS book gives the methods of development and strengthening the latent powers of the mind and the hidden forces of the will by a simple, scientific process possible to any person of ordinary intelligence. The author's first discovery was that Memory, whether mental, visual, or of any other kind, could, in connection with Art, be wonderfully improved, and to this in time came the consideration that the human Will, with all its mighty power and deep secrets, could be disciplined and directed, or controlled, with as great care as the memory or the mechanical faculty In a certain sense the three are one, and the reader who will take the pains to master the details of this book will readily grasp it as a whole, and understand that its contents form a system of education, yet one from which the old as well as young may profit.

Table of Contents:

Popular priced American edition, bound in cloth, 119 pages, postpaid, 50 cents

R. F. FENNO & COMPANY   -   NEW YORK

The Modern Mother

*A Guide to Girlhood,
Motherhood and Infancy*

By Dr. H. LANG GORDON

Size, 6 x 8¾; 278 pages; fully illustrated.   *Price, $2.00*

THIS work marks in its own line the opening of a new epoch. Hitherto such works have been devoted to treatment and a study of the abnormal; here these subjects yield precedence to prevention and a common-sense exposition of the normal. The author, imbued with the spirit of modern preventive medicine, points out the errors and abuses of modern life (so easily avoided and yet so easily yielded to) which affect injuriously the health of women and children. At the same time he clearly assists the mother and others to understand the physiology of womanhood and motherhood, the care of the infant and young girl, and the detection and treatment of common complaints. The subjects of heredity, environment, education and schools, the home-training of children, the physical development of the body and the position of woman in modern life, are among the topics of the day which are touched upon in a new light in this concisely written book. Each of its three sections, *Girlhood, Motherhood* and *Infancy*, provides the mother, the schoolmistress, and the intelligent nurse with a fascinating and easily understood guide and high ideals.

R. F. FENNO & COMPANY
13 East 17th Street   ·   ·   ·   ·   NEW YORK

359